# Blue Collar Resumes, Third Edition

*Steven Provenzano, CPRW / CEIP, President,*
*ECS: Executive Career Services & DTP, Inc.*

[c] 2018

Published by ECS: Executive Career Services & DeskTop Publishing, Incorporated

Library of Congress Control Number: 2011942306

**THIRD EDITION PRINT BOOK**

**ISBN: 978-0-9633558-6-7**


(Third Edition Ebook ISBN: 978-0-9633558-5-0)
(Previous ISBN-13: 978-1-4354-6101-7; ISBN-10: 1-4354-6101-0)

Produced / printed in the United States of America

**Acknowledgments**

Special thanks to all the job seekers represented in this book and everyone who has placed their trust in me and my staff for help finding a new position. Getting to know and assist good people like you over the past 20 years makes my work rewarding and fulfilling.

I'd also like to thank my parents Tony and Doris, brothers Randy, Jim, and Bill, my sister Grace Marie, and the friends who've always been there for me: Jeff Burns, Larry Jesse, Joan Magic, and Diana Klein.

**About the Author**

**Steven Provenzano** is president of ECS: Executive Career Services & DTP, Inc. A former corporate recruiter and author of ten career books, he has written or edited more than 5,000 resumes. Steven has appeared on CNBC several times, CNN, WGN, ABC/NBC in Chicago, and numerous radio programs. He has also been featured in major newspapers, such as *The Wall Street Journal*, *Crain's*, and the *Chicago Tribune*. He is a Certified Professional Resume Writer/CPRW and Certified Employment Interview Professional/CEIP. His work is endorsed by *Chicago Tribune* Career Columnist Lindsey Novak and top executives from Fortune 500 firms such as Motorola and First Data Corporation.

Website: https://Execareers.com.

**<u>Free Resume Review</u>**

For a free resume analysis, you may send your resume in confidence to:
Careers1@Execareers.com

Call toll free: 877-610-6810 or 630-289-6222.

# Introduction

## The Demand for Blue Collar Workers

Greetings job seekers. Now is the time and this is the place to begin your search for a new, or better, Blue Collar position.

At the time of this writing unemployment is at a record low in America, less than 4.5%. Thousands of well-paying, blue collar and administrative jobs remain unfilled, in all types of industries. There's a shortage of skilled and semi-skilled workers, truck drivers, mechanics, you name it. Just about every major company, from UPS and DuPont to GM and Apple, relies on millions of blue collar workers to build, assemble, repair, stock, and deliver what they sell. Without this essential work force--without you--America would grind to a halt, a fact that seems lost to some of the people who run those big companies.

At my resume and career coaching firm, we help people just like you: administrative assistants and customer service staff, factory workers, drivers, and those from a multitude of skilled trades. Industry analysts have spoken for years about the essential role of blue collar and service workers, because in many cases, they have direct contact with the most important person in their business: the customer.

Granted, employers are looking for people with wider skill sets to work longer hours, and they expect higher quality work and devotion to their company. They want more bang for their buck. However, they're also willing to pay for training and internships to build their workforce. My team of career consultants just learned that employers will pay up to $2500 for a local community college to train just one entry-level employee prior to hiring. Some employers are even willing to hire workers at the ground floor – even sweeping the floor – and pay them to learn new skills.

Even with this hiring surge, employers still expect a focused, hard-working team of eight to do what used to be done by ten people just a year before. They also want people with good communication skills, and often the first impression you will give an employer of your communication skills is on your resume, so it had better be good!

## A New Philosophy

Because my staff and I write resumes just about every day, I meet a wide range of people looking for better jobs. After writing or editing more than 5,000 resumes, I'm still amazed at the diversity of jobs all around us. But everybody who comes to me has one thing in common--they all want a better job. They can't, however, get a new job without an interview--and they can't get an interview without a great resume.

People still walk into my office and give me handwritten notes on dirty scratch paper. They scribble out a basic history--where and when they worked and a short outline of their daily duties. I tell them that's a start, and then I ask "The Question":

### *What would you most like to DO in your next job?*

Some people are surprised when I ask this, and you'd be surprised at the answers I get. Many assume they'll keep doing the same work they were doing for their previous or current employer, until they start to really think about this question.

No two jobs, even if they have the same job title, are exactly the same. That's why it's essential to look at the *types* of skills you would like to use on the next job and then create a resume that will get you into that *type* of position.

## A New Approach

Most people think a resume is just an outline of old jobs and educational background. (That's what I call a "job list," or "tombstone" resume, a basic history of your working life). To some extent that's true, because your work history is an essential part of your resume (more on this later). But there's a new approach to resume writing that can help open doors to the really *good* jobs, play a key role in increasing your income, and help you enjoy what you're doing 40 to 50 hours every week. To accomplish this, your resume must consistently:

*Develop and market your skills and abilities.*

This may sound like a simple concept, but think about it. Does the average "job list" resume really develop and sell your skills, your talents, and what you can really bring to your next job? Usually not, and for one important reason-- when you send out a "job list" resume, you're telling people what you've done for your previous employers, but you're not really telling **what you can do for your next employer.**

That's really what this book is all about: helping you *identify* and *sell* your most important and relevant skills, abilities, knowledge, and training on paper. With so many people looking for new jobs in today's economy, it's essential to create a high-impact resume that develops and sells your skills, abilities, work history, achievements, formal education, and on-the-job training to the maximum.

## Simple and Basic? Or Ineffective?

I can't tell you how many people call my office and say they want a "simple" or "basic" resume. For some reason, they think there's something magical about those words. Most people email brief descriptions of their work history and education. Initially, they ask for feedback and maybe a few "tweaks," as if that will quickly result in more job offers.

Whenever I talk to job seekers with this mindset, I stop them in their tracks and tell them, "We'll make your resume *effective.*" Never underestimate the power of a few "basic" words.

## What You're Up Against

Did you know that the average job listing on CareerBuilder or Monster.com can draw thousands of resumes? Research tells us that most of these resumes have only a few seconds to grab the reader's attention, and here's proof.

### A Minute of Your Time?

A survey of 150 executives from the nation's 1,000 largest companies was conducted by Accountemps/Robert Half. Can you believe that 70 percent said they spend two minutes *or less* reviewing an applicant's resume? That's why your resume must become an attention-getting *advertisement* of your best, most important, most relevant skills and abilities, and not just another job history.

## The Resume Screening Process

As a former corporate recruiter and creator of resumes for those in recruiting and human resources, I've learned that resumes are most often used as a tool for "weeding out" potential candidates. No matter how many job openings a company may have, there simply isn't the time or staff to interview every single person who would like to be interviewed. The recruiters in HR, or your potential boss, may sort through hundreds--even thousands--of resumes, by hand or with ATS software, received from internal job postings, employment agencies, and a wide range of advertisements.

When I was assigned to hire new employees, I did what many of my peers did--I sifted through the day's resumes and made three separate piles. I labeled them "Great," "Possible," and "Never." I first called people from the "Great" stack for interviews, and usually ended up tossing not just the "Never" pile, but the "Possible" pile, as well.

Most resumes are quickly scanned for essential *keywords* that relate to their job requirements, such as certifications, software or technical proficiencies, the ability to train others, or overall knowledge of a specific industry. Assuming that's found, they may also check for such items as a steady work history (not too many jobs in too short a time) or educational background and training.

If the initial glance passes muster, the HR representative may pass along your resume, with several others, to the hiring manager. Typically, that manager is the direct supervisor over the open position and will make the final decision about whom to call in for interviews. The initial interviews are then conducted by the HR department, and a short list of candidates is created.

Finally, about three to five candidates will be interviewed by the hiring manager (sometimes with other department managers present) and a decision will be made to offer the position to the candidate who best suits their needs and their payroll budget. As you can see, there are plenty of opportunities throughout the process to eliminate resumes and candidates who don't stand out as strong contenders.

## The Need for Accuracy

Brevity, accuracy, and overall appearance are key to a successful resume. If you're not sure how to spell a word, look it up. If you don't know how to type accurately, hire a professional typist.

### Check and Check Again

Proofread, proofread, proofread! OfficeTeam conducted a survey of 150 human resources and other managers from the nation's 1,000 largest companies. Results revealed that 76 percent said they would not hire candidates who have one or two typographical errors on their resume, and 45 percent said it would take only one typo to eliminate a candidate from consideration. Be careful what you send. Have family and friends proofread your resume from top to bottom and bottom to top.

You may send your current resume directly to our office for free proofreading and feedback; see the last page of this book for details.

## God Is in the Details

Accuracy and quality of writing is essential. Nothing turns off an employer more than basic spelling or grammar mistakes on a resume. The subconscious impression is, "If this person can't even produce a decent resume, how could he or she possibly perform this job well?"

Read this book thoroughly, especially the resume samples, for tips and tricks on layout, design, grammar, and punctuation for a unique, high-impact resume that does justice to your hard-earned skills and abilities.

Whether you have years of experience or are straight out of school, you can choose to present yourself through your resume in an average way or an outstanding way. The difference between a good resume and a *great* resume might just be the "foot in the door" you need to land those job interviews, which will lead to more opportunities for *better* job offers.

## Taking Stock of Yourself

I truly believe that writing an effective resume is a process of self-discovery, so I try to create personal advertisements for the people who trust me with their careers. I assume they have certain abilities, skills, and training that will be useful in their next job. It's my job to dig deeper--to identify all the best talents that person has to offer and then *develop* those talents on paper--otherwise those talents are not much use in the job-hunting process.

Because I'm not sitting across from you, it's your job to take a step back and take an honest look at what you really can and want to bring to your next employer.

You must take stock of your knowledge and accomplishments in your chosen field and decide what to develop, what to downplay, and what to leave out altogether. Relax, the worksheets in Chapter 1, "Get Started: Assessing Your Skills," should help.

This discovery process will prove even more valuable down the road when you start going on job interviews. It will help get you ready for interview questions and can actually create new career choices when you see that your skills may be applicable to entirely new professions or industries.

During my career seminars, I tell people that their resume can be the most important document they will ever have: more important than their driver's license, their passport, or even their birth certificate, because no other document can have such an impact on income and, most importantly, where and how they spend 40 to 50 hours of their life every week. Your resume is one of the few aspects in your job search over which you have complete control, and it is one of your most valuable assets; it's worth doing right.

Of course, emailing or mailing your resume isn't the only way to get an interview. There's personal networking with friends, former co-workers and clients, and cold-calling target companies. Still, a resume is almost always essential, no matter which method you use to land job interviews.

## Who's Really Getting Hired?

After thousands of face-to-face interviews of potential candidates, I've learned one of the most important facts of job hunting: The best person doesn't always get hired. Rather, it's the person who presents himself or herself as the most *likeable* and a good fit with the company culture. Now it's your job to do this with clarity, precision, and impact in your resume, on the phone with employers, and at the interview. Just like a politician, you need to stay "on message" with strong, consistent communications about what you can and want to do for your next employer.

### Leverage Your Contacts

Market studies show that 60 to 80 percent of professionals get their jobs through informal referrals (an essential part of networking). About 15 percent are filled through search firms, 10 percent through mass mailings, and only about 6-8 percent through published advertisements. Like the saying goes, sometimes it's who you know that matters, but you will always need a great resume to pass on through a personal contact. You'll also need an updated online presence, especially on Linkedin (now used by up to 90% of employers) and even Facebook; check out this article by Recruitment expert Fred Coon:

## How Is Facebook Useful In Recruitment and Job Searches?
By Fred Coon, CEO at Stewart, Cooper & Coon, published 2017

***Job seekers who choose to utilize Facebook's search and networking resources should remember to keep their professional online presence as balanced as possible.***

Facebook had 1.94 billion monthly active users as of first quarter of 2017. With so many users on this social network, it's only natural to assume Facebook's advantages in seeking employment.

What are the benefits of using Facebook for a job search?
While often and understandably overshadowed by LinkedIn as far as recruitment and professional networking is concerned, Facebook has shown to provide its own set of benefits to job seekers and employers seeking to hire top talent.

For Job Seekers

**Facebook can help showcase your professional networks.** You can easily highlight and maximize your professional networks on Facebook. Join group congruous to your industry to connect with others in your field. Just make sure you do not belong to any groups that that may be deemed negative or discriminatory to others.
**Facebook can help showcase your work.** If you possess a tangible skill, it's quite easy to share your talents directly to your Facebook page, while also highlighting your work experience. For instance, Facebook can make it possible for job seekers to showcase excellent writing skills or marketing capabilities to prospective employers.
**You can connect with companies you want to work for.** Nowadays, it's rare for companies not to have a Facebook page. By following or "liking" the page of the company for you wish to work, you can show your interest in joining their team. Inviting others to "like" the company or re-sharing a few of the company's interesting posts will also show your commitment to the company. Just remember to be selective, and don't overdo it.
**Facebook allows you to exhibit important social media skills.** Prospective employers can see how you use Facebook to promote yourself in a professional manner. This will give employers a window into your demeanor, as well as your ability to effectively promote their particular product or service.
**The Facebook Marketplace.** The Facebook Marketplace is a feature that provides classified listings within the Facebook forum. Think of it as an online version of your local "Pennysaver". Job seekers may find the Facebook Marketplace an additionally useful resource.
**Freelancers can advertise on Facebook.** Advertising on Facebook is not limited to consumer products. Freelancers can also advertise the services that they offer. All they have to do is choose their criteria (i.e.: companies they want to attract).

**Facebook can help companies gain exposure for recruitment efforts.** Facebook provides a straightforward way for employers to advertise, due partially to its sheer number of active users. Companies may find even more people noticing their recruitment efforts, compared to other networks. Organizations may also want to look into <u>Facebook for Business</u> for further marketing options.

**Facebook provides employers with a diverse recruitment pool.** As with most online resources, Facebook also gives employers access to a global workforce. In an age where remote work and telecommuting are becoming increasingly common, organizations don't necessarily need to limit themselves exclusively to local talent.

**Facebook helps boost a company's image.** When a company recruits through Facebook, potential candidates see this as a sign of the company's willingness to adapt and stay current. This can help attract even more attention to your job postings.

**Companies can gain more referrals through Facebook.** Since Facebook is a social network with almost 2 billion active users, it is easy for companies to gain an extraordinary number of referrals through its messaging and sharing features. You can also boost your recruitment efforts by maximizing your current employees' networks.

**Facebook allows companies to establish a more personal connection to potential recruits.** Through Facebook, companies are able to engage with job seekers on a more direct level. Job seekers appreciate this, and tend to prefer to work for companies that have a personal approach.

**Facebook helps increase brand awareness.** According to a <u>Trustpilot</u> study, <u>29%</u> of respondents believe that brands that have an active social media presence are more "human". In addition, 31% of respondents trust brands more if they have conversations with people on social media, and 20% check a brand's social media activities when they consider making their first purchase of a company's product or service. This also applies to job seekers. They prefer the transparency of companies that respond candidly to their inquiries through social media.

## The New Facebook Job Search Feature

As of 2017, Facebook users in the U.S. and Canada could search and apply for jobs directly from the Facebook website as well as from the mobile app.

How does this new feature work?

Companies publish job postings on their Facebook page. The postings can be found in two places: The company's Facebook page and under the "<u>jobs</u>" section.

When a job applicant sees a posting he or she likes, they can click on the "apply now" button which will lead to a pre-populated page with the applicant's name, education or employment history that he/she has already made public on Facebook. They can then edit the information before sending send details as is. Users cannot upload resumes, but there is a 1,000 character text box that allows you to type a short cover letter. Just hit "send" and the information will be sent to the company through Facebook messenger.

What are the benefits of using Facebook's job search feature?

**This feature enables companies to hire people who like your brand.** People most likely follow you on Facebook because they like your brand. Your followers get notifications whenever you post something on your page. Those who are actively looking for a job will know whenever you have a job opening and will readily apply for a position that suits them; or perhaps spread the word to someone else they know in the job market.

**Your company will receive notifications through messages to your page.** You can check your messages regularly since Facebook sends notifications whenever you receive an application. This allows you to integrate your business into Facebook and Facebook Messenger.

**There is no cost.** As of now, posting jobs on Facebook through your page is free.

**Facebook prioritizes new features in its algorithm.** When Facebook offers a new feature, it prioritizes that feature in its algorithm that determines what users see on the site. If you want to maximize exposure for your company, take advantage of this now.

**It is another way of getting "likes" exposure for your organization.** Job seekers who are interested in working with your company will "like" your page. Others will even recommend it to friends and family.

Are there any drawbacks to Facebook's job search feature?

**This feature may not be helpful for those seeking high-end positions.** If you are in the corporate job market, there is a chance you may have a more difficult time finding suitable job postings or applicants in this forum. Since the feature is free, it may be more helpful for entry level or lower-level job postings, especially for local companies. For high-end job postings, however, there is no guarantee that people applying for top C-level roles will search for jobs on Facebook, or that those seeking to fill those positions will advertise there.

**This feature is not currently available worldwide.** As of now, the Facebook job search feature is only available in North America.

**There is no guarantee that the job search feature will remain free.** As with all free services, there is no assurance that it will remain that way, or that advanced or premium options which require payment will be added. Of course, this is purely speculative.

What should job seekers avoid when seeking employment via Facebook?

- Do not make comments that could be interpreted as discriminatory in any way.
- Remove photos or "untag" images that may be inappropriate. If you want to keep the images, just manage the privacy settings of your albums so that you can control who sees them.
- If any of your Facebook connections have made distasteful comments on your wall, make sure to delete them.
- Check the apps on your profile and delete the ones that may show you in an unfavorable light.
- Check the groups you belong to. If you belong to groups that discriminate or are inappropriate in any way, leave them immediately.
- Don't post anything that you would not want a prospective employer to see.

## Hopeful Statistics

Facebook is a useful resource for job seekers and employers alike, as long as one knows how to properly apply these tools. Here are some statistics that indicate how this particular social network can assist job seekers and how employers can get access to top talent:

- The average user spends one in every seven minutes on Facebook.
- Around 22 million people surveyed admitted they used social media to find their last job.
- Approximately 52% of people seeking employment used Facebook for their job search.
- Eighty-four percent of job seekers are already active Facebook users.

Facebook has evolved from a place where people can connect socially to a platform where anyone can conduct business and/or recruitment efforts.

## To Conclude

Job seekers who choose to utilize Facebook's search and networking resources should remember to keep their professional online presence as balanced as possible. While Facebook certainly has its advantages, LinkedIn is still the leader in professional networking and recruitment.

The same notion also applies to employers. Utilizing the varying services and benefits of several of the most noteworthy networking and social platforms will ensure that job seekers see the open roles you have available within your organization. Our advice is not to merely use one social media outlet, but successfully maintain your presence among all networking sites for the best results.

### *Fred Coon, CEO*

*Stewart, Cooper & Coon, has helped thousands of decision makers and senior executives move up in their careers and achieve significantly improved financial packages within short time frames. Contact Fred Coon – 866-883-4200, Ext. 200*

Remember, your resume will not get you a job - only *you* can do that - but it certainly can prevent you from getting one. If your resume does *not* effectively sell your skills and showcase your experience and achievements, you can bet there are plenty of others in the stack of resumes on the hiring manager's desk that do. An excellent presentation of your talents can increase your chances of getting an interview, where you get the chance to personally sell your qualifications.

A "great" resume is defined differently for everyone, given their particular situation and the job market. That's why there are very few hard and fast rules about the "perfect" resume. What's perfect is what will work best for you in *your* situation. Just because a resume "style" or "format" seems to work for someone you know doesn't mean it will work for you.

## Interview Yourself

You must now become your own professional writer. Because I can't sit across from you and ask questions about your experience and education, (unless you call our office), you must do it yourself. This requires honesty and objectivity. Are you really proficient at *everything you* do? Of course not. On the other hand, don't take any of your applicable skills for granted. It can be a huge mistake to assume an employer knows what you can do simply because they're already in that particular business.

## A Word About Professional Resume Services

If you give it your best shot and still have trouble writing your resume, a Certified Professional Resume Writer (CPRW) may help. CPRWs must pass a challenging test and meet rigid criteria before receiving certification from the Professional Association of Resume Writers (PARW).

Throughout my career in writing, I've created resumes for technical writers and professional journalists who were amazed at the results. That's because I make resumes my specialty. If I needed written documents on integrated circuit design or computer programs, I'd hire a technical writer. If I needed someone to run a company, I'd hire the best executive I could find.

A good CPRW may be able to write better about you simply because that person is *not* you. The best ones know what employers want to see and may have experience in recruiting or corporate human resources. The writer can take an objective look at your background, ask you numerous, in-depth questions, and create a marketing piece that has a strong chance of impressing an employer and increasing your chances of getting a personal interview.

When considering a professional resume writer, ask about CPRW certification, years of experience, any publications, and whether the writer can give you good references. Make sure the person works out of a regular, full-time office, and that this isn't just a sideline business. Additional experience in human resources, recruiting, or top management is a plus, but these are some of the same people we write for every day.

If the writer offers you a flat fee over the phone, remember that this can easily change when they actually see the work involved in writing your resume. The writer should offer a free resume analysis and not even try to quote prices without seeing what's required to create your resume.

## Making the Most of This Book

*Blue Collar Resumes, Third Edition* is designed to help you discover, organize, and market your skills and abilities to employers with the goal of landing interviews. Using sample resumes and the latest ideas about effective resume writing, you should be able to sift through your entire work history, then extract and develop key points about your talents and sell them to the reader—your prospective employer.

Chapters 1 through 7 will walk you through the process: from helping you evaluate past work experience, education, and skills to translating them into powerful selling points. You'll also learn the most effective way to format and organize your achievements, design the finished product, and leverage basic techniques for making job contacts.

Additionally, this book includes more than 100 resume examples, based on resumes that helped my clients land jobs. Of course, the names and particulars have been changed, but the circumstances of each resume represented in this book are "real life." Read through the resumes and study the different formats, designs, and presentations. You can pick and choose elements you like and create your own job-winning resume.

The resume examples in the book were chosen to reflect a spectrum of careers and job descriptions. You may note that some of the jobs represented are not traditional "blue collar" jobs. That's because the definition of "blue collar" has changed over the years. The term used to be interchangeable with "manual labor." However, with advances in technology, traditional blue collar workers--factory workers, assemblers, and construction laborers--are often required to perform technical tasks that have little to do with manual labor.

For instance, an automobile assembly line worker may now need to program and operate complex robotic and CNC equipment for a specific assembly line operation. In the past, products were assembled with basic tools--hammers, socket wrenches, handheld welders, and soldering equipment. Today, high-tech assembly lines require trained personnel to program and operate advanced equipment for high-speed production and quality control. Of course, these workers still get their hands dirty every day, but, for the most part, many jobs that were once labeled "blue collar" require less brawn and more brain.

Many of you reading this book may aspire to jobs in fields not traditionally considered "blue collar." Perhaps you're looking to use newly acquired skills in staff management, quality control, or computer systems. That's why I've included a wide range of examples--executive secretaries, customer service representatives, data entry clerks, and clerical positions--that indeed blur the traditional lines of white collar and blue collar, until the collar becomes somewhat "gray."

People in these "gray collar" positions tend to have more direct contact with both customers and white collar workers within the company, such as executives and sales representatives. These workers, often categorized as "clerical," "support staff," or "customer service" workers, are becoming more recognized as essential to a company's bottom line success. As stated previously, they often deal with the most important person in the corporate food chain--the customer.

I've also included resumes that represent jobs outside the traditional blue collar spectrum. You'll find resume samples for dancers, caterers, travel agents, and medical workers.

No matter what income level you're at, or what type of work you do, this guide is designed to help you increase your income through career advancement. Go ahead and make notes in the margins, fill out the worksheets (or make copies of them so you can change, update, and improve as necessary), or circle phrases and ideas that apply specifically to your situation, as long as this isn't a library book. The point is this--*use it!* The more you involve yourself in this process, the better you'll understand what makes a successful resume--and the better your chances of getting hired for the job you deserve.

# Chapter 1

# Get Started: Assessing Your Skills

Whenever I write a resume, I think about what runs through the minds of prospective employers as they read the resume:

### *What can you do for me?*

Employers must see clear, concise reasons to consider you as soon as they pick up your resume. Keep throwing reasons at them, especially relevant keywords related to your skills and industry preference. The more you give them, the better. Put yourself in their shoes and pretend that you're reading a resume from someone you've never met. Is it enough to write that you're "skilled" in customer service? Or do you need to be specific? Compare a simplistic statement on your resume to this one: "Personally communicate with staff, management, and customers regarding company procedures and product lines."

Take some time to think about how you would answer employers' questions regarding your communication skills, leadership talent, technical knowledge, computer systems, ability to train and motivate others, and how you can produce results.

In the following pages, you'll find worksheets to help you identify your skills, work experience, and achievements – in detail. This may be the most important step in developing your resume. Completing these forms will help you pull out and develop your most important transferable skills, training, work duties, and accomplishments to answer some of the most common questions of prospective employers. The forms will help *you* learn more about yourself and make you more confident as you pursue exciting new opportunities and walk into job interviews.

Take some time as you work through these pages. If necessary, review performance evaluations from previous jobs, ask co-workers for honest assessments of your skills and strengths, and give some thought as to which aspects of your work you're best at and, most importantly, love the most.

# Get Started: Assessing Your Skills

## YOUR PERSONAL INVENTORY

**Name**

First ___

Last ___

**Address**

Street _____

City _____ State _____ Zip

**Telephone:** Area Code _____ / _____

**E-mail Address:** _____

**Desired Position or Industry:** _____

**EMPLOYMENT (List most relevant jobs first)**

From Company _____

____ **19** ____ City and State _____

To _____ Type of Business

____ 19 ___ Product or Service

Positions or Titles _____

Responsibilities and Duties ____

Supervisory Duties: _____

Accomplishments or Major Achievements _____


From Company _____

____ **19** ____ City and State _____

To _____ Type of Business

____ 19 ___ Product or Service

Positions or Titles _____

Responsibilities and Duties ____

Supervisory Duties: _____

Accomplishments or Major Achievements _____

**EMPLOYMENT**

From          Company _____

____19___City and State ____

To          Type of Business_____

___ 19___Product or Service_____

Positions or Titles_____

Responsibilities and Duties ____

Supervisory Duties_____

Accomplishments or Major Achievements_____


From          Company _____

____19___City and State ____

To          Type of Business_____

____19___ Product or Service_____

Positions or Titles_____

Responsibilities and Duties ____

Supervisory Duties_____

Accomplishments or Major Achievements_____

**EMPLOYMENT**

From          Company _____

____19 __City and State ____

To          Type of Business_____

____19___Product or Service

Positions or Titles_____

Responsibilities and Duties ____

Supervisory Duties_____

Accomplishments or Major Achievements_____


From          Company _____

____ 19___ City and State ____

To        Type of Business

_____19____Product or Service

Positions or Titles_____

Responsibilities and Duties _____

Supervisory Duties

Accomplishments or Major Achievements_____

**EDUCATION (Most recent first)**

**College**_____

**City/State**_____

Degree_____Year_____

Major_____Minor_____GPA_____

Coursework/Studies_____

Achievements/Activities_____

**College**_____

**City/State**_____

Degree_____Year_____

Major_____Minor_____GPA_____

Coursework/Studies_____

Achievements/Activities_____

**Awards/Scholarships**_____

**Seminars and Special Training**_____

**Vocational/Trade School**_____

**City/State**_____

Certificate_____Dates Attended_____

Awards/Achievements_____

Special Jobs/Equipment_____

**Vocational/Trade School**_____

**City/State**_____

Certificate_____ Dates Attended_____

Awards/Achievements_____

Special Jobs/Equipment_____

High School_____

Dates Attended _____

City/State_____

Achievements/Activities_____

**Military Service_____**

Dates Enlisted_____

Special Skills/Training_____

Awards/Achievements_____

Honorable Discharge? _____Rank_____

## PROFESSIONAL MEMBERSHIPS

Organization_____Dates_____

Offices Held_____

Duties/Responsibilities_____

Skills Acquired_____

Organization_____ Dates_____

Offices Held_____

Duties/Responsibilities_____

Skills Acquired_____

Organization_____ Dates_____

Offices Held_____

Duties/Responsibilities_____

Skills Acquired

Organization_____ Dates_____

Offices Held_____

Duties/Responsibilities_____

Skills Acquired

## COMMUNITY SERVICES and VOLUNTEER ACTIVITIES

Organization_____

Offices/Titles Held_____

City/State_____Dates_____

Specific activities in which you were involved and skills utilized

Organization _____

Offices/Titles Held_____

City /State_____Dates_____

Specific activities in which you were involved and skills utilized_____

Organization_____

Offices/Titles Held_____

City/State_____ Dates_____

Specific activities in which you were involved and skills utilized_____

**PERSONAL INTERESTS, SPORTS, and HOBBIES**

_____

_____

_____

# References

**Business:**

Name_____Title_____

Company Name _____

Company Address_____

Telephone, Office_____ Home (optional) _____

Name_____ Title_____

Company Name _____

Company Address_____

Telephone, Office _____Home (optional) _____

Name_____ Title_____

Company Name _____ Company Address_____

Telephone, Office_____ Home (optional) _____

**Personal:**

Name_____Profession_____

Telephone, Office_____ Home (optional) _____

Name_____Profession

Telephone, Office_____ Home (optional)_____

Name_____Profession_____

Telephone, Office_____ Home (optional)_____

# Chapter 2

# Organize Your Resume for High Impact

A resume is your opportunity to promote and sell your talents, and put yourself in the very best light to communicate your unique achievements, special skills, and one-of-a-kind experience.

Because each of us has different experience, skills, and achievements, there isn't *one perfect way* to organize a resume. In this chapter, we'll take a look at the three most common resume formats to determine which may work best for *you.*

1. **Chronological format.** The chronological format is the most commonly used resume format. It emphasizes your work history, positioning it either first on the resume or following the Job Objective section or Title. The employment history is listed in order of the most recent job first. Most people use this format because it is simple and straightforward – and it is what most human resources professionals are used to seeing. If you've had a steady work history, and you've gained skills and achievements as you have progressed, this might be a good format for you.

   The main problem with this format, however, is that it emphasizes most *recent* experience. So, if you're applying for a position as a manicurist, for example, and your most recent job was in retail sales, your resume might get tossed in the reject pile before the reader notices that you'd been doing nails for 15 years prior to your last job.

   The chronological format may also be troublesome for the person who has had an erratic job history – gaps in employment are made apparent by the chronological listing of jobs, and may raise questions in the reader's mind.

2. **Functional format.** A functional format begins with a listing or summary of your skills, combined with duties and achievements from your various positions. The idea is to communicate abilities and strengths that the prospective employer might be seeking. The only details about job history will be as they relate to the skills you highlight, and they may not include work dates or names of employers.

   For example, if you were seeking a job as a cook for a catering company, you might list that you'd cooked meals for 400 people for a six-month period while at sea. You wouldn't, however, mention that this was part of your tour of duty in the Navy 12 years ago.

   Often, job seekers use this format to downplay gaps in work history or the fact that they're jumping into a new career. Homemakers or military personnel returning to the workforce often use this format. However, studies have shown that the functional format is the *least liked* among employers and recruiters. That's because it groups all your skills, job experience, and achievements *out of context,* with no clear explanation of when and where they took place. A functional resume can send up red flags to readers--who may suspect that you're trying to hide something.

3. **Combination format.** Here's the one I like the most, because it's a combination of what's best of the functional and chronological formats. Typically, a combination resume begins with a strong Profile/Experience section to sell your skills and abilities that are directly related to the job you're seeking. (You may or may not include the word "Profile" or "Experience" to introduce this section on your final document.) Then you can demonstrate how you applied or acquired these skills by following it with a Job History/Employment section (sometimes called the "Experience" section, if "Profile" is used for the skill section above), and Education/Training sections, if applicable.

This is the format that typically works best for my clients. It develops and markets your skills up front, which are then reinforced with job duties and accomplishments in context. This approach reassures the reader that you have nothing to hide by offering details about work history. In the combination format, you may also incorporate volunteer jobs and non-paid experience into your chronology of jobs and experience. This is fine, as long as you don't try to lead the reader into thinking they were paid positions. We've found the combination format to be a winning format for most people. Many clients tell us they've received a 10-percent to 20-percent response rate. In other words, many will get one or two interviews for every 10 resumes they send out.

Note that throughout the samples in this book, I've used the word "Experience" for your employment history; then I use "Profile" for the skill-oriented section on top. The words are interchangeable. You may omit any title for your Profile section and use "Experience, Employment, or Career History" for your job section.

## Job Search Facts

## You Are Not Alone

A recent *Business News Daily* study found that 84% of workers are unhappy in their current position and will look for a new job this year (2011).

# Reaching for the Ideal Position

Imagine yourself in the ideal position. What would you actually be *doing* day to day and hour to hour? When I was an HR director and reviewing resumes, my requirements were simple--the candidate had to:

-- Demonstrate on paper that you have considered the requirements of the position.
-- Effectively pre-sort your transferable skills and specific work duties/experience in terms of relevance.
-- Clearly spell out those relevant skills and abilities at the very top of your resume, typically in your Profile/Experience section.
-- Write clear, high-impact job descriptions, developing and quantifying your duties and achievements at each position.

Because time is tight during a job search, and the competition can be intense, the trick is to get as much *relevant* information across to the reader as quickly as possible. In most cases, the best ways you can do this are the following:

-- Match your skills and abilities to those demanded by the job.
-- Back this up with evidence, in context--your on-the-job achievements and accomplishments.

# Keeping Your Resume "Honest"

Remember that hiring managers are often in a hurry to get someone on the job. When they come across too many adjectives, or get a sense that an applicant is trying too hard to sound perfect or discuss their softer, personal attributes (best developed in the cover letter) rather than communicate business-related skills and qualifications, they may just assume you don't have them. They'll go on to the next resume in the stack and look for essential items.

If you find yourself embellishing too much, maybe you need to look closely at what your skills really are. When employers come across too many "fluff" words, such as "self-motivated," "computer literate," or "hard working," they may simply not read the Profile/Experience section at the top of your resume and just quickly scan your jobs. Then all that expensive paper and typesetting were for nothing! That's why I always remind people that it's *content* that matters most.

There's another reason for leaving out the "fluff." If employers think you're trying to embellish too much in your writing, they may wonder, "What is this person trying to cover up? A lack of genuine skill? A rocky job history?"

Never lie on your resume. Someday your boss may ask you to do something you can't do, and there goes your credibility and your job. You must be able to back up everything on your resume during an interview, so it's up to you to develop your most important and relevant skills in light of the work you're seeking, and that's much easier to do when you give yourself credit for your real talents, spell them out simply, and then position them to their best advantage.

## Job Search Facts

## Identify and Market Your Best Attributes

Starting to feel underqualified? Don't worry, because here are four more reasons why your Profile/Experience section can be so helpful. According to a survey by the American Society of Training and Development, the top four qualities employers are looking for today are the following:

1.  The ability to learn.
2.  The ability to listen and convey information.
3.  The ability to solve problems in innovative ways.
4.  The knowledge of how to get things done.

# Resume Essentials

You already gathered all the details you'll need to begin writing your resume when you filled out the worksheets in the previous chapter. But before we begin, let's review the definitions and importance of all the different pieces of information your resume may include:

1.  **Name, address, email and phone number--preferably your cell phone/home number.** Hard to believe, but as a corporate recruiter, I actually received resumes without phone numbers! Needless to say, those applicants didn't get far with our company. Be sure you've listed all your contact information correctly. Avoid listing your work number if still employed, unless your boss knows you're leaving, or you can speak in private.
2.  **Job titles.** These titles can be changed to be understood by as many employers as possible. For instance, "Entry-level Landscaper" can simply be written as "Landscaper." Don't, however, give yourself a "promotion," listing a title that implies more responsibility than you actually had.
3.  **Company names and dates.** Unless you've had four or five jobs shorter than one year and are writing a purely functional resume, include company names and the locations (city *and* state, unless they're local). Use months as well as years, or omit months if it helps you leave out jobs or cover your tracks, but be consistent! Notice different ways of listing dates throughout the resume samples in this book.
4.  **Job duties.** Identify key duties in your jobs, including an overall "big picture" of your daily responsibilities; then include more specific job functions. Follow this section with bulleted achievements--quantified when possible--and how you exceeded job expectations. Include part-time employment when it applies to the position desired. You may also include part-time jobs or volunteer work that shows initiative, self-motivation, and leadership, as well as organizational and communication skills.
5.  **Licenses and certifications.** Include items most relevant to your career goals or that demonstrate initiative, a desire to learn new ideas, or self-motivation. You might include CDL Driver's

Licenses, certifications for operating vehicles such as forklifts or construction equipment, or insurance and real estate sales licenses, in addition to other applicable credentials such as "HAZMAT Certified." Additionally, include civil service or government grades and classifications when appropriate for the type of job you're seeking.

6. **Education.** List the highest level reached first. Avoid listing high school if you have a college degree. Education becomes less important as your hands-on work experience grows. Place your Education section following Employment when you have several years of applicable work history. You may include college attendance and course completions even if no degree was earned. Additional professional training should be included, especially if sponsored by an employer; it shows the firm had confidence in your ability to learn and succeed. List which firms sponsored the seminars or college courses. You may also include whether you "self-funded" college costs, if there's space on the page.

   If you're right out of school with no applicable work experience, present your education right after your Profile/Experience section.

7. **Languages.** Fluency in a foreign language may be extremely valuable on the job. List your level of proficiency: "Speak conversational French," "Fluent in Spanish," "Read and write Italian," "Familiar with Russian." These can be mentioned in a communications bullet in your Profile/Experience section or near the bottom in a Personal section, as shown in some of the resume samples in this book.

8. **Professional memberships.** List trade and professional groups if they're relevant to your future job. This demonstrates an active interest in industry developments and that you share ideas with others in your field. These affiliations can prove very valuable in your job search when you get to personal networking.

# Eliminate from Your Resume

What you leave out of your resume is just as important was what you include. I get asked about these items all the time. They're best discussed with potential employers, rather than included on your resume, as they stand more chance of working against you than for you.

1. **Salary requirements/history.** When employers want to know your salary requirements, they generally want to know if they can afford you--or how cheaply they can get you. They also want to make sure they don't end up paying more than they need to fill the position. If this is requested in the job posting or advertisement, you may include it, but on a separate "Salary History" sheet and never on the resume itself.

## Job Search Facts

## Send It Anyway

Writer and manager Stan Wynett conducted one of my favorite surveys, and it was printed in the *National Business Employment Weekly.* According to his survey of more than 200 employers who posted job openings stating, "Resumes without salary history will not be considered," more than 90 percent said they would *still call* a candidate if they thought they were right for the job, even if salary history or requirements were not included! Essentially, if they like you enough, they'll call, if only to learn more about your salary requirements. Then when you have them on the phone, you can ask about other factors or benefits, such as insurance, a company car, location, advancement potential, and so on.

If salary information is not requested, then do not offer it; you could be knocked out of consideration for being over- or underpriced. Another option is to mention a salary range in a cover letter ("I am seeking compensation between $60,000 and $67,000"), or state a range that you would be willing to accept. It's best, however, to avoid discussion of salary until you've hooked the employer. Once you get an offer, *then* you can negotiate compensation.

2. **"Resume" at the top of the page or "References Available Upon Request" at the end.** If the person reading your resume can't tell it's a resume, you don't want to work for them! As for references, create a separate References sheet, with three or four names, titles, and phone numbers of previous supervisors, if you are sure they will give you a positive reference, and make sure they know that you're using their name. You should print these on the same paper stock as your resume. Bring this page, along with your resume, to complete the job application.

   The personnel representative or hiring manager may want to call a former employer; usually someone will check with you before contacting your current employer. Double-check this at the interview if you are concerned about keeping your job search confidential.

3. **Reasons for leaving a job.** Never include this information on your resume--you want to highlight positives, not negatives. The only exception to this is if you were promoted or transferred within a company. Why? Because this shows continuity and growth--*positive* reasons. Even if your reasons for leaving a company are good (another company or headhunter sought you out and hired you away), you don't want a prospective employer focusing on this and wondering whether you'll be a loyal employee.

   You may be asked why you left a particular position during the interview, and you should be prepared to answer these questions then. Rehearse a concise response with as positive a spin as possible. Check these two chapters: *At Last: The Interview* and *Motivation and Inspiration, Get Your Career in Gear,* later in this book.

4. **Religious or political groups.** This type of information has a chance of working against you, so don't offer it unless you know it will be perceived positively. Try to put business considerations first. What do these associations have to do with the position you're seeking? Like anything else, if it won't actually help you get in the door, leave it out.

   If you have little or no job history, but lots of experience with churches, synagogues, schools, or service groups, (Kiwanis, Boy Scouts, and so on), then you should develop and include this background on your resume. You may also extract your best communication, organizational, and leadership skills used with these groups and paraphrase them in your Profile/Experience section.

5. **Any negative information.** Remember that to many employers, resume reading is a process of elimination, so don't give the reader any reason to take you out of the running. Never mention a bad experience with a former supervisor and avoid including any item that could be seen as affecting your performance on the job--for example, the fact that you were unemployed for two years because of an illness. True, this information may be disclosed to the employer at some point, but you don't have to "spill your guts" up front in your resume.

6. **A photograph.** Unless you're applying for a job as a model, don't include a picture or any other physical description of yourself. First, while it may be both illegal and unethical to select employees based on looks, if you provide a photo you open yourself up to being considered based on your appearance. Don't subject yourself to the personal biases of the HR department or hiring supervisor.

# Optional Items

1. **Title.** If you're applying at a large company that may be hiring for many positions at the same time, this component will help to quickly match your position to the job you're seeking. If, however, you are *more* interested in getting hired by the company, and less interested in what job you are hired for, you might consider dropping the title.

2. **Objective.** This element helps define and summarize your job goals so that the reader can quickly determine what you're seeking. It also, however, focuses on what *you* want. That's fine, as long as

you know for certain that what you want matches *exactly* with what the employer wants. Objectives are best when they're specific and focused rather than broad and vague.

3. **Military service.** You should include any positive experience in the military, especially technical skills acquired. If you're seeking a position with a firm involved in defense contracting that hires former military personnel, you may be just what they're looking for. Include highest rank attained, supervisory experience, and applicable training. For technical positions, include systems and equipment operated, repaired, or maintained.

   If your only applicable work experience was in the military, then this must be developed like any other job. On the other hand, if you're looking for work that's completely unrelated to skills gained during your time in the military, you may only list highest rank attained and city and state of deployment.

   Your Profile/Experience section is a great place to extract and develop your best, transferable skills *out of context* for the reader. In other words, develop skills in this section without mentioning military-specific items. Write them using business-oriented language, in terms the hiring manager can understand and apply to his or her business needs.

4. **A "Personal" or "Interests" section.** If you need to fill room at the bottom of the page, include two to three lines outlining your interests. But make sure the interests you choose match in some way the skills and responsibilities demanded by the job. For example, if you're applying for a job as a clerk in a fabric store, definitely add "sewing" as a hobby.

   The interests you list may also represent *indirect* skills that may reflect positively on your potential. For example, playing on a recreational sports team may indicate that you work well with others--you're a "team" player and you live a healthy lifestyle. Your involvement in Big Brothers or Sisters shows you may be a good role model and have leadership potential.

   Omit items that have no connection to tackling the job, especially pastimes that might be considered controversial or in conflict with the job. (You're applying for a job at the humane society? Probably not a good idea to mention your passion for taxidermy.)

5. **Age and marital status.** Legally, these two items should have no bearing on whether you're called in for an interview. But let's face it--some employers still discriminate based on age and marital status. Revealing your age can label you as too young or too old. What if you're twice as old as the president of the company or half as old as the average manager? You may be perfect for the job, but such prejudice can run deep. Leave out your age altogether, and get the reader to focus on your relevant skills and abilities.

   Omit marital status, unless this will demonstrate a certain stability and improve your chances of getting an interview, or if you are applying for a job that specifically requests a husband-and-wife team, such as cross-country truckers, bed-and-breakfast managers, etc.

# One Page or Two?

Contrary to popular belief, one page is not always best. Two-page resumes earned a bad reputation years ago because people were putting too much useless information on them. They were writing long, irrelevant job histories or expanding too much on their personal likes and dislikes, hobbies, and so on.

Remember to think in terms of relevance rather than the number of pages. We write plenty of two-page resumes for our Blue Collar clients. Unless you have an extensive and relevant work history, or a detailed technical background of more than five years, try to keep your resume to one page--just don't leave out important skills simply to force your resume onto one page!

Remember, what counts most is the *content* of your resume. So think in terms of an advertisement. You want to grab your reader's attention by highlighting the benefits that your experience and skills will bring to the position. Whether that takes one page or two depends upon how many benefits you have to offer.

# Chapter 3
# Using a Title or Objective

Expert resume writers disagree about the value of including job Objectives or Titles in resumes. Some people claim the two elements are unnecessary and just take up space. Others believe such components add focus to the resume and quickly tell a busy employer exactly what position or type of work the applicant is seeking. First, let's define each element, and then we'll examine its merits and weaknesses.

## The Title

The more straightforward of the two elements is the Title, and its purpose is self-explanatory. It's two to four words that define the exact title of a position or *type of work* you're looking for, centered at the top of your resume, and typically presented in all-caps. A Title sets the tone of your resume; it quickly tells a busy reader what you'd like to do for them--and how to think about you while reading your resume.

When using a Title to apply for a specific position, use the exact words presented in the advertisement or job posting. For example, in previous jobs you may have been called a Line Supervisor, but if a position is advertised for "Production Team Captain," *that's* what you want to use as your title, because that's *the exact job you're going for.* Note that if you think you can tackle the position, it's OK to use those words in your Title, even if you've never had that exact title on a job.

On the other hand, if you're merely interested in working for a company in any capacity, and would explore other job openings with them, then don't limit yourself to a specific job title. In that case, use a wide-ranging, general Title such as **PRODUCTION OPERATIONS** or **MANAGEMENT / OPERATIONS.**

The Title is easily changed with every resume you send out, and it should be tailored to suit the job opening. Examples include the following:

-- CARPENTRY / CONSTRUCTION
-- PRODUCTION MANAGEMENT or MANUFACTURING / OPERATIONS
-- MECHANIC: Production Equipment (update type of equipment as needed)
-- WAREHOUSING / DISTRIBUTION or WAREHOUSE OPERATIONS
-- ROUTE DRIVER or ROUTE SALES REPRESENTATIVE

## The Objective

An Objective is simply a short statement that describes the job you want--or what you can *and* want to do for your next employer. It appears at the top of the resume, directly after your name and contact information.

Objectives have been criticized for being too long, wordy, self-oriented, and subjective. I believe, however, that there are times when it can enhance your resume. For example, if you know exactly what you want to do and your job goal matches perfectly with the job you're applying for, then by all means introduce your resume with a targeted Objective that zeroes in on the job.

An Objective may also be important if your current job goal doesn't exactly match your past experience. Perhaps your past three jobs have been in retail sales, but you're applying for a position as a daycare worker. Without a short, well-written Objective at the top of your resume, the resume screener may discard your resume as he or she scans your experience and doesn't see a connection.

Because it's so important that the Objective and prospective job responsibilities are in agreement, it's best to customize the Objective for each resume you send out.

The best Objectives are specific, including a job title and indicating clear focus. Here are some examples:

**OBJECTIVE:**          Quality Control Supervisor: A position where leadership and profit-building skills would be utilized.

This example lists a general department, Shipping and Receiving, but not a specific job title.

**OBJECTIVE**:          A position in Shipping and Receiving, where proven abilities in packing, distribution, and accurate record keeping would be of value.

Here's an example that mentions an overall industry: Construction, but not a specific job title in that industry:

**OBJECTIVE:**          A position utilizing 11 years in Construction (or plant) operations, where a strict attention to detail (or profitability) would be of value.

Of course, you may always omit the heading "Objective" and jump right in, with a descriptor below the initial 1-4 word Title:

### *TRANSPORTATION / LOGISTICS*

A position leveraging skills in cost-effective freight routing, warehousing, and transportation.

Because a company may be hiring for many different positions, an Objective or Title will quickly help the reader understand what job you're shooting for. If you're interested in a broad range of jobs within a given company, you may consider omitting these components. If so, use a TITLE, followed by a Combination format, and be sure the first Profile/Experience bullet gives the reader a big picture of the types of skills and knowledge you offer. This puts additional importance on the Profile/Experience section of your resume, as discussed in Chapter 2.

# Pack Action into Your Resume

To pack the most punch into your resume, you must think like an advertiser: the product is *you* and your *hard-earned skills.* Use words that add strength to descriptions of your work experience, abilities, and training. As the Madison Avenue types would say, *"Make it sizzle."* True, your statements and listings will tend to be written in short, brief, and succinct phrases, but that doesn't mean they have to be boring or passive.

# Professional Writer's Tip

It's okay to use sentences that take "I," "we," "he," "she," and other pronouns for granted and omit these words altogether, except in the cover letter. Use the abbreviated third-person form shown in the Profile/Experience sections in this book. This is more direct. It helps you get straight to your qualifications and *sell* them. When space is tight, however, or if you must have all of your qualifications on one page, you can reduce the Profile/Experience section to one or two short paragraphs with bullets.

Go for strong, action-oriented words when describing your experiences. Avoid passive-sounding verbs such as "did," "was," and "used." Use more powerful descriptors like "exceeded," "increased," "accomplished," and "directed" whenever possible. Try to vary the words you choose; while "achieved" is a terrific word to describe your accomplishments on the job, it loses impact if you repeat it in each bulleted listing.

When developing your resume, keep a dictionary and perhaps a thesaurus by your side. A thesaurus will help you find synonyms for commonly used words when you're searching for a fresh way to describe a similar experience.

The following list includes some powerful, high-impact words you might find helpful when writing your resume:

| | | | |
|---|---|---|---|
| Achieved | Demonstrated | Introduced | Reinforced |
| Adapted | Designed | Investigated | Reorganized |
| Administered | Developed | Maintained | Researched |
| Advised | Drafted | Managed | Restructured |
| Amended | Eliminated | Modified | Reversed |
| Analyzed | Established | Monitored | Reviewed |
| Approved | Evaluated | Motivated | Revised |
| Assigned | Expanded | Organized | Saved |
| Assisted | Expedited | Participated | Scheduled |
| Budgeted | Focused | Performed | Screened |
| Built | Forecasted | Planned | Solved |
| Collected | Formulated | Prepared | Spearheaded |
| Compiled | Generated | Processed | Streamlined |
| Computed | Guided | Produced | Strengthened |
| Conducted | Implemented | Promoted | Structured |
| Controlled | Improved | Proposed | Supervised |
| Coordinated | Increased | Provided | Supported |
| Created | Initiated | Purchased | Taught |
| Cut | Innovated | Recommended | Trained |
| Decreased | Instituted | Recruited | Trimmed |
| Delegated | Interpreted | Reduced | Updated |

# Chapter 4

# The Profile / Experience Section: Market Your Skills

The Profile/Experience section--sometimes known by the weaker term "Summary" --appears at the top of your resume, immediately following the Objective or Title. While there are many ways to "summarize" your background, the type of section I recommend here gives the reader a high-impact, big picture of your most relevant, most important skills and abilities. It gives you the chance to develop and sell your skills in the first 30 seconds, when readers are most interested in knowing what you can do for them.

Your Profile/Experience section may include skills gained in non-paid positions, as well as knowledge acquired through education and training. This is an excellent opportunity to translate all your relevant skills and experiences into transferable skills and abilities. It is a key component of the Combination format, where other sections, such as Employment or Education, serve to support it with facts and figures about your on-the-job work experience, results, and achievements.

# Why Use a Profile / Experience Section?

Some people think it's enough to list their jobs on their resume. However, when you sift through your transferable skills and spell them out for the reader, right on top of your resume, you'll always have a better chance of getting your foot in the door. With a strong summary, you're in charge of what you want the employer to know about you. As stated, your work history typically follows this section (unless recent training or college work is more relevant to your goals) to support your statements with evidence and detail.

Here's an example of how effective a summary like this can be. I once wrote a short Profile/Experience section--only six lines of text--for a new college graduate. He sent out 20 resumes and received four job offers in just the first two weeks! (See Larry Capp's *Graduate* resume.

A well-written summary section gives you control over what direction to market yourself: what skills to emphasize, what skills to downplay, and what key words to include. Without it, you're at the mercy of your job history or education, and your resume is like a ship without a rudder.

Your Experience section may contain marketable skills and abilities, *whether or not you've used them on the job*. Spell out your most relevant skills and abilities, regardless of where you learned those skills. You can list just about any skill, aptitude, or training with the right qualifying words. Start with the skills you deem to be most relevant and thus most valued by the prospective employer--*and* that are your strongest.

Use data from the worksheets in Chapter 1, and think about how best to extract and present your skills and abilities from your actual work duties and training. Think of it this way: you use your skills to *do things* on a job; now it's time to *isolate and develop* those skills apart from job duties at the top of your resume.

This section should be kept to one to three bulleted paragraphs for a one-page resume, and two to five bulleted paragraphs for a two-page resume.

# Professional Writer's Tip

The very first bullet or paragraph of your Profile/Experience section should act as an umbrella over your specific skills. It gives the reader a snapshot of where you're coming from and what type of strengths and abilities you will bring to the new position.

Begin your Profile/Experience section with that umbrella statement about overall skills and industry knowledge that best matches the type of work you're seeking.

These might be analytical skills (production line setup, systems, or familiarity with specific equipment) or communication skills (written, speaking, reporting, or creating graphs and charts).

Here's a list of sentence starters with stronger words near the top:

- ▶ Proficient in...
- ▶ Comprehensive experience in...
- ▶ Experience in...
- ▶ Extensive knowledge of...
- ▶ Skilled in...
- ▶ Proven abilities in..
- ▶ Perform...
- ▶ Plan and conduct...
- ▶ Plan and implement...
- ▶ Train and supervise staff in...
- ▶ Utilize...
- ▶ Knowledge of...
- ▶ Familiar with...
- ▶ Trained in...

Think about how your qualifications can be shaped into phrases that your prospective boss would appreciate. Write down everything you think of--then narrow it down and make a short list of those items you feel are most applicable to the desired position.

# Keep It Relevant

The main goal here is to keep your Experience section relevant to both your needs and the employer's. This section is about overall ability. A trainee, intern, or new entrant into the job market may have many abilities and very little work history. I've found that one of the best ways to get someone in the door for an interview is to market all of his or her relevant ability and knowledge, regardless of where it was attained.

If you're still having trouble starting this section, simply think of the type of skills or training you have that would be useful or relevant, or shows an aptitude for the next job. Then extract those skills and develop them. Here are some examples:

-- Skilled in the repair and maintenance of mechanical (or electrical) systems, including pumps and conveyors for plastic molding systems.
-- Assist in report preparation and analysis, data compilation, and review.
-- Plan and conduct written and oral presentations in a professional manner for work crews and supervisors.
-- Familiar with production line setup, streamlining, teardown, and quality control for a Fortune 500 company specializing in automotive parts.

This information, combined with your education and knowledge of the field, will all help project you as able to walk in, tackle the responsibilities, and succeed in your new job.

# Group Similar Skills Together

When you have more than a few skills to highlight, always try to group those skills together. Here are some examples of bullet points for your Profile/Experience section, organized into skill sets. Notice how each paragraph attempts to build on the previous one. You may use such groupings as the following:

## Mechanical skills

- Skilled in the setup, repair, and daily maintenance of production, packaging, and product testing equipment.
- Strong aptitude in the repair and maintenance of mechanical systems, including industrial packaging and CNC manufacturing equipment.
- Comprehensive experience as Journeyman Carpenter, including rough frame construction, trim work, and quality control for custom-built homes and commercial structures.
- Trained in the operation and repair of punch presses, slitters, shrink wrappers, and conveyor systems.

Here's another example of a Profile/Experience section. Have you ever helped train, supervise, motivate, or simply orient or coordinate production staff? If so, your next bullet in the Profile/Experience section may use some or all of the following items:

## Training skills

- Assist in staff training and supervision in production line setup, assembly operations, quality control, and packing and shipping.
- Skilled in group and individual training of work crews and support staff (and supervisors), with full responsibility for the design of training and performance testing programs.

In all cases, try to avoid overused, general statements such as, "excellent communication skills" and instead give the reader specifics. Without details and examples, your statements could read as "fluff." For instance, in the following example, the writer offers specific applications for good communication skills, both written and oral:

## Communication skills

- Plan and conduct written and oral presentations in a professional manner.
- Assist in staff training, performance reviews, and written documentation.
- Compile and present production status reports to management regarding quality, cost overruns, defects, and shortages.
- Closely monitor and report on quantities, parts, components, component/finished good prices, labor costs, and quality levels.

With a strong Profile/Experience section as the backbone of your resume, you have an excellent opportunity to summarize and showcase your strengths. It's a great way to demonstrate your written communication skills, and it quickly tells the reader that you're a candidate worth getting to know better. Take the time to carefully craft this section--the potential payoff is well worth the effort.

# Chapter 5

# Employment: Build an Impressive History

The Employment section has been the heart of all traditional resumes. In the Chronological format, it comes up front, following the name and contact information and the Objective or Title.

In the Functional resume, however, the Employment (job chronology) section may be replaced by a modified Profile/Experience section, which highlights and summarizes job duties, achievements, and various skills out of context--not listed under company names or locations. That's why I don't recommend a purely Functional resume because employers typically want to know when and where you worked, and what you did at specific jobs. The Functional resume sidesteps this important element, and employers may think you're trying to hide a rocky job history.

In any case, a clear, chronological Employment section (sometimes called an *Experience section,* if the word Profile is used for your summary on top) is one of the most structured elements of your resume. This is where you tell the reader what you've done or achieved at other companies, in context. Here's where you back up and verify the statements about skills and abilities in your Profile/Experience section. Almost always, your previous jobs are listed in reverse chronological order--that is, your most recent work experience is listed first, below that the previous job, and so forth.

Each separate job listing in your Employment section will include the following components:

-- **Company name.** Use the complete name, avoiding nicknames or abbreviations that may not be familiar to the reader.
-- **Company location.** Use city and state only, and don't list the company phone number--you want the employer to call *you* first.
-- **Your job title.** You might consider "translating" your title to a more universal title if the internal label is unusual or unfamiliar to other work environments. Just don't "promote" yourself to a job level you didn't really have.
-- **Dates of employment.** Use year *and* month. However, you may omit the month, particularly if you have a history of longevity--staying with employers for many years. In this case, as long as the years are correct for the jobs you're listing, you could leave out irrelevant jobs lasting only a few months.
-- **Brief job description.** Don't take a lot of space to do this. One to three sentences should be enough to give the reader a general idea of what you do. Also, chances are the prospective employer has a good idea of what the job involves, especially if you're applying for the same type of position.
   Be specific whenever possible. For example, if you supervise people as part of your responsibilities, indicate how many employees report to you. If you're in charge of a budget, include the amount. If there is anything unique or unusual about the job that the title or general description doesn't reveal, be sure to mention that as well (for example: "Travel to offices in Mexico six times a year.").
-- **Achievements at each position.** Here's where you get to brag a little. Employers love to see achievements, accomplishments, and results that demonstrate excellence and self-motivation on the job. Here you can list awards and explain their meaning. Typically, this information will appear in a list or bulleted format, which helps catch the reader's eye and break the monotony of gray type throughout your resume.

   -- Ranked #1 in quality control among 18 QC representatives and earned a vacation to Hawaii.
   -- Increased this department's profit margin from 18% to 21%.
   -- Developed more effective production techniques, reducing downtime by 12% and slashing defects by 80%.

Check the resumes in this book; they're loaded with achievements and quantifiable, verifiable results. Did you increase the efficiency of operations? Reduce downtime? Speed production or inventory turns? How much money did you save the company by introducing a new maintenance procedure, system, operation, or piece of equipment?

Try to give the reader a scope and perspective to understand your achievements. What percentage of overall revenues? How many others were you competing with for the top sales award? Do this without misrepresenting yourself and without using generic language or vague wording like "excellent communication skills," "self-motivated," or "computer literate."

When you proofread your resume, ask yourself whether your descriptions of achievements could apply to just anyone or uniquely yourself. Step back and look deeper into your skill sets. What *measurable* results did you bring about in your previous jobs in terms of dollars saved or earned, time saved, or production increased?

Think about what you really mean by phrases such as "excellent communication skills," for example. Does that mean you can research and write (or produce) status reports for staff and management? If so, on what subjects or topics: product or material costs, finished goods, labor costs, or quality? And how did you perform them in your previous job? Did you win awards? Get promotions? Improve conditions?

If you find yourself trying to stretch the truth, then maybe you're not right for the position you're shooting for. It's time to reassess and look at yourself more objectively.

Are your talents transferable to other fields or markets? Someone with strong mechanical skills should be able to learn how to repair and maintain different types of equipment.

Following are two examples of high-impact job descriptions. Note the overall layout, including placement of dates off to the right (to de-emphasize) and the company name emphasized with an underline. This emphasis creates an "umbrella" effect over the job title and description. Also note that the bullets are used sparingly and only for emphasis of various key achievements. In addition, the first sentence gives an overall, big picture description of daily duties. Following is a breakdown of specific duties.

EXPERIENCE

Mitsubishi Semiconductor America. Inc., Durham, NC                                          1/85-3/09

**Quality Assurance Operations / Test Production**
Performed functional, electrical, in-process and final inspections on a wide range of semiconductor materials and devices. Responsible for detailed, quality-level checks and visual audits on modules; assembled and tested devices during various production processes.
Conducted group and individual training for up to 16 workers in all production line testing and quality control procedures.

- Trained team members on statistical process control and electro-static discharge.
- Operated x-ray machines, microscopes, digital calipers, component testers and lead bend machines, as well as tape & reel for discreet devices and Topaz soldering equipment for PC boards.
- Directly involved in packaging, assembly lines, and topaz line procedures; utilized acoustic and other precision measurement instruments in a class-10 clean-room environment.

In the next example, the applicant had originally supplied a vague description, something like "Level I Shop Assistant." So I changed it to something more descriptive, to give the reader a better sense of what he did:

EMPLOYMENT:          Dreisilker Electrical Motors. Glen Ellyn, IL          7/76-Present
                     **Shop Repair and Maintenance**
                     Responsible for training and supervising up to 4 in all shop procedures, including

the complete teardown, repair, assembly and test running of electrical motors. Gained extensive skills with a wide range of equipment, including the troubleshooting and maintenance of:

- Sleeve and ball-bearing motors up to 5,000 h.p.
- Medium and large generators, slip-ring motors and vertical high-thrust hollow shaft pump motors.
- AC and DC motors up to 5,000 h.p.
- Medium and large induction synchronous motors, as well as eddy current clutch motors.

- Repair special grinder and hermetic motors, including removing stators and installing medium and large vertical motor thrust pumps.
- Install and braze rotor bars and connect end rings.
- Inspect and measure shafts and bearing housings.
- Produce status reports for management.

Remember that bullets add white space, give the eye a focal point, and help break up gray blocks of type - but don't use bullets on every line, or they lose impact. In the Employment section, you should be concentrating on specific job duties and achievements, measured as much as possible in terms such as dollars, percentages, and numbers. For example, if you helped revise a procedure that saved the company time or money, then you should indicate how many hours, days, or months, and significant dollars or percentages.

A note about dates: If you've been working for a long time, we sometimes move job experiences that occurred 18 or more years ago into a section labeled "Prior Experience." Of course, an employer will be most interested in your most recent experience. If your "ancient" work history is irrelevant or adds nothing to your credentials, you may want to leave it off entirely. But if those experiences do enhance your overall value, you can still mention them, but just minimize them so you have space to focus on your current skills and experience.

Your employment history isn't the only measure of your experience that prospective employers will want to know about. They'll also need to know about your education, special training, certifications, and other credentials that provided the skills and knowledge you need for your next job. The layout and design of your Education section is explored in the next chapter.

# Chapter 6
# Education: Develop Your Strongest Credentials

How should you list your formal education, training, special courses, and required certifications? This all depends on relevance. Remember, your resume is your "advertisement," your personal marketing piece; you want to *lead* with the information that will put you in the best light and play up your strengths. So, if your education is your strongest suit, put that at the beginning of your resume.

For example, perhaps you are applying for a job as a photographer's assistant. If all your work experience has been in retail sales, but you recently completed several photography courses, you'll list your Education below a Profile/Experience section developing your overall knowledge of photography and above your Employment section.

For most of us, however, our work history may be more relevant or recent than our education. That's why you'll see that most resumes include the Education section toward the end.

# It's About Growth

Regardless of high unemployment rates, new jobs are being filled every day in the U.S. The market for blue collar workers is expected to grow. The Bureau of Labor Statistics has estimated that between 2004 and 2014 there will be 40 million job openings for workers without a bachelor's degree. That's more than twice the number of jobs for people graduating from four-year colleges and universities.

Following are a few examples of Education sections that I developed for clients. Note that the layout is consistent with the Employment sections illustrated in the previous chapter, however the EDUCATION and other titles may be centered or left justified, depending on space available and your personal preference. Whatever format you choose to present your work history and education, you should be consistent from section to section. For example, I typically **bold** the names of degrees.

### EDUCATION

Judson College, Elgin, IL
**Associate Degree:** Electrical Systems          Graduated 12/08
Successful completion of courses in electrical system configuration, wiring, industrial fuse-box installation, line testing and troubleshooting.

OR:

Elgin Community College, Elgin, IL          Spring, 2005
Completed various liberal arts courses.

Grand Canyon University, Phoenix, AZ     Fall, 2010
Completed one year's studies in liberal arts.

If you have not earned a degree, it's still to your advantage to indicate that you have or are taking courses, even listing specific classes that may be relevant to your job goals.

# EDUCATION

Bergen Community College, Paramus, NJ                                    1/15
Successful completion of courses related to (or in) Business Administration.

Plaza School of Technology, Paramus, NJ                                  7/16
Trained in CAD versions 11 and 12 (Computer-Aided Drafting.)

National Education Center, Rets Campus, Nutley, NJ                       4/18
**Associate Degree:** Electronics Engineering Technology

**CERTIFICATE:** HAZMAT Certified by the State of Illinois, 2017

Some clients ask me, "Should I include my high school information?" I tell them yes, if there's no other indication that you've graduated from high school. In other words, if you list that you've earned a bachelor's degree or associate's degree, it will be assumed that you graduated from high school. Without this additional educational experience, you are wise to add that you graduated from high school.

As for dates, I sometimes advise leaving off the date of graduation--whether for high school or college. Sadly, age discrimination still exists and often older workers are the targets of this bias. But remember, if you omit the dates for one listing, you must leave them off for all.

For example, if you choose to list that you earned an associate's degree, but leave off the fact that you did so in 1982, then you should also leave off the date for your recent completion of a certification program.

I recommend listing certifications and training programs following formal education listings, such as college. However, you may also mention your most relevant certifications in the Profile/Experience section on top.

If you have a minimal amount of formal education, your certifications, as well as workshops, seminars, and other professional training you've gathered become more important. When you list these, be sure to point out any pertinent subjects covered in the training and make note that you "completed" or "graduated" from the course.

**EDUCATION:**        Successful completion of a **CAD/CAM seminar** by Hewlett
                      Packard Corporation.

                      Completed seminars by Anthony Robbins and Zig Ziglar related
                      to communication, sales, and self-motivation.

Always give yourself credit for any kind of training, formal or informal. This communicates more than the fact that you've acquired a certain level of knowledge. It also conveys to the reader that you are self-motivated, have a desire to learn more about your field or industry, and that you want to grow and advance, traits that all savvy employers are looking for.

# Chapter 7

# Design Your Eye-Catching Resume

The "look" of your resume may be as important as the content, at least in the first few seconds when it must grab the reader's attention. Your resume must appear flawless; this marks you as a professional who is attentive to detail. A clean, light look is ideal, because it gives the impression that your resume will be easy to read and extract important information.

You can achieve this appealing look through the effective use of a variety of elements, including type (size and style), white space, margins, and special treatments such as bullets, indenting, italics, underlining, and boldface type. By checking the samples in this book, you can greatly enhance the overall appearance of your resume by how it is created and printed.

## Computer, or Professional Resume Writer?

Your first decision is to determine how you'll create your resume. Perhaps you're a two-finger typist and would rather write something longhand and have a professional person lay out, design, and typeset the final document.

Of course, if you put yourself in the hands of a professional resume writer, this will be your easiest course of action. But if you want to develop your own resume, I recommend that you use the samples in this book and a common word processing software such as MS Word. Not only will you be able to get a much more professional look, but you'll also have a greater choice of type styles and design elements to create a more attractive, readable look. You'll also be able to store your resume, modify it, update it, and customize it with each job you apply for, which I highly recommend.

If you don't have a computer, there are plenty of options for finding one. Most libraries offer computer time free to the public, not to mention schools and business centers such as FedEx offices.

## What Typeface? What Size?

Typefaces used for text are either *serif* or *sans serif.* Serifs are the "hands" and "feet" at the top and bottom of letters. Serif typefaces, then, are fonts such as the one you're reading now that have such "hands" and "feet." Sans serif type faces utilize letters without these extensions.

**This is an example of a sans serif typeface.**

Which should you use? Serif types are recommended for most printed materials. Just about every major newspaper uses serif type. Serif type is easy to read; the theory is that serifs help the eye move along from word to word more easily. If you are in a creative or high-tech field such as graphic arts or design, or your resume copy is minimal, you might consider a sans serif face such as Helvetica, Kent, or New Gothic, which are generally larger fonts, even in the same point size as serif type.

Keep your type size between 10 and 12 points. I've found that 11-point type is best; anything smaller is hard for the eye to scan and anything bigger can seem excessive. Fill the page with essential information; then adjust the size of type and the margins and tabs to make it all fit.

One of the best and most common ways to make your resume attractive and readable is to use "white space." Break up blocks of text and add white space to your resume with bulleted text and healthy margins and indents. This helps the highlights of your background stand out, while giving the eye a focal point.

I usually indent (tab) after each bullet, and there are many different types of bullets.

Another way to add white space is to use a return at the end of every sentence and to add blank spaces between groups of text. There are plenty of samples of white space in the following resume examples.

Yet another method of adding white space, used in just about every resume in this book, is to indent each paragraph after the appropriate heading (such as Experience, Employment, and so on). I prefer an indent of 1.5 to 2 inches.

**EXPERIENCE:** ▶ Extensive background in the assembly and installation of electrical components and machine parts, on job sites and production lines.

▶ Skilled in troubleshooting and taking prompt corrective action; read and interpret blueprints and bills of materials; adhere to safety policies, procedures and codes.

▶ Utilize ARC and MIG welders, micrometers, air gun nailers, torque wrenches, hammers, screwdrivers, drill presses, shears and Whitney presses; operate forklifts and cranes in a safe, professional manner.

You may also use a simple dash or asterisk, but as you can see, these don't stand out as well as the computer-generated bullets:

*   Skilled in the total rebuilding and fabrication of custom and stock engines, differentials and gears, as well as blown gas and alcohol motors.

—   Proficient in boring and honing blocks and heads; skilled in the use of lathes, mills, grinders, and all general shop equipment.

Use "frills" such as boldfacing, underlining, italics, bullets, or dashes only now and then, and not on every line. These graphics lose their impact when they're overused. They should only be used to make major points stand out or to set items apart and break up type. Avoid using all the elements: boldfacing, underlining, or italics in the same resume. Choose a combination of any *two*. My personal favorites are bolding and underlining. I may then use italics only for a short description of the company, but pick whichever one you like.

Some of these techniques may seem trivial, but it's the minor details that make up a great resume. Without attention to detail, you will end up with yet another data-sheet resume that won't work very well. The techniques presented here will distance you from the pack and help you win the resume game.

# Line Length

The resumes I design for my clients follow a simple format. The body copy is usually indented about 1.5 inches from the left margin. This allows for shorter lines and makes the resume more scannable to the eye. This also gives greater white space and an excellent place to put your section headings (Objective and Experience, for example). Margins should be 1 inch all around, but they may be shortened to .75 inch or widened up to 1.5 inches as needed to fit your information on one or two pages. Again, don't be afraid to use two pages if that's what it takes to develop and market your skills!

If you still need more or less space than margin shifting allows, change your type size by one-half point, but try to keep it around 11 points.

Avoid violating your margins or hyphenating words at the end of a line; however, you can make an exception to this rule for compound words such as self-employed, when the line ends after "self."

Don't worry about squaring off (fully justifying) your lines unless space is really tight. Many resumes in this guide are fully justified and use the entire page width to pack more information on each page, but notice that you should still always place a return at the end of each individual sentence. Doing this automatically adds white space between lines, and your resume avoids that "tombstone" look with big blocks of gray type.

# Placement of Dates

I recommend the placement of dates directly across from the job title or company name, flush right. An assistant director for alumni career services at a major university said she liked to see dates placed immediately after the company location: "Chicago, IL, 8/03-1/04." I agree with this if you'd like to hide or mask dates of shorter positions.

# Printing Your Resume

Chances are, your computer is connected to a printer that will produce good-quality originals as you need them. Be sure to use only a high-quality laser or inkjet printer.

As for photocopying your resume, remember that no copy machine can reproduce the print quality of a typeset original. Avoid photocopying more than 12 resumes at a time, because you'll almost certainly want to make edits and changes down the road.

If you don't anticipate wanting to customize your resume for different job opportunities, visit a FedEx office or the copy department of a major office supply store. These stores use high-quality photocopiers; you can typically choose to do it yourself, or ask for help from an assistant. Either way, run a sample before you print the entire order - you want to make sure there are no black or gray streaks, or spots on your resume. This will also give you a chance to adjust the lightness or darkness of the copier.

# What Color Paper?

I advise my clients to stick to white, off-white, or ivory colors of paper, as these are good, easy-to-read colors. Avoid grays or dark beiges because they reduce contrast between paper and ink. Lighter paper works much better when your resume is faxed to an employer or scanned into a database. Also avoid the splotchy parchment papers or those with unusual textures. If you want your resume to stand out on a desk of white papers, use a natural or ivory color. Check the linen designs such as Classic Linen Avon Brilliant White or a smoother paper, such as Strathmore, available in white or natural colors.

The professionals I write for receive actual laser prints of their resume on their choice of paper. (I usually recommend a smooth, white linen.) I also provide them with a laser master on plain white paper, which they can duplicate at a good print shop.

# Proofread, Proofread, Proofread!

Before printing or sending out a single resume, always proofread it slowly and carefully. Check *everything,* including dates of employment, the spelling of company names, and your name and address. One trick that helps catch typos is reading your resume backwards. Start with the very last word and read to the first. This forces you to focus on the words individually. Have relatives and friends read over your resume, too. After all, you may be too close to it to catch errors that may be obvious to a more objective reader.

You'd be surprised what can slip by in the finished version. This is your life, your career, your future on paper--it must be as close to perfect as possible. Here's a quick item in the Job Search Facts that gives excellent motivation for making the effort to create an excellent resume:

## The Dreaded Typo:

An OfficeTeam survey revealed that 76% of executives polled *"would not hire a candidate with 1-2 typos" on their resume;* 45% said it would take only *one* typo to eliminate a candidate. You might be surprised how common this is. I see typographical or grammar errors in virtually all resumes I see. Always have your resume checked for errors by family, friends, or your office staff.

# Chapter 8
# Secrets of Electronic Resumes

Your resume may very well be viewed by an HR representative, and if approved by that person, the hiring manager. However to save time, a growing number of companies are using computers to scan and sort through the hundreds, even thousands of resumes they may receive. Two such companies that use computers to scan resumes in the Midwest are Motorola and First Card, one of the largest credit card processing companies.

If you send your resume via email, attached as an MS Word or plain text (.txt) file, then it's already in digital format, and will be added to the company's (or recruiter's) database.

OCR (Optical Character Recognition) comes into play initially when a paper resume is scanned into a computer. If mailing or faxing your resume, you can assume it will be placed on a scanner, converted to a digital file, and loaded onto a large computer database. Employers can then use special scanning software to find certain "keywords" or "hits" on your resume for a match.

# Keywords

*Keywords* refer to those words or phrases used in automated searches of resumes to match your resume to an employer's criteria. Keywords tend to be more of the noun or noun-phrase type (for example, Total Quality Management, UNIX, Bio-Chemist, training, budgeting, technical teams), which are often linked with power action verbs (skilled in, developed, coordinated, empowered, organized, and so on).

The keyword resume must contain an adequate description of the job seeker's skills, abilities, characteristics, and industry-specific experience, presented in terms to accommodate the electronic/computer search process. Try to build your Profile/Experience, Employment, and Education sections with as many keywords as possible.

**Examples of keywords may include types of computer software or systems, such as:**

| | |
|---|---|
| Windows 7/XP | Macintosh |
| QuarkXpress | Lotus |
| MS Office | MS Word or PowerPoint--elements of MS Office |

**Keywords may include your knowledge of various duties or operations, such as:**

| | |
|---|---|
| Accounts payable | Inventory control |
| CNC equipment repair | Staff training and supervision |

**Keywords may include industry-specific terms, such as:**

| | |
|---|---|
| Automotive | Electronics |
| Food and beverage | Carpentry |
| Retail | Manufacturing / Production |
| Mechanic | Warehousing |

**Keywords may identify the level of employment, such as:**

| Manager | Supervisor |
|---|---|
| Executive | Assistant |
| Entry-level | Intern |

# Formatting Tips for Electronic Resumes

Resume management systems search databases for keywords and rank resumes using multiple (10-20) criteria. This reliance on resume management systems, coupled with the downsizing of human resource departments, has resulted in a situation where many resumes are never seen by human eyes once they enter these systems.

Of course, nothing is perfect, and that holds true for document scanners. If your resume is scanned from paper into a computer system, letters and entire words may be read incorrectly. Underlining, italics, and certain typefaces can be misinterpreted, and essential keywords may not be picked up.

The best way around this problem is to bypass the paper scanning procedure and email your resume directly to the employer. That way, your resume is already in digital format, and there's very little chance of words being misread.

The lesson here is to make your resume as computer- and scanner-friendly as possible, so that its life in a database will be extended, and its likelihood of producing "hits" is improved.

If you send your resume via email because you know a particular employer prefers to receive and store resumes electronically, then attach a fully formatted MS Word or PDF version of your resume. If you're not sure the employer accepts or can open MS Word or PDF files, then save a copy of your resume as a separate text-only file on your computer. When responding to job openings online, you can modify and then cut and paste this resume into an email or fill-in-the blank form, such as those found on Monster.com or CareerBuilder.com. Remember, though, that you can only use this cut-and-paste technique with a text-only file. Use this format only when you're not sure if the employer or website will accept the fully formatted MS Word attachment of your resume, like the samples in this book.

To create a stripped-down, text-only file, open it in MS Word or any other word processing software and click Save As. You should then be able to select "text only" or .txt format. Before you press Save, rename this text version of your resume, such as "MyResumeTextVersion" and then click Save. Now, close and then reopen this new text version; it should now have no lines, underlines, or special font formatting, and might appear in a basic Courier or other such font.

To be certain your resume can be downloaded and seen by target companies, you may also attach your resume as an MS Word file, in addition to a cut-and-paste text version in the body of the email.

Use these tips to format your basic text resume and then click Save:

- -- Left-justify the entire document.
- -- Remove tabs and indents.
- -- Remove italics, script, underlining, graphics, boxes, outlines, bold or shading.
- -- Remove horizontal and vertical lines.
- -- Remove parentheses and brackets.
- -- To highlight achievements, use asterisks (*) or greater than (>) signs as bullets, followed by two spaces.
- -- Adjust compressed lines of print (typesetting and proportional spacing may cram too much into one line if there's a long word near the end of the sentence).
- -- Again, save the file in a basic Courier or similar font.

## Signed, Sealed, Delivered

While email is the most common form of delivering resumes these days, you may also send it by fax or snail mail. Many employers believe that sending a customized, printed resume with a signed, personalized cover letter through "snail mail" shows a candidate has extended great effort to tailor his or her information to the needs of the target company. In addition, such elements as the choice of paper, quality of printing, and style or design will give insight to the employer about your overall professionalism.

# Snail Mail

Even in the electronic age, you're safe in sending a paper resume in most cases. When you do, just be sure to send it unfolded with a customized, signed cover letter in a 9 x 12 envelope so it arrives flat and neat. (Most people grab the largest pieces of mail first--don't you?)

Now that your resume has been created, you need a plan--a job-hunting strategy that will allow you to maximize all that information and win some job interviews. That's what the next two chapters are all about.

# Chapter 9

# Using Your Resume to Speed Your Job Search

Perhaps you're at the beginning of your job search--you may have just been laid off. Maybe you're doing fine at your current job, but you want more challenges, a better salary, or a new direction. Whatever your reasons for seeking a new job, job-hunting can be hard work, but the payoffs are well worth it. And the good news is that now you've developed the most important tool in your job-hunting arsenal--your resume.

Your next step is to seek out those job opportunities. There's a world of possibilities out there, and you need to explore every avenue in search of your ideal job. So where do you find out about job openings? Let's consider these options.

## Your Current Employer

If you're lucky, your next great job could be with the company you're now working for. Most companies have a human resources department that posts job openings, and current employees are typically given priority consideration for such positions. These jobs are posted to employees before they're advertised; in fact, most job openings are never advertised, and are filled from within, or through word-of-mouth referrals from staff and managers.

When you hear of a new position at your current company, you have a rare chance to get your resume in and schedule an interview *before* the deluge of interviews and responses. Keep an eye out for such job postings, but go further in your search for internal opportunities. Talk to co-workers in other departments to learn about upcoming changes and expansions. Seek out opportunities to work on interdepartmental projects that put you in contact with other supervisors and managers. You'll be in a better position when an opening comes up.

## Your Company's Competitors

What better place to find job openings for positions that reflect your experience and skills than other companies just like the one you work for? In most cases, these companies will be considered "the competition" for your current employer. Unless you've signed some sort of agreement not to work for a competitor within a period of time after you leave your current position (such as a non-compete clause), these companies can be great sources of job opportunities.

## Trade Organizations and Networking

To learn about new positions before they're heavily advertised, consider joining trade organizations where you can meet with employees from various companies. Include some of these individuals in your "network" and touch base with them regularly to learn of opportunities. These groups may be organized on a national or local level. There are opportunities for regular meetings and special events, where you can meet and get to know others in your industry or area of expertise. Most organizations have regularly published newsletters or magazines that may include job listings.

You should join at least one such organization. Often, your employer will have a policy of paying for all or part of your membership and will encourage you to be active in the group. And if you're currently not employed? All the more reason to be a member of a trade organization, so that you can stay in touch with others in your industry and keep your knowledge and skills up to date.

Search for new or potential opportunities at other companies through online resources (check the appendix in this book; virtually all companies have a website with promotional information and/or job openings) and resources found in the reference section of any public library.

# Employment Agencies

The function of an employment agency is to match job seekers like you with employers. When you enlist the services of an employment agency, you typically fill out a profile and interview with an agency representative, who then takes the information and seeks a match among their client companies.

Many employment agencies specialize in a particular industry or field. For example, some may focus on placing secretaries, administrative assistants, and office workers; another may focus on medical technicians.

When considering working with an employment agency, be sure you understand what your financial commitment might be. It's more common for the employer to pay any agency fees if a job match is made. However, you may be asked to pay the agency for its services, and the terms of payment vary from agency to agency. For example, you may be required to pay an amount equivalent to one month's salary. I don't recommend ever paying an agency, and when seeking their assistance, make sure you understand all the terms and conditions before you sign an agreement.

# Online and Newspaper "Want Ads"

You've probably read the statistics that as many as 80 percent of all job openings are never advertised. While this may be true, it certainly doesn't make sense to ignore the classified ads, both online and in your community newspaper. Sunday's edition is typically categorized by field. Keep a few things in mind as you check off possibilities to contact on Monday morning:

Blind box ads are used by companies that don't want to be identified, and they pay extra for the privilege. Respond to blind ads if the position seems right for you, but don't expect much. Often, companies will place such ads simply to check the pool of available talent. (Be wary, too, that the blind ad you read hasn't been placed by your current employer! You can usually submit a response to the box office number and ask that it not be passed on to certain firms.)

Advertisements in trade journals and magazines related to your field may be more targeted. Of course, that means that others responding to the ad may have more targeted experience as well, so your competition may be stiffer. Typically, these ads tend to draw the biggest deluge of resumes. Just like you, every other job seeker looking for the same type of work will likely respond. Advertisements on CareerBuilder.com or Monster.com can receive thousands of resumes within a few days of posting. Yet statistically, only about 6-8 percent of all jobs are filled through such large, online job boards, while 60-70 percent are filled through personal networking - people who've heard that you're looking for a new position. That's why you must build your network

# Build Your Network!

I used the term "network" a few times in the previous sections. What exactly is a network? It's your collection of relationships: co-workers, colleagues, industry connections, friends, and relatives who may connect you to your next job opportunity.

Many people think of networking as meeting strangers in social circumstances, shoving a business card in their hand, and then calling them up to ask for a job.

Networking, however, should *never* be a forced action, but rather the slow building of relationships. As you build these relationships, you'll share information about yourself, help your contacts when you can, and turn to them for advice and help when you need it.

You may turn to one of your networking contacts from a trade association and ask about potential opportunities, or for advice related to your job search. It's just as likely that you'll offer that contact some good advice--or that they'll introduce you to someone who provides you with knowledge that helps you do your job better and leads to a promotion, which leads to interest from an outside employer. Like they say, what goes around comes around.

The secret is to make your network broad and inclusive. Join business organizations, volunteer in a community effort, participate in your kids' school activities, and get to know others in your company better. You never know where important connections will take your career.

# College Placement Offices

If you're poised to graduate and enter the "real world" soon, be sure to contact your school's placement office by the beginning of your last semester of school. Often, such placement offices have some good connections with desirable employers looking for top-notch, entry-level candidates.

Even if you've been out of school for a number of years, it might be a good idea to contact your *alma mater*. You never know where this may lead. My alma mater, Northern Illinois University, provides a wide range of career support services to its graduates.

# Job Fairs

Similar to online and Sunday newspaper want ads, you'll be competing with a large pool of candidates at job fairs. This can be a great opportunity to drop off resumes with many companies and save time, travel, and postage. You won't have to provide a cover letter and--if your timing is right--you might have a chance for an impromptu interview right on the spot. If your particular department head isn't at the fair, ask the representative for his or her name so you can send a personalized resume and letter, or have that representative forward your resume to your potential manager when he or she returns to the office.

Check the Sunday classified section for listings of upcoming job fairs. They're common in college towns, as well as major cities. Most job fairs are free, but occasionally you may run across one that charges admission.

# How to Pursue That Job Lead

Once you've learned about a job opportunity, whether it's through a networking contact, an online job board, or a trade publication, you aren't necessarily ready to zap off your resume yet, and here's why.

## Know the Target Company, Their Needs, and How You Can Fill Them

An OfficeTeam survey revealed that 60% of employers said that applicants rarely indicate company or industry knowledge in their cover letters; 38% said this remains a problem during interviews.

Before you do anything, *research, research, research!* Whenever possible, call the company to find out exactly what they do and the name of the person who would be your supervisor. Visit your local library to read up on the company.

This cannot be overemphasized, because applicants who show knowledge of a company stand a much better chance of being hired--or at least interviewed--by that company.

Don't forget, there may be hundreds of others applying for the same position you are. You want to do everything in your power to set yourself apart.

Learn everything you can about the company, the position, and your supervisor. Then you can customize your resume, your cover letter (see Chapter 13, "Resume and Cover Letter Examples"), and your responses in the interview to closely match the needs of prospective employers, as discussed in the next chapter.

# Chapter 10

# At Last: The Interview

By now, your resume should be starting to generate job interviews. As I've said before, a resume won't get you a job, but it can get you interviews, where you get the chance to make a personal connection with the people you hope to work with. It's your opportunity to go for the *close,* as they say in the world of sales. However, before you agree to any interviews, it's essential to get the information and skills you need to *make* that close.

Books have been written on the topic of interviewing, but in this chapter, I'll offer some of the key tips and secrets for conducting a job-winning interview:

## Research the Company and Position

In the previous chapter, I stressed the importance of learning as much as possible about the job opportunities you're pursuing *before* developing and sending out your resume and cover letter. I can't overemphasize how important it is to walk into the company with a clear understanding of the corporate culture and, specifically, the job environment you'll be working in.

Not only do you want to know facts such as the size of the company, locations, chief activities, annual revenues, and plans for the future, but you'll also want to know about the *culture* of the company. For example, if you walk into the interview knowing that this is a very traditional company, you'll present yourself as more conservative, perhaps focusing on your traits of steadfastness and reliability, or your long tenure at previous jobs. You may dress in the traditional "interview" attire: a dark suit. Avoid talking about the value of radical change and how you pushed for cutting-edge management changes in your previous job.

Researching the prospective employer will also help you formulate some good questions for your interviewer regarding a typical day on the job, long-term prospects given current economic trends, and potential for advancement.

## Practice Your Answers

While it's true that you can't predict exactly what you'll be asked in the interview, you should have some idea of the types of questions to prepare for, such as "Tell me about yourself," "What do you like best about the work you do?" or "What are your weaknesses?"

At the very least, you should prepare a response to the question, "Tell me about yourself." Often, what interviewers are assessing with this question is your ability to communicate what's *important.* If you go off on a tangent about where you were born and what your hobbies are, you're not really focusing on your interviewer's interests. Prepare a brief speech - no more than a couple minutes - that sums up your work experience for the person you're talking to. Check the article by Scott Ginsberg in Chapter 12, *Motivational Articles, Get your Career in Gear,* for tips on answering the "Tell Me About Yourself" question.

Additionally, if you feel you need help in preparing for other commonly asked interview questions, check the Appendix, "Job Hunt Resources Materials, at the end of this book for some great books and resources on the topic.

# Present a Professional Image

Often, the dark-suit model of professional dress does not apply to situations in which work is primarily physical, or "blue collar." So, why, then, wear a "white collar" to an interview for such a job?

This is another reason to research the company prior to the interview. What is the corporate "climate"? Is it ultra-casual? Even though you may apply for a job as a laborer, you may have to interview with supervisors or upper-level managers.

In some cases, dressing more casually for an interview for a blue collar job will be entirely appropriate. After all, you may be seeking a job in which you'll wear a uniform. However, if you dress "up" for the interview, it's unlikely to work against you, and it just might work for you. It's usually safe to wear a suit - whether for women or men - to an interview, regardless of the position. If you don't own a suit, or can't afford a new one, ask a friend if you can borrow theirs or check some of the larger, well-stocked secondhand stores, which have some excellent items. Be sure all your clothes are cleaned and well pressed before the interview.

Whatever you choose to wear, make sure that your appearance is flawless--your clothes are clean and pressed, and you're well groomed, down to your fingernails.

# Arrive on Time

To employers, your punctuality is an important indicator of your reliability. Do whatever you must do to arrive at the interview on time. In fact, try to get there about 15 minutes early. This will give you time to collect yourself, review your notes and resume, and enter into the meeting with a calm and positive attitude.

## Speak Up!

An Accountemps/Robert Half survey polled 150 executives from the nation's 1,000 largest companies. Can you believe that a third said that during interviews, applicants are often *too humble* in recounting their own achievements? Don't take anything for granted or assume that employers already know how great you are. When you're called in for an interview, don't overwhelm the listener and brag about yourself, but by the same token, don't downplay your abilities.

Practice answering basic interview questions with friends and family, or if possible, hire a career coach. Being able to express yourself clearly is essential in all social situations.

# Be Positive

No matter what happens before the interview - you were given horrible directions, the office was hard to find, traffic was terrible - start your interview with a positive attitude. Your interviewer wants to talk to someone who conveys enthusiasm, optimism, and eagerness. Regardless of what kind of day you've had, keep a smile on your face and think positive!

# Don't Be Nervous

An interview is not a life-or-death situation; relax and be yourself. Remember that you're not the only person who will be interviewed for the job. The employer may be interviewing other candidates who come across more relaxed and confident but don't have the skills and experience you have. Don't let them get your job!

The interview is another chance to discover and market your potential, while learning more about what the employer really wants. Keep in mind that you're there to interview the company as well. You shouldn't feel as if the burden is all on your shoulders to make a good impression.

Any decent interviewer understands that you may be nervous, especially if it's one of your very first interviews. The interviewer should know how to put you at ease right from the start with some light conversation, rather than put you on the spot - but don't count on it.

Some interviewers actually enjoy intimidating candidates with out-of-this-world questions or impossible situations to see how you react under pressure. Just keep in mind that it's all a show to see what you're made of. Retain your composure as much as possible, thoughtfully consider your replies, and maintain eye contact with the interviewer when responding.

## Timing Is Everything

When is the best time to book an interview? Believe it or not, it can make a difference. An Accountemps survey, published in *The Chicago Tribune,* polled 200 executives. It found that job applicants who interview in the morning may be viewed more favorably than those with interviews later in the day. Fully 83 percent of those responding said they preferred to interview candidates between 9 a.m. and 11 a.m. No other time of day even came close, probably because it's before hiring managers have been overwhelmed with work or a heavy lunch.

# Keep Your Personal Life out of the Interview

You may be aware that your interviewer is prohibited by law from asking certain questions about your personal life. Questions that attempt to ascertain your ethnic background, marital status, sexual activity, and physical or mental health are off limits.

There's a reason for this. So, in the course of the interview, be careful not to *offer* personal information. The interview is not the place to talk about how excited you are about your upcoming wedding, or how eager you are to supplement your family income so you can start a family.

Of course, you're not perfect, and that's really not what employers expect. Sometimes, they just want to hire someone who seems to have the right kind of skills, the right type of background, and who they think they can train in their way of doing things.

I can guarantee that employers are more interested in hiring someone who seems reliable, trainable, and a "good fit" with their company culture. A company can always train you in a specific task or procedure, but they can't give you a positive attitude, change your personality, or make you "fit in" to their work environment.

Above all, the interview is your chance to show the interviewer that you would indeed "fit" with the personality of the company, as well as those you'll work with.

This chapter has a weird box in it that I couldn't get rid of. You'll see it and know to delete it. Thanks, Steve >

# Chapter 11

# Motivation and Inspiration: Get Your Career in Gear

As a member of LinkedIn and a dozen other sites, organizations, and professional groups, I come across great articles that reflect my own ideas on the overall job search. Topics range from self-motivation and attitude adjustment to resume writing, personal networking, and interview techniques.

With permission from the authors, I'm including some of the best articles here.

I think you'll find them uplifting and useful. There are three main categories that focus on Inspiration/Motivation, Networking Tips and Strategies, and Interview Techniques.

I'll start with a few of my favorite quotes. As always, feel free to send your own questions, feedback and comments to my personal, direct email at: Careers1@Execareers.com.

*"People become really quite remarkable when they start thinking that they can do things. When they believe in themselves, they have the first secret of success."*

--Norman Vincent Peale

*"The world is more malleable than you think, and it's waiting for you to hammer it into shape."*

--Bono

*"What lies behind us and what lies before us are tiny matters compared to what lies within us."*

--Ralph Waldo Emerson

*"A happy person is not a person in a certain set of circumstances, but rather a person with a certain set of attitudes."*

--Hugh Downs

*"We judge a man's wisdom by his hope."*
--Ralph Waldo Emerson

# Inspiration / Motivation

## You Are Not Alone

Mike Robbins, author/speaker, www.Mike-Robbins.com

We're never truly alone, even when we feel that way. Most of us have important, loving, and caring people in our lives who are there to support us--if we're willing to open up, ask for, and receive their help. And, regardless of how many people are around us, what our current relationship, family, or work situation may be, or any of the other external circumstances in our life--each of us has access to a higher power, whether we call it God, Spirit, Source, or anything else.

One of the deepest and most basic fears of being human is the fear of loneliness--no one to be with us, love us, accept us, support us, and take care of us if and when we need it. Although this fear seems very real and there's nothing wrong with us for feeling it, the paradox is that we aren't ever really alone--we're surrounded by love and support all the time, from others and, of course, from God. The idea that we're alone is simply a "story" we tell ourselves, especially when things get difficult, scary, or both.

Here are some things you can do to let go of this "story" of being alone when it shows up in your life:

1. **Open Up Vulnerably:** Acknowledging, owning, and sharing your deepest truth is one of the best ways to liberate yourself and connect with other people in an authentic way (hence, reminding you that you're not alone). So often we think that if we really let others know how we feel, what we fear, and what's truly going inside our head and our heart, they will judge us, reject us, or not understand us. In most cases, the exact opposite is true.

2. **Ask For Help:** As the saying goes, "the answer is always 'no' if you don't ask." When we have the courage and vulnerability to ask for the help and support we need, a few important things happen. First of all, we're liberated from the pressure of trying to take care of everything ourselves. Second of all, we give other people the opportunity to contribute to us and be of service (which most people love to do). And finally, we're able to tap into the energy, brilliance, and creativity of other human beings, which is almost always helpful and is also a good reminder that we have access to a great deal of love and support.

3. **Allow Yourself to Be Supported:** Being "supportable" is something many of us, myself included, struggle with. Even if we're vulnerable enough to tell the truth about how we really feel and ask for the support we truly want, it takes a certain amount of maturity, self-respect, and humility to allow other people to support us. Even if it's scary and feels uncomfortable at first, practicing and expanding your capacity to receive the support of others is both generous (as it allows other people to make a difference) and wise (you don't have to work so hard and struggle so much).

4. **Have Faith**: Faith is the belief in things not seen or proven. At some level, our ability to grow, expand, and evolve in life is directly related to our ability to live with a deep sense of faith--in ourselves, others, and a higher power. In our lowest moments, when it feels like we truly are alone and that things will never turn around, work out, or go the way we want them to in life, our faith is what can pull us through. Waiting for a "guarantee" or until we think we're "ready" or "deserving" of support sets us up to fail and creates more fear and anxiety. Having faith in ourselves, others, life, and God is what can remind us, in an instant, that we're not alone--because we're not!

# An Introduction to...

## The Absolutely Last Job Hunting Guide You'll Ever Need!

© James C. Gonyea

*Career/job development specialist, author, and host of the Internet Career Connection (www.iccweb.com)*

As a career and job development specialist for 40 years, I am keenly aware that finding employment in today's competitive job market is difficult, if not impossible for some job seekers. More than ever before, job seekers must use proven, effective strategies if they expect to get hired. In past years, a simple strategy comprised of sending your resume to advertised positions was usually all that was required. Those days are gone!

So, what should an effective job search campaign look like? First, it must address the following issues:

1. What talent do I have to offer?
2. Which employers need my talent and why?
3. How can I convince employers that I'm the best candidate to meet their needs?

In addition, your campaign must follow a well-proven plan of action--one that will focus your time and energy on marketing your talent to the right buyers. Listed below are eight steps that I recommend every job seeker follow when trying to find employment.

**Step 1:** **Define your talent.** Identify your employment value. Clearly understand and be able to articulate what it is that you can do that employers need. (Note: If your talent is not as good as it should be, additional training may be necessary before you undertaken a job search.)

**Step 2:** **Identify the employers who need your talent.** Determine where you are most likely to find employment. Research employers to target the best prospects.

**Step 3:** **Determine why each targeted employer needs your talent.** What value can you bring to each employer? What needs can you satisfy? How can you contribute to the employer's bottom line?

**Step 4:** **Document your talent.** Prepare the necessary materials (resumes, portfolios, cover letters, letters of recommendation, etc.) that can be used to convey your value to employers.

**Step 5:** **Pitch your talent.** Using various communication options (mail, email, face-to-face conversations, etc.) offer your talent to those employers who need it and request an interview to discuss how you can be of value.

**Step 6:** **Discuss your talent and negotiate a deal.** Using the interview, illustrate how you can be of value to the employer and solicit an offer of employment.

**Step 7:** **Evaluate the job offer (or your job hunting strategy).** If you're offered employment, determine if it's right for you and then communicate your acceptance or rejection of the offer, or renegotiate the offer. If after repeated attempts you are not offered employment, re-evaluate how you are conducting your job search, correct it, and continue.

**Step 8:**      **Thank everyone!** Do the right thing! Personally thank all the people who helped you find employment. You may need their help again in the future!

(For a complete copy of the above article, please email the author at jcg@iccweb.com.)

# How to Retrain Your Brain for Change

*By M.J. Ryan*

Big changes are happening for you. But it's (literally) easier to resist change than go with it. Your brain needs to create new pathways to perform a new behavior. Follow these tips on changing without draining your brain.

"I'm going to get better at networking."

"I'm going to increase my personal productivity."

"I'm going to learn to delegate more."

At some point we've all vowed to make some big change--or had to as a result of the huge changes around us. But all too often, our good intention soon gets pushed aside. Not because we lose motivation, but because we just don't know *how* to change. Especially when it comes to a career change.

## Changing your behavior takes work.

Our brains have enormous "plasticity," meaning they can create new cells and pathways. But our brains also create strong tendencies to do the same thing over and over.

Here's why: the brain cells that fire together wire together. Meaning, having run in a certain sequence, they are more likely to run that sequence again until it becomes a habit. It's one of the ways the brain conserves energy. By now, you've got a deeply grooved pathway to doing what you've always done. That's why change is hard; you've got to practice enough to create a new pathway that is strong enough to compete with the old one.

According to many brain scientists it can take six to nine months to create that new automatic behavior. But it can be done. I just finished working with a micromanaging executive who no one believed could stop meddling. His goal was to have his employees rate him great at delegating in six months. He succeeded--and so can you at whatever you want to change.

## Three limiting beliefs that curb a job seeker's ability to change their behavior:

1.  **Bad habits can't be broken.**
    Executives don't understand that the change process is not about getting rid of bad habits. The pathway to your current behavior is there for life. Instead, you want to focus on the new, more positive habit and keep at it no matter how many times your brain jumps the tracks and goes back to the tried and true.
2.  **I'll forget.**
    Executives fail to put reminders in place in the beginning. Unless you have a trigger from the outside, like a Blackberry reminder, a note on your computer, or a coach or buddy, it's virtually guaranteed you'll keep defaulting to the old behavior.
3.  **I want it all.**

Executives are not concrete enough about what they want and are unrealistic about what they can reasonably ask themselves to change. Here's what an executive client of mine said he wanted to change in three months: "To be more positive with co-workers, staff, and colleagues, to be more creative and productive, and to take better care of myself." "How about create world peace while you're at it?" I replied. "And what does `more' mean anyway?" As this client demonstrated, we expect too much of ourselves, and we expect to change overnight. When that doesn't happen, we resign ourselves to staying the same, convinced that we are weak or unmotivated.

These beliefs can make us even more stuck in a rut. But there are even more ways to shake these excuses and retrain your brain.

**Ways to retrain your brain**

1. **Make it nonnegotiable.**
   Promise yourself that you are absolutely going to do it. When you do it, where you do it, and how you do it can, and most likely will, change according to circumstances. But that you *will* do it is not open for consideration. Making it compulsory is a tool for overcoming backsliding after your initial enthusiasm fades.

2. **Make it actionable.**
   You have to know what actions you're going to take: 10 cold calls a day, for instance. Or asking more questions. Then be sure to track yourself so you can tell if you're succeeding.

3. **Come up with solutions for your usual excuses.**
   Instead of just hoping it will be different this time, write down your typical rationalizations and create coping strategies in advance. That way, you won't get stopped in your tracks and lose forward momentum when they arise. And yes, they will!

4. **Schedule it in.**
   Want to have blue sky thinking time? Block it out on your calendar. Want to work out? Schedule it. Make a specific, time-bound appointment with yourself, and you'll be much more likely to do it.

5. **Do it daily.**
   The more you make what you want part of your everyday life, the more it will become so routine that soon you won't even have to think about it. If you want to get better at networking, for instance, do something every day: one email, call, or meeting.

6. **Focus on the horizon.**
   Take a tip from high performance athletes. Look at how far you've come, not how much you have left to do. Scientists call this the horizon effect. It creates encouragement--"I've done twice as much as a week ago!" and builds determination--"I've made it this far; I might as well keep going." Don't forget to ask yourself how you've accomplished the task, so you can mine your success for ideas on how to keep going.

7. **Don't turn goof-ups into give-ups.**

   You will mess up or forget. Remember, you're learning. How many times does a baby fall before learning to walk? When you treat yourself as a learner, you don't collapse into shame or guilt, but can try again with greater wisdom. Keep at it no matter how many times you blow it.

The ability to have a change of pace is one of our greatest capacities as leaders, particularly in these turbulent times. When you have this invaluable tool in your arsenal, you'll be empowered to bring anything you want into reality and be better equipped to help those around you change too.

*The author of many best-selling books, M.J. Ryan is a consultant with Professional Thinking Partners where she specializes in coaching high performance executives and leads training in effective teamwork in corporations, nonprofits, and government agencies. Her latest book is* AdaptAbility: How to Survive Change You Didn't Ask For. *Visit her website at* www.mj-ryan.com *for more change survival tips.*

# Networking Tips and Strategies

## Adopt These 10 Traits, and You'll Have People Knocking Down Your Door Trying to Do Business with You

*By Ivan Misner, Ph.D.*

Networking is more than just shaking hands and passing out business cards. Based on a survey I conducted of more than 2,000 people throughout the United States, the United Kingdom, Canada, and Australia, it's about building your "social capital." The highest-rated traits in the survey were the ones related to developing and maintaining good relationships. For years I've been teaching people that this process is more about "farming" than it is about "hunting." It's about cultivating relationships with other business professionals. It's about realizing the capital that comes from building social relationships. The following traits were ranked in order of their perceived importance to networking. They're the traits that will make you a "master networker."

1.  **Follow up on referrals.** This was ranked as the No. 1 trait of successful networkers. If you present an opportunity, whether it's a simple piece of information, a special contact, or a qualified business referral, to someone who consistently fails to follow up successfully, it's no secret that you'll eventually stop wasting your time with this person.

2.  **Positive attitude.** A consistently negative attitude makes people dislike being around you and drives away referrals; a positive attitude makes people want to associate and cooperate with you. Positive business professionals are like magnets. Others want to be around them and will send their friends, family and associates to them.

3.  **Enthusiastic/motivated.** Think about the people you know. Who gets the most referrals? People who show the most motivation, right? It's been said that the best sales characteristic is enthusiasm. To be respected within our networks, we at least need to sell ourselves with enthusiasm. Once we've done an effective job of selling ourselves, we'll be able to reap the reward of seeing our contacts sell us to others! That's motivation in and of itself!

4.  **Trustworthy.** When you refer one person to another, you're putting your reputation on the line. You have to be able to trust your referral partner and be trusted in return. Neither you nor anyone else will refer a contact or valuable information to someone who can't be trusted to handle it well.

5.  **Good listening skills.** Our success as networkers depends on how well we can listen and learn. The faster you and your networking partner learn what you need to know about each other, the faster you'll establish a valuable relationship. Communicate well, and listen well.

6.  **Network always.** Master networkers are never off duty. Networking is so natural to them that they can be found networking in the grocery store line, at the doctor's office, and while picking the kids up from school, as well as at the chamber mixers and networking meetings.

7.  **Thank people.** Gratitude is sorely lacking in today's business world. Expressing gratitude to business associates and clients is just another building block in the cultivation of relationships that will lead to increased referrals. People like to refer others to business professionals that go above and beyond. Thanking others at every opportunity will help you stand out from the crowd.

8.  **Enjoy helping.** Helping others can be done in a variety of ways, from literally showing up to help with an office move to clipping a helpful and interesting article and mailing it to an associate or client. Master networkers keep their eyes and ears open for opportunities to advance other people's interests whenever they can.

9.  **Be Sincere.** Insincerity is like a cake without frosting! You can offer the help, the thanks, the listening ear, but if you aren't sincerely interested in the other person, they'll know it! Those who have developed successful networking skills convey their sincerity at every turn. One of the best

ways to develop this trait is to give the individual with whom you're developing a referral relationship your undivided attention.

10. **Work your network.** It's not net-sit or net-eat, it's net-work, and master networkers don't let any opportunity to work their networks pass them by. They manage their contacts with contact management software, organize their email address files, and carry their referral partners' business cards as well as their own. They set up appointments to get better acquainted with new contacts so that they can learn as much about them as possible so that they can truly become part of each other's networks.

Do you see the trend with these 10 points? They all tie in to long-term relationship building, not to stalking the prey for the big kill. People who take the time to build their social capital are the ones who will have new business referred to them over and over. The key is to build mutually beneficial business relationships. Only then will you succeed as a master networker.

*Ivan Misner is co-author of the New York Times bestseller* <u>Masters of Networking</u>. *He is the founder and CEO of* <u>BNI</u>, *the world's largest referral organization with more than 2,400 chapters in 13 countries around the world. He also teaches business courses at California State Polytechnic University, Pomona, and resides in Southern California with his wife and three children. Dr. Misner can be reached at* <u>misner@bni.com.</u>


# Harness the Power of Networking©


## Four Essential Steps to Make Your Connections Count!

By Susan Fignar

With today's topsy-turvy economy and uncertain job market, the one thing you want to be able to count on is support from business colleagues, clients, vendors, and even family and friends. It's not only who we know, but what we know about them and how we can help each other. Remember, even the Lone Ranger couldn't do it alone. He had his trusty partners Tonto and Hi Ho Silver!


# Networking vs. Partnerships

Networking is only the tip of the iceberg in furthering career aspirations. If not managed properly, it can soon become a numbers game based on how many events attended, business cards collected, speaking engagements given, and associations joined. While networking brings visibility, it doesn't necessarily bring credibility. However, business partnerships, which are built on a higher level, can bring credibility, trust, integrity, and a positive reputation. The important thing to remember is that it's not how visible you make yourself, but how you are perceived.

So, how can you stop the numbers game and build a quality network to develop/strengthen your business partnerships?

# The Partnership Factor: Build and Strengthen Your Business Partnerships

Strive to become a **connector** vs. a giver or taker; focus your efforts to develop and deepen relationships, not contacts. Simply meeting people is not the best use of anyone's time. It's better to be known by fewer people who can speak to your unique capabilities and abilities and will work on your behalf. Building trust with key individuals is the first priority and will take time, so be patient. Listed below are four proven tips to move you closer to building and strengthening successful business partnerships:

1. **Be approachable and proactive.** Look open and initiate conversation rather than wait for others to approach or contact you via email, telephone, and/or in person.

2. **Participate only in organizations and events that are relevant to you and your business** vs. trying to be in too many places.

3. **Concentrate on leadership roles** vs. membership. You will get more out of an organization if you volunteer to be on a committee or take on a board position, rather than being a regular member. It's better to be seen and singled out as a leader in one or two organizations than to be a passive member of several groups.

4. **Follow through with your commitments**. If you take on a volunteer role, be sure to deliver what you promised. The quickest way to develop a negative reputation is to fail to follow through. Commit to those activities you have the time and ability to accomplish.

**Take Action:** Partnerships take time. You don't build solid relationships/partnerships overnight! If your partnerships are not mutually beneficial, it's time to re-evaluate them, move on, and to replace the ones on your A and B list that are not mutually beneficial.

Following are a few questions to explore:

1. List three to five steps you can take to build/strengthen your business partnerships (for example, colleagues, clients, vendors, prospects).

2. What do you know about the person's skill set and reputation you want to partner with for business purposes? Are they complementary or do they overlap with your services?

3. What strengths/core values/personality attributes are important to you and to the individual(s) you would like to partner with?

4. How many introductions have you made on behalf of others over the past three months, and how many introductions have others made on your behalf? Remember, we judge others and they judge us on our actions, not our words.

**Track your progress**: Over the next 12 months, record and share your progress and any challenges you may experience along the way with an accountability partner who is known for their ability to successfully relate and connect to others. For the first 60 days, track your progress weekly; after that, bi-monthly or monthly. You will be pleasantly surprised by your successes and lessons learned along the way.

your firm are interested in learning how to develop and strengthen your professional network, contact: Susan Fignar, Pur-sue Inc., specializing in executive presence and relationship management at www.pur-sue.com | sfignar@pur-sue.com

# Interview Techniques

# 10 Good Ways to Tell Me About Yourself'

"If Hollywood made a movie about my life, it would be called..." and nine more memorable answers to this dreaded job interview question."

By Scott Ginsberg

You know it's coming.

It's the most feared question during any job interview: Do you think I would look good in a cowboy hat?

Just kidding. The real question is: Can you tell me about yourself?

Blecch. What a boring, vague, open-ended question. Who likes answering that?

I know. I'm with you. But unfortunately, hiring managers and executive recruiters ask the question. Even if you're not interviewing and you're out networking in the community--you need to be ready to hear it and answer it. At all times.

Now, before I share a list of 10 memorable answers, consider the two essential elements behind the answers:

**The medium is the message.** The interviewer cares less about your answer to this question and more about the confidence, enthusiasm, and passion with which you answer it.

**The speed of the response is the response.** The biggest mistake you could make is pausing, stalling, or fumbling at the onset of your answer, thus demonstrating a lack of self-awareness and self-esteem.

Next time you're faced with the dreaded, "Tell me about yourself..." question, try these:

1. **"I can summarize who I am in three words."** Grabs their attention immediately. Demonstrates your ability to be concise, creative, and compelling.
2. **"The quotation I live my life by is…"** Proves that personal development is an essential part of your growth plan. Also shows your ability to motivate yourself.
3. **"My personal philosophy is…"** Companies hire athletes--not shortstops. This line indicates your position as a thinker, not just an employee.
4. **"People who know me best say that I'm…"** This response offers insight into your own level of self-awareness.
5. **"Well, I Googled myself this morning, and here's what I found…"** Tech-savvy, fun, cool people would say this. Unexpected and memorable.
6. **"My passion is…"** People don't care what you do--people care who you are. And what you're passionate about is who you are. Plus, passion unearths enthusiasm.
7. **"When I was seven years old, I always wanted to be…"** An answer like this shows that you've been preparing for this job your whole life, not just the night before.
8. **"If Hollywood made a move about my life, it would be called…"** Engaging, interesting, and entertaining.
9. **"Can I show you, instead of tell you?"** Then pull something out of your pocket that represents who you are. Who could resist this answer? Who could forget this answer?
10. **"The compliment people give me most frequently is…"** Almost like a testimonial, this response also indicates self-awareness and openness to feedback.

Keep in mind that these examples are just the opener. The secret is thinking how you will follow up each answer with relevant, interesting, and concise explanations that make the already bored interviewer look up from his stale coffee and think, "Wow! That's the best answer I've heard all day!"

Ultimately, it's about answering quickly, it's about speaking creatively, and it's about breaking people's patterns.

I understand your fear with such answers. Responses like these are risky, unexpected, and unorthodox. And that's exactly why they work. Otherwise you become (yet another) non-entity in the gray mass of blah, blah, blah.

You're "hireable" because of your answers. When people ask you to tell them about yourself, make them glad they asked.

Let me ask you this: How much time did you dedicate this week to becoming more interesting? Let me suggest this: For the list called, "61 Stupid Things to Stop Doing Before It's Too Late," send an email to me, and you win it for free! scott@hellomynameisscott.com

# The Name of the Game
# Acing the Interview by Avoiding Seven Deadly Sins

By Dani Ticktin Koplik

The numbers say we're officially out of the recession and hiring is up over last year. But employers have been spoiled and are now crazy selective: in the scramble for internships and fulltime jobs, candidates need every advantage they can get.

So, let's assume you've scored the interview and, for argument's sake, so have a number of other candidates. How can you stand out and gain a competitive edge? Aside from having the right qualifications, the single most important thing you can do is control *how you show up*. This is serious business. To underscore the importance, I've come at it from the sinful dark side, on the premise that drama, dysfunction, and disaster (can you say Charlie Sheen?) sell better than good intentions and milquetoast check lists.

For an interviewing edge, beware the Seven Deadly Sins:

### Sin #1:

*Do not* make the interviewer dig through your resume or cover letter to find your objective, your relevant skills, and what benefits you bring to the party. That would only clear a fast path to the trash. Inundated with resumes, recruiters are looking to eliminate bodies so *do not* make it easy. Resumes with objectives or titles up front. Cover letters without the words "I" or "me," 150 words. Have someone else proofread for format, grammar, spelling, and typos. Otherwise, trash!

### Sin #2:

*Do not* undervalue proper etiquette or your personal "presentation." Etiquette should never be an afterthought; in fact, it's increasingly necessary for smooth interactions in a diverse workplace and global marketplace.

### Follow the three "P's":

-- **Punctuality:** Doesn't mean on time; it means 15 minutes early. Arriving late is not only disrespectful but it's irresponsible and signals a lack of interest.
-- **Presence:** Good posture, a great handshake, an easy smile. Keep in mind the phrase "be here now." Presence communicates confidence, engagement and appreciation. Don't overwhelm but definitely express enthusiasm.
-- **Polish:** Appropriate attire (email me for specifics), proper grooming, eye contact, and good manners. *No* calls, texting, tweeting, peeking. And offer to excuse yourself if the interviewer gets an outside call.

Absolutely follow up, ideally with a handwritten note, to convey thanks as well as your interest in the position. Include a touchstone from your conversation, a pearl that demonstrates your thinking and again, show enthusiasm. Personality counts for a lot.

### Sin #3:

*Do not* arrive unprepared. ***Do your homework!*** Using all tools at your disposal, research the company, the industry, and the competition, understand why they open their doors every day, know who the top execs are, read their policies. Be prepared to engage topically and ask thoughtful, interesting questions. Avoid asking "time clock" questions or anything that can be answered on the website.

### Sin #4:

*Do not* make it about you or your quest for personal growth and professional development. Not their problem, at least not initially. Hiring you is about one thing and one thing only: how quickly you will contribute value. Understand this, show initiative and train your focus on the company and how you can best serve.

**Sin #5:**

*Do not* focus only on the task. The new global economy requires a host of skills separate and apart from technical proficiency, which, by the way, is the bare minimum. Process functions that are rational, analytical, and logical can be outsourced or automated; instead, the value is in interpretive, contextual, and innovative thinking, which ideally results in better decisions and solutions. If this hasn't yet made your radar, make it your business to make it your business. You will definitely stand out.

**Sin #6:**

*Do not* forget to listen. Communication is a tentpole skill--without it, nothing else matters. The key to being a great communicator is being a great listener--generally if you really listen, people, clients, interviewers will tell you everything you need to know. It takes discipline but it really truly pays off. When speaking, avoid verbal traps and tics. For example, lose the "like," eliminate upspeak (ending declarative sentences with a question mark), use complete sentences, and don't meander--get to the point. Again, this shows both respect and focus.

**And the DEADLIEST sin of all, #7:**

*Do not* bring your parents! They should remain "of counsel" and in the shadows. Having them schedule your appointments or otherwise show up on site, by phone or in negotiations is highly inappropriate. You'll be perceived as high-maintenance and unable to think on your own. Plus you'll royally upset the interviewer.

*Dani Ticktin Koplik, a career management coach, is expert in extracting peak performance from her corporate and private clients. She can be reached at dtk@dtkResources.com or 201.724.2145.*

# Chapter 12
# Before and After Resume Examples

Following are graphic examples of how three job applicants can be presented in a completely different light. The "Before" resumes were written by the job seekers themselves or other resume writing companies. We're often called upon to rewrite resumes from companies such as Internet job boards attempting to write resumes as a sideline. As with all resumes in this book, applicant and company names have been changed.

Notice the new Titles used on each example. The first example is specific: ***Manufacturing & Logistics Associate.*** The new Title targets an overall industry where Dean seeks to utilize his talents: ***Manufacturing / Logistics.***

In the second example, I replaced a general Objective statement with a shorter, more specific Title: ***Construction Operations / Supervision.*** I also replaced Jason's subjective summary section about personal attributes with high-impact skills and abilities he is likely to use on the job.

In the third example, I replaced Jorie's Summary with a Title, ***Accounting Operations: AP / AR,*** followed by a keyword skill section that paints a picture of her most important talents. I removed all subjective statements, while interpreting and developing her knowledge up front, for quick scanning by both employers and computers. Job sections required improved grammar and punctuation, as well as stronger, more complete sentences.

*Before:*

# Dean DeValle

Current Address:
85 Country Lane
Inverness, Illinois 60007

dean@gotmail.com
Cell: 555-555-1291

## MANUFACTURING & LOGISTICS ASSOCIATE

➤ 5 years experience in manufacturing with warehouse, shipping and inventory control competencies.
➤ Knowledge expert in the production shipping process from preparing customer orders to loading shipping trucks.
➤ Proficient with UPS systems.
➤ Computer Skills: Data Entry and skilled in Microsoft Office - Word & PowerPoint.
➤ Certified Forklift Operator.
➤ Recognized by supervisors for working independently and for continuously recommending ideas to improve safety and quality. Consistently completes work accurately and on-time.
➤ Exceptional attendance record. Familiarity with production reporting.
➤ Experience training new hires and completing behavioral and safety audits.

## EXPERIENCE

Tredegar Corporation, Lake Zurich                                    May 2010 – April 2017
**Support Technician**
Responsible for the set-up process designed to produce plastic film for TV's, computer monitors, diapers and paper towel binding.
→ Accurately led the set-up for >30 finished goods or product packaging directives using resin, cores and packaging supplies.
→ Responsible for the change over process from completing a finished film product to restarting a new production run.
→ Certified forklift driver, loading and unloading trailers. Perfect safety record.
→ Plant recognized for quality and safety excellence.
→ Received hiring bonus for recommending a new hire.

UPS, Palatine, IL                                                  August 2009-May 2010
Responsible for key components of the international shipping process.
→ Managed the quality control process to ensure shipments were defect free. Audited billing information and corrected invoicing errors.
→ Loaded and unloaded trucks efficiently to ensure shipments were on time and complete.

Jim Coleman, Ltd., Palatine, IL                                    September 2007–May 2010
**Warehouse Associate, Inventory Management**
Responsible for the customer fulfillment process.
→ Received materials from UPS, tracked and pulled inventory, shipped and loaded orders to meet product and inventory specifications.

## EDUCATION

Harper College courses                                             2007 - 2008
Fremd High School                                                  2006
Certified Fork Lift Driver                                         2010

# Dean DaValle

85 Country Lane
Inverness, IL 60007

dean@gotmail.com
Cell: 555-555-1291

## *MANUFACTURING / LOGISTICS*

➤ Skilled in manufacturing, logistics and warehousing, including shipping and inventory control for a wide range of operations.

➤ Experience in various production environments; assist in coordinating systems, procedures and processes with managers and supervisors.

➤ Accurately prepare customer orders for cost-effective loading of shipments; proficient in UPS systems; Certified Forklift Operator.

➤ Utilize Windows systems including MS Office, Word and PowerPoint for account tracking and updating, data entry and status reports.

➤ Personally train and motivate new employees; plan and conduct audits related to safety and staff performance; excellent record of safety and attendance; self-motivated and energetic.

## EXPERIENCE

**Tredegar Corporation**, Lake Zurich, IL                    5/10–4/17
**Support Technician**
Performed all aspects of production setup and support in the manufacture of plastic film for TVs, computer monitors, diapers and paper towel binding.

• Accurately led set-up operations for more than 30 finished goods and product packaging directives using resin, cores and packaging supplies.

• Responsible for the changeover process, from completing a finished film product to starting a new production run.

• Loaded and unloaded trailers via forklift, with a perfect safety record.

• Recognized for quality and safety excellence by plant managers.

• Earned a hiring bonus for recommending a new hire.

**UPS**, Palatine, IL                    8/09–5/10
**Shipping Manager**
Responsible for key components of the international shipping process.

• Managed the quality control process to ensure shipments were free of defects.

• Audited billing information and corrected invoicing errors.

• Loaded and unloaded trucks efficiently to ensure shipments were completed on time.

## EDUCATION

**W.R Harper College,** Palatine, IL; completed various liberal arts courses    2007-2008
**Fremd High School,** Palatine, IL; Graduate                    2006
Certified Fork Lift Driver                            2010

*Before:*

**Jason Alba**
**674 N. Leaf Avenue**
**Broadside, Il 60041**
**555-555-9660**
**127@getmail.com**

**Objective:** Obtain full time employment with construction company.

**Summary:**

- **Communications** -- Good written and verbal presentation skills. Use proper grammar and have a good speaking voice.
- **Organization** -- Strong organization skills and common sense.
- **Computer** –Good knowledge of Microsoft Office systems
- **Interpersonal Skills** -- Able to get along well with co-workers and accept supervision. Received positive evaluations from previous supervisors.
- **Flexible** -- Willing to try new things and am interested in improving efficiency on assigned tasks.
- **Attention to Detail** -- Concerned with quality. Produce work that is orderly and attractive. Ensure tasks are completed correctly and on time.
- **Hard-working** – Often worked extra hours when required.
- **Reliable** -- Excellent attendance record.

**Education**
Lane Technical High School, 1996 -2000.

**Other**
In the construction industry of 7 years, I have learned discipline, teamwork, how to follow instructions and work hard. I am ambitious, outgoing, and reliable and have a solid work ethic.

**Job history**

Certified Chimneys  - April 09 to June 2009  Laborer
Damico Consulting  -  March 2005 to present  carpenter/painter/handyman
Relm Properties - Sept 2007 to Dec 2007 carpenter/painter/handyman
Don Bauer Enterprises - Summers 2007 to 2008 carpenter/painter/handyman

**References available upon request**

*After:*

**Jason Alba**
**674 N. Leaf Avenue**
**Broadside, IL 60641**
**555-555-9660**
**127@getmail.com**

## *CONSTRUCTION OPERATIONS / SUPERVISION*

> More than 7 years in commercial and residential construction, including carpentry, basic plumbing/electrical work and painting for a wide range of projects.

> Assist in team training, supervision and motivation; ensure high-quality work, on time and under budget, resulting in a strong referral clientele.

> Familiar with blueprint reading and interpretation; create accurate, clear correspondence, including memos, work orders and contracts; utilize Windows systems including MS Office: Word, Excel and Outlook.

> Plan and conduct written and oral presentations in a professional manner, primarily for architects, builders, contractors, vendors, suppliers and property owners.

> Skilled in the use of all major construction tools including hand and table saws, drills, routers, grinders, sanders and painting/finishing materials.

## EXPERIENCE

Damico Consulting, Chicago, IL                                                    3/05-Present
**Carpenter/Painter/Handyman**
Perform virtually all aspects of construction for a wide range of home renovations, buildouts and room additions for residential and mid-sized commercial structures.
Responsible for basic plumbing and wiring, including sink/shower installations and wiring for overhead lights and ceiling fans.

* Consistently recognized by staff, managers and customers for attention to detail and personal     service.
* Corrected a flaw in purchasing procedures, reducing costs by up to $10,000 annually.

Relm Properties, Schaumburg, IL                                                   9/07-12/07
**Carpenter/Painter/Handyman**
Worked directly with customers to determine and meet their specific needs, primarily for room additions, essential repairs and indoor/outdoor painting projects.

Don Bauer Enterprises, Hoffman Estates, IL                              Summers: 2007-2008
**Carpenter/Painter/Handyman**

## EDUCATION

Lane Technical High School, Niles, IL 1996 -2000

*Before:*

## JORIE ANN HOSSA

674 N. Leaf Avenue • Broadside, IL 60041
847-555-5555 • JeSuis7@mail.com

## QUALIFICATIONS SUMMARY

Self starter, highly motivated, enthusiastic and professional with over 20 years experience in customer service in several different financial industries.

- Ability to prioritize daily workload and respond to requests promptly.
- Common sense and excellent customer service skills.
- Strong interpersonal and organizational skills.
- Strong knowledge of Microsoft Office System.
- Track record of assisting in the implementation of application procedures that reduce labor costs.

## PROFESSIONAL EXPERIENCE

**HENRI STUDIO– Wauconda, IL**                                04/2010 to 1/2017
**Accounts Payable Clerk**
- Managed daily workflow of A/P department.
- Maintained relationship between the company and vendors.
- Responsible for processing invoices and check runs.
- Participated in implementing new paperless process, resulting in streamlined operations.

**Accounts Receivables Assistant**
- Duties include billing of invoices and creating credit memos, applying cash from all incoming lockbox, credit card, ACH and wire payments and processing credit card payments on automated system.

**Customer Service Representative**                           07/2009 to 04/2010
- Responsible for addressing telephone and email problem resolution.
- Provided support to sales team.
- Processed sales orders.

**Shipping Clerk –Temporary**                                03/2009 to 06/2009
- Responsible for paperwork necessary for factory operations.,
- Prepared shipping documentation (bill of lading, packing slips, shipping labels).
- Assist with inventory management.

**DAMICO CONSULTING/ALLBANK MORTGAGE– Ingleside, IL**         03/2005 TO 02/2009
**Loan Processor/Office Manager**
- Assist Loan Office with the processing of applications and obtaining the required documentation from prospective borrowers.
- Processed loan submissions and follow up through several different Lender websites.
- Discussed and prepared credit dispute and problem resolution correspondence for clients.
- Managed daily workflow and accounts payable.

## Professional Experience Continued

**THE HORTON INSURANCE AGENCY** –Orland Park, IL                    09/1993 to 11/1998
**Personal Lines Customer Service Representative**
- Provided support to managers and agents.
- Prepared insurance quotes for prospective customers.
- Addressed telephone and written inquiries.
- Processed claim requests for clients.
- Trained newly hired customer service representatives
- Participated in implementing new paperless process, resulting in streamlined operations.

**FIDELITY INVESTMENTS INSTITUTIONAL SERVICE COMPANY**– Boston, MA        02/1991 to 07/1993
**Client Service Representative/Team Leader**
- Oversee the Capital Markets Trading Team.
- Act as liaison with other institutional departments.
- Coordinated daily workflow, telephone coverage, problem resolution and special projects.
- Implemented team building and training needs with management.
- Prepared quarterly performance reviews for team members.

**FIDELITY INVESTMENTS INSTITUTIONAL SERVICE COMPANY**– Boston, MA        09/1989 to 01/1991
**Client Service Representative**
- Provided client and marketing support for Bank Wholesale Clients.
- Acted as primary operations representative in problem resolution.
- Executed trade transactions.
- Performed daily reconciliation and settling of trades.
- Prepared monthly load compensation reporting.

**PARAGON CABLE**– St. Petersburg, FL                    08/1988 to 08/1989
**Customer Service Representative**
- Addressed incoming telephone inquiries and problem resolution.
- Prepared daily work orders for technicians.
- Processed customer billing.
- Trained newly hired customer service representative.

## PROFESSIONAL DEVELOPMENT

Licensed Loan Originator – State of Illinois – 2005 to 2009
Licensed in Property and Casualty Insurance – State of Illinois –1994 to 1999
Completed NASD Series 6 and 63.
Attended Dr. Dennis Waitley's positive thinking course "The Winners' Edge".

## JORIE ANN HOSSA

674 N. Leaf Avenue • Broadside, IL 60041
847-555-5555 • JeSuis7@mail.com

### *ACCOUNTING OPERATIONS: AP / AR*

➤ Skilled in all aspects of general accounting, bookkeeping and office administration, including personal customer service and executive support in a wide range of industries.

➤ Perform all aspects of accounts payable/receivable and general ledger maintenance; update inventories and communicate with vendors and suppliers for cost-effective purchasing.

➤ Utilize Windows and Microsoft Office systems, including Excel, Word, Outlook and PowerPoint for data compilation, spreadsheets, graphs, charts, presentations and correspondence with staff, managers and C-level clients.

➤ Establish and organize accounting systems and procedures; determine and meet the specific needs of constituents with speed and accuracy, using personal, yet professional communication skills.

### EXPERIENCE

Henri Studio, Wauconda, IL                                                    04/10-1/17
**Accounts Payable Clerk**
Managed all daily activities in the Accounts Payable department, including contract negotiations with vendors, suppliers and contractors.
Accurately processed and filed invoices; developed payment plans to accommodate customers.
Processed and delivered bank deposits, and printed/distributed bi-weekly pay checks to staff and managers.

➤ Researched and implemented a new paperless process, resulting in fast, accurate, streamlined operations.
➤ Improved collections by 25%; wrote and implemented new telephone scripts for collections staff.

**Accounts Receivable Assistant**
Duties included billing and invoice distribution; created credit memos and applied cash from all incoming lockbox, credit card, ACH and wire payments.

➤ Utilized Excel and QuickBooks to process credit card payments; produced and presented monthly status reports to senior management.

**Customer Service Representative**                                           07/09-04/10
Responsible for addressing telephone and email problem resolution.

➤ Provided critical product information and support to the sales team and processed orders, including account servicing and troubleshooting.

**Shipping Clerk**                                            Temporary Position, 03/09-06/09
Updated and processed a wide range of tracking reports and invoices related to factory operations.
Prepared all required shipping documents, including bills of lading, packing slips and shipping labels.

➤ Updated and maintained accurate inventories.

Damico Consulting / Allbank Mortgage, Ingleside, IL                    03/05-02/09
**Loan Processor / Office Manager**
Assisted Loan Office staff and managers in processing loan applications.
Communicated with customers in a professional, yet personal manner to obtain and process all required documentation from borrowers.
Managed daily workflow and all accounts payable procedures.
Processed loan submissions and worked closely with numerous lender websites.
➢ Discussed and resolved credit disputes and various problems, corresponding with clients on a daily basis.
➢ Reduced delinquent accounts by 21%.

The Horton Insurance Agency, Orland Park, IL                    09/93-11/98
**Personal Lines Customer Service Representative**
Provided full support to managers and agents, including the preparation of accurate insurance quotes for prospective customers.
Processed claim requests for clients and answered a wide range of telephone and written inquiries.
➢ Effectively trained, mentored and supervised new customer service representatives.
➢ Involved in creating and implementing a new paperless process, resulting in streamlined operations.

## PRIOR EXPERIENCE

Fidelity Investments – Institutional Service Company, Boston, MA
**Client Service Representative/Team Leader**
Trained and supervised the Capital Markets Trading Team in daily workflow, personal customer service and a wide range of special projects.
Chosen to act as Liaison with other institutional departments.
Coordinated and oversaw telephone coverage and problem resolution to maintain excellent quality and customer satisfactions.
➢ Implemented team building and training standards with management.
➢ Interviewed team members and prepared quarterly performance reviews for managers.
➢ Promoted to this position from:

**Client Service Representative**
Communicated daily with key clients, providing client and marketing support for bank wholesale clients.
Acted as primary operations representative for problem resolution.
Performed daily reconciliations and the execution and settling of trades; prepared load compensation reports.

## PROFESSIONAL DEVELOPMENT / TRAINING

**Licensed Loan Originator** – State of Illinois – 2005 to 2009
**Licensed in Property and Casualty Insurance** – State of Illinois –1994 to 1999
**Completed NASD Series 6 and 63.**
Completed Dennis Waitley's positive thinking course **"The Winners' Edge".**

# Chapter 13

# Resume and Cover Letter Examples

# The Cover Letter

You should create a custom cover letter using key facts about the company's market, product lines and current condition. Even if you only change the first two lines of your cover letter, this helps differentiate you from the pack of applicants who seem to send resumes to every company on earth. Of course, research isn't possible with blind ads, but you can still write a letter emphasizing keywords used in the job posting.

The cover letter is a great place to clarify situations that might be confusing to the reader. Let's say your resume indicates years of experience as a teacher, and you are pursuing a job as leader of a crafts shop. You might use your cover letter to explain that your favorite aspect of the current job is leading and planning craft projects for your students.

The one thing your cover letter should *not* do is repeat the exact same information found in your resume. However, you can certainly elaborate on various points made in your resume by re-writing certain items and adding a new, personalized spin to each item; check the cover letter samples below for creative ideas.

## Who Are They Hiring?

Research shows that up to 65% of recruiters and hiring managers *do* read cover letters. A cover letter is a great place to develop your personal attributes and "soft" skills: self-motivation, personal reliability, dedication to your profession, desire to serve customers, why you like the work you do, and so on.

How long should a cover letter be? As you'll see in the examples below, never more than one page. Begin with a catchy introduction that quickly tells the reader the type of work you're seeking, and why you want to work for them, specifically. Follow this with two-four points that outline skills and achievements most relevant to that particular employer.

Expand on communication skills, or the ability to work well in groups or independently. Remember, for those who do read the letter--either before or after they read the resume--it's critical that the cover letter be as powerfully written and professionally presented as your resume.

Finally, conclude with an action plan, such as: "I'll follow up next week to schedule an interview or answer any questions you may have." If that's not possible, ask the reader to call you to arrange an interview or discuss mutual interests *at their convenience,* or if there's any further information they may require.

**Roger A. Marlin**
2645 Fish Avenue
Schaumburg, IL 60193
847/555-0596
Fishalot@hipster.com

March 5, 2018


Clyde Franklin
Team Manager
Northwest Airlines
Minneapolis-St. Paul International Airport
St. Paul, MN 55111

Dear Mr. Franklin:

I am seeking a position as Aircraft Dispatcher with your company, and have enclosed my resume for your review. Specifically, I would like to better utilize my experience in aircraft dispatching, flight and ground instruction, and ground operations with a major commercial airline such as Northwest Airlines.

- As Aircraft Dispatcher/Crew Scheduler at UFS, Inc., d/b/a United Express, I'm in charge of daily dispatch operations coordinating ATP commuter flights. In addition, I schedule crews on a rotational basis, and am currently a part-time instructor at the Aircraft Flight Dispatcher Training Center.

- Prior to UFS, I worked as an intern at American Flyers, where I gained a solid foundation in ground operations and flight/ground instruction, after having earned an Associate of Science Degree in Business Aviation.

Throughout my career, I've proven my ability to learn new systems and procedures with speed and accuracy. I would welcome the chance to discuss mutual interests, and how my skills may be leveraged to benefit your excellent airline. Thank you for your time and consideration, and I look forward to hearing from you soon.

Regards,



Roger A. Marlin

Enc.

*JOSEPH SLAVICEK*
406 South State Street
Elgin, IL 60123
847/555-8017
JoesPlace@Forklift.com

Mr. Tony Boxit
Total Shippers, Inc.
2345 N. Locust Street
Itasca, IL 60148

Dear Mr. Boxit:

I am pursuing opportunities with Total Shippers, Inc. in Distribution or Warehouse Operations. My background includes Distribution Management, with extensive experience at both line and staff-level supervision in union and nonunion environments.

Throughout my career, I've been deeply involved in creating and managing RF materials management systems, and have directed all aspects of RF, from implementation to training and enhancements to second-generation upgrades.

Most importantly, my peers would tell you I am skilled in providing ongoing team training and development, with a strong commitment to quality and results.

I am available for an interview at your earliest convenience, and can provide solid references at your request. Please let me know when we may meet. I look forward to your response, and thank you for your time and consideration.

Sincerely,


Joseph Slavicek

Enc.

**EDWARD GRABBER**
67812 Castlewood Lane
Bartlett, IL 60109
708/555-9649
Bestmail@motown.com

Dear Hiring Manager:

I am exploring new opportunities in production assembly with your company. Specifically, I am seeking to better utilize my experience developed in positions at various manufacturing and construction companies.

Throughout my employment, I've proven my ability to work effectively with management and staff at all levels of experience. I have also developed an excellent knowledge of assembly tools and equipment, including MIG robotic welders. I can read and interpret blueprints, while keeping a sharp eye on details and results.

Most importantly, I have demonstrated my ability to meet a wide range of product quality and technical specifications.

Please let me know as soon as possible when we may schedule an interview and discuss how my skills can benefit your company.

Thank you for your time and consideration, and I look forward to hearing from you.

Sincerely,


Edward Grabber

**JOSEPH L. LADLE**
5687 Woodview Drive
Medinah, IL 60157
708/555-3819
Spoon@mail.com

May 10, 2018

Mr. Rich Charles
Motorola, Inc.
1303 East Algonquin Road
Schaumburg, IL 60173

Dear Mr. Charles:

In the interest of exploring opportunities with Motorola, I am enclosing my resume for your review. Specifically, I'm seeking to better utilize my experience in the Culinary Arts as a Chef or Sous Chef.

- My career has included full responsibility for the setup of banquets and catered events at Indian Lakes Resort, as well as fine dining for up to 700 guests per day.

- Throughout my career in food service, I have hired, trained and supervised staff in virtually all kitchen operations, while ensuring cost-effective purchasing and inventory control. My peers would tell you I'm self-motivated and energetic, and communicate well with management and staff at all levels of experience.

Because my resume is only a brief outline of my abilities, I would welcome the opportunity to meet with you to discuss mutual interests. In addition, I can provide excellent references on request.

I look forward to speaking with you soon, and thank you for your time and consideration.

Sincerely,


Joseph L. Ladle

**THOMAS G. MINO**
661 Pinewood Lane
Bloomingale, IL 60108
708/555-3052
TomMail@mailit.com

August 22, 2017


Samuel Haber
K.L. Smith Company
724 Eden Way
Elgin, IL 60120

Dear Mr. Haber:

I am exploring new and challenging opportunities with your company and have attached my resume for your review. Specifically, I would like to better utilize my experience in transportation as a Driver/Courier, or in a similar position.

Throughout my career, I've proven my ability to work effectively with management and staff at all levels of experience. Most importantly, I can provide exceptional transportation service in fast-paced environments.

*   I'm detail-oriented, carefully checking delivery instructions and make corrections when necessary to expedite shipments.
*   My background includes full responsibility for the timely and accurate delivery of confidential and sensitive materials.
*   I am self-motivated and energetic, and communicate well with staff, managers and customers.

I can provide excellent references, and am available for an interview at your convenience to discuss how my experience can benefit your company. Please contact me at the above number to arrange a meeting.

Thank you for your time and consideration, and I look forward to hearing from you.

Regards,


Thomas G. Mino

Enc.

**THOMAS P. MUNICH**
118 North Rockwell
Chicago, IL 60659
312/555-5179
Muni@tom.com


September 13, 2017

Sylvia Rothman
Oasis Heating and Cooling, Inc.
7127 Sherwood Drive
Forest Park, IL 60130

Dear Ms. Rothman:

Given the expanding need for home renovations in the Chicago metropolitan area, the demand for quality HVAC installations and repair has never been greater. I recently received Certification in HVAC systems, and am certain my education in state-of-the-art equipment can benefit your customers and your company.

My previous experience and training from the Environmental Technical Institute has provided expert skills in:

► The teardown and troubleshooting of air conditioners, gas and electric furnaces, and a wide range of equipment including humidifiers.

► Communicating with a wide range of customers to determine and meet their needs in a friendly yet business-like manner.

Throughout my employment, I've proven my ability to work well with staff and customers to provide quick, professional service. My co-workers and customers would tell you I'm very self-motivated, with an excellent record of reliability customer satisfaction.

I am enclosing my resume for your review, and would like to meet for an interview to discuss how my skills will benefit your company. I may be reached at the above number, and look forward to hearing from you.

Regards,


Thomas P. Munich

Enclosure

# WILLIAM T. BACKUP

---

## REFERENCES

Curt Fort
Sales Manager / Vice President
Waterfield Financial
11115 Kenwood Road
Cincinnati, OH 45242
513/555-5400


Mindy Semiloff
Ford Consumer Finance
4034 Woodthrush Drive
Grosbeck, OH 45251
513/555-4784


John Donovan
908 Meadowland Drive
Cincinnati, OH 45255
513/555-7022

# WILLIAM T. BACKUP

*Salary History*

(Annual basis)

<u>Vallen Safety Supply Company,</u> **Warehouse Supervisor,** $43,500

<u>Preferred Meal Systems,</u> **Warehouse Manager,** $44,000

<u>Panasonic,</u> **Assistant Manager,** $38,000

<u>Quality Distribution,</u> **Warehouse Manager,** $35,000

<u>Wayco Foods Corporation,</u> **Night Superintendent,** $30,000

<u>Superior Coffee,</u> **Warehouse Superintendent/Production Manager,** $28,000

## *HEWITT A. STREAMLINE*

33188 West Schick
Bloomingdale, IL 60108                    hewfixit@aol.com                              708/555-8047

## *AIRCRAFT MECHANIC*

- ▸ Licensed Airframe and Powerplant Mechanic; with hands-on training
- ▸ in structural repair and composites.
- ▸ Experience in A&P inspections, including the repair and maintenance of systems for the DC-10, DC-9, 747 and 727. Simulators include the 707 cockpit procedural trainer and 747 and L2X maintenance videos.
- ▸ Performed repairs on the Cessna 150, 152, 172 and 172RG.
- ▸ Conversant in Spanish; familiar with Windows 7 and MS Office.
- ▸ Skilled in the use of lathes and standard shop equipment, as well as:

  - • Fiberglass and bonded honeycomb repair
  - • Weighing and balancing of control surfaces
  - • Removal and replacement of skin panels and aircraft fasteners
  - • Manufacture and testing of control cables
  - • Comprehensive modification of aircraft structures
  - • Corrosion control and aircraft painting

## EDUCATION

Southern Illinois University, Carbondale, IL
**B.S. Degree: Aviation Management,** Graduated 5/92

**A.A.S. Degree: Aviation Maintenance Technologies,** Graduated 12/90
▶ Alpha Eta Rho, Professional Aviation Fraternity

## EXPERIENCE

Tapco Corporation (ASLS / Manpower), Wood Dale, IL          2014-Present
**Warehouseman**
Responsible for data entry/retrieval on a proprietary database, as well as production scheduling.
Duties include the shearing of copper-clad laminate for printed circuit boards.
Occasionally supervise up to six employees in stocking, inventory control and forklift operation for truck loading and unloading.

Rice Heating, Hoffman Estates, IL
**Heating / Air Conditioning Service**          Part-time, 9/92-Present

Tim's VW Restoration, Carbondale, IL          1987-1992
**Technician / Assistant Manager**
Performed engine/body rebuilding and inventory control.

# TERRY B. SAFE

2645 Marlin Avenue
Schaumburg, IL 60193   SafeTown@mailit.com   847/555-0596

*AIRCRAFT DISPATCHER*
**Aircraft Dispatcher Certified**

**PROFILE:** Coordinate crew/flight routings and prepare dispatch releases, utilizing the Apollo System and Kavouras weather tracking system, in compliance with FARs and company policies/procedures.

Skilled in decision making and problem solving; effectively handle multiple priorities.

*Additional Certifications:*

| | |
|---|---|
| Flight Instructor-Instrument | December 1994 |
| Flight Instructor-Airplane | December 1994 |
| Commercial Pilot | November 1994 |
| Instrument Rating | February 1994 |
| Private Pilot | June 1989 |

## EMPLOYMENT:

**FS, Inc., d/b/a United Express,** Chicago, IL  2006-Present
**Aircraft Dispatcher / Crew Scheduler**
In charge of daily dispatch operations for nine UFS-owned ATP 64-seat aircraft, including weather checks, routing, crew/aircraft selection and fuel loads for this commuter airline. Generate dispatch releases and secure final signoffs from assigned Captains. Maintain crew schedules for 180 crew members.

**The Hertz Corporation,** Chicago, IL  1995-2006
**City Revenue Manager**
Hired, trained, scheduled and managed 80 counter representatives and 50 shuttle bus drivers in providing rental car services, with responsibility for daily sales.

**Yankee Flyers,** West Chicago, IL  1993-1995
**Internship / Operations Manager and Flight / Ground Instructor**
Scheduled flight students, instructors and aircraft for daily flight training lessons. Administered flight/ground instruction operations within budget guidelines.

## EDUCATION:

**Airline Flight Dispatcher Training Center, Inc.,** Elk Grove, IL 1996
**Certificate: Aircraft Dispatcher**

**Inver Hills Community College,** Grove Heights, MN  1993
**Associate of Science Degree in Business Aviation**

# JOHN B. URBAN

702 Kool Avenue
Streamwood, IL 60107                    Urban@zipit.com                    708/555-0412

## *ASSEMBLY/DISTRIBUTION*
A position where skills in inventory control, tracking and
hydraulic valve assembly would be of value.

**PROFILE:**
- ▶ Comprehensive skills in the assembly of hydraulic valves from as few as three parts to as many as 20.
- ▶ Experience in the setup and organization of warehousing and distribution operations; utilize Fourth Shift data entry software.
- ▶ Perform staff training and supervision in warehousing and distribution procedures.
- ▶ Skilled in Windows 7 and the full MS Office suite.
- ▶ Fluent in Spanish; communicate well with staff, vendors and customers.

## EMPLOYMENT:

Sterling Hydraulics, Inc., Schaumburg. IL                    8/01-present
**Shipping and Receiving Clerk**
Responsible for the accurate inventory, shipping and receiving of hydraulic valve parts for this $7 million company.
Compile and maintain all records of receivables on a daily basis.
Trained and supervised a crew in shipping/receiving and distribution operations.
Assemble various hydraulic valves.
Set up procedures for arranging stock room at the end of each shift.
Ensure the orderly setup of valve parts.
Prepare all paperwork for shipping via UPS and Federal Express.
Operate forklift for truck loading/unloading, stocking, picking and cycle counting.

- ▶ Utilize Excel and Outlook for data entry and inventory control; develop graphs, charts and spreadsheets.

Amp, Inc., Schaumburg, IL                    1998-7/01
**Shipping and Receiving Clerk**
Handled prompt receiving, shipping, order picking/packing and storage of supplies.
Operated forklift for loading/unloading trailers on a busy dock.

First Impressions, Elk Grove Village, IL                    1997-1998
**Shipping and Receiving Clerk**
Performed general warehouse duties including receiving and picking/packing.

## EDUCATION:

Harold Washington College, Chicago, IL
Completed one year of courses in Law Enforcement

Prosser Vocational High School, Chicago, IL                    Graduated 1997

**ZACK BEACH**
67812 Castlewood Lane
Bartlett, IL 60109
708/555-9649
MailZach@beach.com

---

*ASSEMBLY/ PRODUCTION OPERATIONS*

**PROFILE:**
► Extensive background in the assembly and installation of electrical components and machine parts, on job sites and production lines.

► Skilled in troubleshooting and promptly taking corrective action; read and interpret blueprints/bills of materials; adhere to safety policies, procedures and codes.

► Utilize ARC and MIG welders, micrometers, air gun nailers, torque wrenches, hammers, screwdrivers, drill presses, shears, Whitney press; operate forklifts and cranes.

**EXPERIENCE:**

Beardsley and Piper, Inc., Chicago, IL                1/06-Present
**Assembler**
Primarily assemble foundry machines and roofing lines for clients in diverse regions including China and Vietnam; adhere to blueprint and bill of materials specifications.

Coiltech, Schiller Park, IL                10/02-12/05
**Service Representative**
Installed, connected, tested and adjusted new electrical equipment including coils, stackers and slitting lines for large-scale machinery.
 * Traveled to customer sites in the Midwest and West.

Beardsley and Piper, Inc., Chicago, IL                1/97-9/02
**Assembler**
Operated a crane and standard pallet forklifts to assemble and install such parts as large overhead frames.
Performed shipping/receiving activities including packing crate boxes for domestic and international orders.

Littel, Inc., Chicago, IL                4/95-12/96
**Assembler**
Operated automated equipment to assemble and inspect a variety of products including pop cans and automobile hoods, doors and fenders.

**EDUCATION:**

Lincoln Technical Institute, Norridge, IL                Graduated 1994
**Diploma: Automotive and Diesel Mechanic**

Weber High School, Chicago, IL                Graduated 1992

# RICHARD L. SMASH
2358 Aberdeen Court
Schaumburg, IL 60194
Smashmouth@aol2.com
847/555-7056

---

## *AUTO COLLISION REPAIR / SHOP MANAGEMENT*

**PROFILE:**

▶ Extensive background in virtually all aspects of automotive collision repair and operations management, including production, sales and office functions in compliance with industry standards.

▶ Skilled in salesmanship, troubleshooting, billing/job cost estimating, materials/parts procurement and inventory control; well-versed in preferred insurance practices.

▶ Hire, train and supervise technicians in mechanical craftsmanship, technical applications, quality control and flagship customer service.

▶ Utilize Mitchell, ADP and CCC estimating systems; ASE certified in body paint, steering/suspension and AC, and in AC recovery and repair; efficiently operate Chief frame machines, the electronic Chief Genesis measuring system and the FMC four-wheel alignment system.

## EMPLOYMENT:

Wally's CarStar, Des Plaines, IL                              1999-Present
*A collision repair franchise with $1.25 million in average annual revenues.*

**Production Manager**                                             1/94-Present
Supervise up to seven body and paint technicians in daily job assignments, with strict attention to detail to meet delivery deadlines and quality standards.
Provide on-the-job training, schedule and assign jobs, and evaluate worker performance.
Handle customer inquiries and troubleshooting; communicate with technicians and insurance companies to resolve problems with speed and accuracy.
Order parts/supplies and monitor inventory levels.

Write up estimates for customers; work closely with State Farm and American Family insurance staff to process claims.
Process all daily cash, including cash reconciliations and bank deposit preparation.
Track and document information on used parts in accordance with Illinois Secretary of State regulations.

▶ Rated #1 in office operations in 1994 for CarStar nationwide.

## EDUCATION:

Denver Diesel and Automotive College, Denver, CO
Certificate: Basic Collision Course

Maine East High School, Park Ridge, IL

# VICTOR A. WHEEL

3241 Thorn
Keeneyville, IL 60134                708/555-0954                Wheel@carz.com

## AUTOMOTIVE MECHANIC
A position where hands-on skills would be utilized.

## EXPERIENCE:

- Skilled in the repair and maintenance of auto and truck gas and diesel engines and transmissions.
- Handle diagnostic testing on computerized systems; experience in complete teardowns and rebuilds.
- Repair and maintain light and medium duty trucks, autos, mowers, pumps and tractors.
- Utilize Windows 7 and MS Office, including Word and Excel for correspondence writing, spreadsheets and status reports.

## EMPLOYMENT:

Krimson Valley Landscape Co., Roselle, IL                2009-Present
**Mechanic**
Responsible for repair and ongoing maintenance for up to 25 trucks and automobiles, as well as landscape equipment such as mowers and tractors.
Organize job and maintenance schedules.
Previously supervised up to 10 employees in professional landscaping operations.

► Work effectively with staff, management and customers to diagnose, explain and expedite a wide range of repairs.

4B RV - Recreational Vehicles, Streamwood, IL                2008-2009
**Mechanic**
Repaired all types of RV motors and drive trains, as well as internal systems for plumbing and HVAC.
Performed all mechanic's duties for used cars and campers.

Long Chevrolet, Elmhurst, IL                2004-2008
**Line Mechanic**
Responsible for all types of repair on new and used automobiles.

Ray's Arco, Bensenville, IL                2002-2004
**Mechanic**
Worked on all makes and models of small trucks and cars.

## EDUCATION:

Southern Illinois University, Carbondale, IL                2002
**Certificate:** Auto Mechanics

Driscoll High School, Addison, IL                Graduate

# DON BOOKMAN
22616 Plamondon
Addison, IL 60101
650/555-6650
Books@readit.com

---

## *BINDERY OPERATIONS*

**PROFILE:**
- ► Extensive background in virtually all aspects of finishing operations for printed materials, including sales, production and office supervision responsibilities in team environments.
- ► Train and supervise staff in cutting, folding and stitching activities, as well as daily equipment/tool maintenance and repair; maintain quality standards and compliance with customer specifications.
- ► Operate machinery including Lawson, Siebold and Polar paper cutters; Muller Martini, McCainn, Omega and Consolidated stitchers; Baum and MBO folders; 3-knife book trimmers and RB-5 Perfect binders.

## EMPLOYMENT:

Kelvin Press, Broadview, IL                                                10/02-Present
**Finishing Supervisor**
Coordinate and schedule 12 employees in finishing activities for a wide range of commercial jobs, for this printer with sales revenues of $12-$ 15 million.
Provide on-the-job training; evaluate and document individual performance.
Work closely with Sales to assess and meet customer specifications.
Procure, setup and maintain equipment in accordance with job requirements.
- ► Requested by Muller Martini to demonstrate its saddle-stitching machinery to a prospective client.

Olympic Bindery, Broadview, IL                                          1/95-10/02
**President / Co-Owner**
Responsible for the setup and operation of this binding company, as a member of a two-partner team, with responsibility for sales, administration and production.
Hired, trained and managed up to 32 employees in cutting, folding and stitching.

- ► Negotiated the lease for an 18,000 sq. ft facility; configured the layout and purchased/installed the equipment.
- ► Handled a variety of jobs such as AMOCO credit card applications,
- ► PERT crack 'n peel stickers and Ed McMahon/Clearinghouse sweepstake materials.
- ► Key clients included Soodik Printing, Berlin Industries and XX Collins.
- ► Achieved $1 million in sales and developed a client base of 100 accounts.

Progressive Bindery, Clyo, IL                                            4/91-12/94
**Foreman**
Supervised up to 30 employees in production activities.

Bell Litho, Elk Grove Village, IL                                        3/89-4/91
**Combination Operator**

# JAMES A. HOUSEMAN
2357 North Sheridan Road, #SB
Chicago, IL 60660
708/555-0257 or 312/555-2004
Housedude@when.com

---

**Building Maintenance**
A position where maintenance and mechanical expertise would be utilized in a team environment.

**EXPERIENCE:**

► Proven ability to maintain buildings and mechanical equipment, including contracting outside services, troubleshooting and professionally handling tenant requests.

► EPA Certified for Type I maintenance; expert in HVAC systems such as refrigeration, air conditioning, heating and electronics.

► Skilled in various trades and maintenance; repair and installation services include:

| | |
|---|---|
| ► Plumbing | ► Electrical |
| ► HVAC | ► Carpentry |
| ► Drywall | ► Tile |
| ► Pest Control | ► Floor |

**EMPLOYMENT:**

Village Park, Westmont, IL                                      2004-Present
**Building Maintenance Supervisor**
Responsible for maintaining plumbing, electrical systems, boilers, lighting and other repair and mechanical work for a 400-unit apartment complex.

233 East Walton, Chicago, IL                                   1999-2003
**Building Engineer**
In charge of maintaining common areas of this first-class condominium building, including heating, ventilation and other utilities; assisted tenants in repairs and maintenance.

El Lago Condominium Association, Chicago, IL                   1997-1998
**Building Maintenance Technician**
Responsible for general maintenance of boilers, circulating pumps and cooling towers.

Malibu East Condominium Association, Chicago, IL               1992-1997
**Building Maintenance Technician**

**CERTIFICATION:**

EPA Certification, Type I                                       1991
Air Conditioning Contractors of America

**ADVANCED TRAINING:**

HVAC Systems, Janitors Local #1                                1992

# THOMAS SLICER

2204 Oak St.
Roselle, IL 60172        Chopper@block.net        708/555-1858

**OBJECTIVE:**  *BUTCHER / MANAGER*
A position utilizing expertise meat and food merchandising, as well as personal customer service.

**EXPERIENCE:**

■ Proven abilities in all aspects of butchering, retail meat processing and merchandising, including quality control, sanitation and staff management.

■ Train and motivate meat processing personnel; conduct training sessions on meat products and consult/communicate with senior retail managers and store owners on merchandising.

■ Develop and implement cost-effective inventory control procedures and policies; plan and prepare product displays.

## EMPLOYMENT:

Dominick's Stores, various positions and locations:

Buffalo Grove, IL
**Meat Cutter**        6/03-Present
Responsible for solving meat department operational problems; handle meat product processing; train department personnel.

Two Hoffman Estates, IL
**Meat Department Manager**        1996-6/03
Directed and supervised entire meat department operation, including processing and quality control; set up product displays, trained and supervised up to 10 employees.

Several Chicago-area suburban stores
**Meat Processing Training Specialist**        1992-1996
Planned and conducted training sessions in meat product management and merchandising for meat department managers and line personnel.

## EDUCATION:

J.B. Conant High School, Hoffman Estates, IL        Graduate

# HAMMER T. NAIL
2811 Amelia
Addison, IL 60101
Nailit@board.com
708/555-9335

---

## *CARPENTRY / CONSTRUCTION*
A position where proven skills would be of value.

- Skilled in Carpentry, Woodworking and Cabinetry, including project supervision from excavation to final trim.
- Train and supervise work crews in commercial/residential remodeling and new construction projects; coordinate schedules, staff, laborers and managers from all the major trades.
- Handle material and supply ordering, as well as vendor/customer relations and quality control.

## EXPERIENCE

J.S. Adams, Inc., Des Plaines, IL                                    1994-Present
**Journeyman Carpenter**
Responsible for all types of carpentry, including framing and final trim work for commercial and residential remodeling and new construction projects throughout the Chicagoland area.
Supervise up to 50 carpenters and other professionals in electrical work, plumbing, brick laying, roofing, HVAC, concrete forming and excavating.
Order materials and blueprint updates; consistently meet strict time constraints.
Experience with hundreds of projects including:

* Addition: A major nursing home.
* Remodeling: Emergency Room, Michael Reese Hospital.
* Addition/Remodeling: A major food processing plant.
* Remodeling: A major youth academy.
* Addition: A 30-door loading dock for a major bread company.

Mayfair Construction, Chicago, IL                                    1993-1994
**Commercial Carpenter**

Tureck Construction, Chicago, IL                                    1986-1993
**Residential Carpenter and Trim Foreman**
Supervised a wide range of carpentry and trim work for custom-built homes in Lincolnshire, IL.
Supervised up to 20 employees in all procedures.

Corona Furniture, Chicago, IL                                    1982-1986
**Custom Furniture Maker**
Responsible for complete fabrication of custom, ornate furniture, including replicas of desks and cabinets.
Operated and maintained all tools in a complete mill shop.

**PERSONAL:**        Self-motivated and professional.
                     Willing to begin at entry-level and advance within a well-run company.

# WATTS T. DEAL
1249 Grant Circle, Apt F
Streamwood, IL 60107
Deal@Watts.com
Cell: 708/555-0835

## *CASINO OPERATIONS / HOSPITALITY SERVICES*

**PROFILE:** ► Extensive background in customer-oriented service operations and business development, including sales, marketing, promotions and cost control.

► Excellent communication skills; maintain positive relations with staff and customers in high-volume, fast-paced operations.

► Proven ability to handle currency and financial transactions accurately; resolve discrepancies promptly; licensed by the Illinois Gaming Board.

► Familiar with Windows 7, MS Word, Excel, QuickBooks, and the specialized systems MUTUALINK and KRONOS; utilize the TRW system to run credit checks.

**EMPLOYMENT:**
Grand Victoria Casino, Elgin, IL                                    9/04-Present
**Cage Supervisor**
Responsible for up to 100 employees including 74 cashiers, four soft count supervisors and 13 soft count clerks in cashiering for this riverboat casino.
Monitor the KRONOS payroll reports for payroll information.
Utilize Quattro Pro to schedule cashiers and track cash over/short counts.

Run customer credit requests through the TRW credit report system.
Monitor transactions for zero-tolerance adherence to the Illinois Gaming Board regulations.
Prepare currency transaction reports (CTR) as required under Chapter 31.
Submit incident and credit fraud reports to Security personnel.

- Trained in the Trace Miller Company reservation booking system.
- Promoted from Cage/Ticketing Supervisor.

Casino Queen, East St. Louis, IL                                    2003-2004
**Main Banker / Cashier**
In charge of all aspects of cage/bank operations for this riverboat casino.

First State Federal Credit Union, Dover, DE                         2001-2003
**Head Teller**

Army & Air Force Exchange Service, Ramstein Air Base, Germany        1999-2001
**Central Checkout Supervisor**

**TRAINING:** ■ Frontline Leadership, Principles of Management and CUNA Star (Customer Service) Modules Training.

# Timothy A. Watcher

112 Lexington Drive #306
Mt Prospect, IL 60056                     Watch@tim.net                          847/555-1041

## *CATV LINE MAINTENANCE / SWEEP*

**PROFILE:**    ▶  Skilled in all aspects of MATV and CATV line sweep, configuration and maintenance, from head-end and nodes to fiber optic connections, cabling and indoor/outdoor installations to multiple TVs.

▶  Proficient in the fine-tuning of amps and the use of taps and connectors; splice from nodes to term taps and proof prints for upgrades.

▶  Experience in staff hiring, training and supervision in all major operations, including customer communications, status reporting and quality control.

## EXPERIENCE:

Contracts with TCI Cable Co., Mt. Prospect, IL

**Contractor:** ANS, Inc., Westminster, PA                          4/08-9/08
Performed walkouts and proofed prints for high-quality upgrades.

**Supervisor:** Voltelcon, Rancho Cuca Monga, CA                2/05-3/08
Trained and supervised up to 12 in CATV upgrades, including a 750 mhz MATV upgrade for FOX Broadcasting and an upgrade for Time Warner.
Utilized prints and processed node orders; routed all work and processed staff time sheets.
Produced end-of-day update prints and updated all production logs.
Worked with vendors and suppliers; ordered all materials and processed payroll.

▶  Directed the MATV/CATV system setup at Fox Broadcasting in Los Angeles, including all routing, splicing and activation for numerous on-site monitors.
▶  Acted as liaison with Fox executives and maintained all work schedules and quality control.
▶  Lead Person with Time Warner executives for their CATV system in Oahu, HI.

**Contractor:** R.S. Services, Barrington, IL                          9/04-2/05
Performed system upgrades including splicing and activation.
Supervised a CATV upgrade project for Continental Cable in Romeoville.

**Prior experience** with the City of Chicago installing CATV Install and Service Technician for Lakes Cable; installed underground and aerial systems.

## EDUCATION:

Completed NCTI courses:
Installer, Installer Tech. and Service Tech.

McHenry High School, McHenry, IL                          **Graduate**

# JOSEPH L. LADLE

5687 Woodview Drive
Medinah, IL 60157
708/555-3819
Spoons@soup.com

## *CHEF / SOUS CHEF*

**EXPERIENCE:**
- Diverse experience as Chef or Sous Chef, including full responsibility for staffing, inventory control, cost-effective purchasing and all kitchen operations.
- Experience with a wide range of American, Italian and Asian cuisine, as well as French Fine Dining.
- Skilled in the complete setup and management of banquets, cafeterias and kitchens for high-volume breakfasts, luncheons and dinners.
- Effectively hire, train and supervise all levels of kitchen staff in food preparation and state-of-the-art presentation; fluent in Spanish.

## EMPLOYMENT:

The Point Supper Club, Bloomingdale, IL       12/94-Present
**Sous Chef**
Prepare a wide range of soups, appetizers and specialty dishes for this fine dining restaurant with banquet service for up to 200.
Assist in interviewing, hiring and scheduling up to 20 staff.
Handle food ordering, inventory control and kitchen supplies.
*     Create and prepare daily specials ranging from Asian, Seafood and Steak to Health-oriented dishes.

Indian Lakes Resort, Bloomingdale, IL       4/88-11/94
**Head Chef**       6/93-11/94
Responsible for 10 employees and all operations of the Frontier Grill, specializing in American Cuisine.
Supervised breakfasts, lunches and dinners for up to 700 meals per day.
Coordinated stocking, inventory control and payroll in a cost-effective manner.
*     Organized all work schedules and trained/managed personnel, including a Sous Chef, Line Cooks, Pantry Chefs and Dishwashers.

**Sous Chef:** On-The-Pond Restaurant       7/92-6/93
Effectively hired, trained and supervised up to 20 employees in the preparation of French Fine Dining and American Cuisine. Maintained inventories and purchased food and supply. Handled a wide range of food service and banquet duties.
*     Managed the employee restaurant, with up to 600 meals per day.

**Sous Chef, Lead Line Cook and Pantry Chef**
Frontier Grill       4/88-7/92

## EDUCATION:

Washburne Trade School, Chicago, IL
**Culinary Arts Degree**       4/92

Davea Vocational School, Addison, IL
**Culinary Arts Program**       Certificate: 6/90

Current Member: **Culinary and Pastry Arts Advisory Council**

**MARK C. HAMMER**
2266 Augusta
Elgin, IL 60120
708/555-0627
Handle@wood.net

## CONSTRUCTION MANAGER / SUPERINTENDENT

**EXPERIENCE:**

■ More than 10 years in construction supervision including accurate takeoffs, estimating, budgeting, contracting, purchasing and invoicing.
■ Experience in full on-site construction management and land development; effectively schedule, monitor and inspect all work from start to customer orientation.
■ Work effectively with architects, engineers, developers, bankers, contractors, inspectors, city officials, decorators, agents and home buyers.

**EMPLOYMENT:**

Pulte Home Corporation, Hoffman Estates, IL          7/07-Present
**Superintendent**
Responsible for contractors and all activities on site for single family and townhome projects.
Schedule, monitor and inspect all work from start to customer orientation.
*   Maintain budgets, process invoices and control overhead costs.

J.H. Darnell & Sons, Dallas, TX          8/03-7/07
**Joint Venture**
Researched and selected subdivisions lots for custom homes valued up to $1 million.
Involved in interim finance acquisition, budgeting, contracting and interface with architects on design.
Accountable for all activities from start to customer orientation.
*   Assisted in sales activities; Texas Real Estate License.

**Superintendent**          8/01-1/03
Responsible for scheduling, monitoring and inspecting all custom home work from start to finish.
Performed customer service and orientations in a professional manner.
*   Directed the construction of homes valued up to $2 million.

U.S. Home, Dallas, TX          3/96-8/01
**Superintendent**
Budgeted and contracted work on condominium projects.
Scheduled, monitored and inspected all work from start to completion; handled customer orientations.
Processed invoices and directed the service department for the project.

**EDUCATION:** University of Wisconsin, LaCrosse, WI Major: Management Minor: Marketing

U.S. Home, Inc., and Pulte "U", Pulte Home Corp.
Completed Management Development Programs.

# RICK RODRIGUEZ

2161 W Schaumburg Road #137
Phoenix, AZ 20193        Rickmail@guez.com        708/555-9010

## *CONTRACTOR / CARPENTER*

**PROFILE:** More than 12 years in building and construction operations, including nine years in all aspects of carpentry for homes valued up to $ 1 million.

Supervise and coordinate carpenters in rough framing, interior trim and exterior elevations; maintain excellent quality and work closely with carpenters, builders and subcontractors.

Perform lumber takeoffs and estimate, purchase, and schedule materials in a cost-effective manner; interpret blueprints and work with building inspectors.

## EMPLOYMENT:

Sun Contractors, Inc., Schaumburg, IL        2000-Present

**Owner / Operator**
Responsible for high-quality construction of homes, room additions and numerous remodeling and construction projects.
Trained, supervised and motivated crews of up to 10, including wage determination, assignments, and terminations. Successful experience in all aspects of custom home carpentry, including full contractor duties, with a variety of builders including:
- Carpentry Foreman for Artisan Development Group, Barrington, IL
- Calia Development, Wilmette, IL

Two homes in South Barrington and Long Grove, IL, valued at $500,000 and $600,000 respectively.

- JWW Builders, Barrington, IL; $900,000 home.
- Affinity Corporation, Arlington Heights, IL; $800,000 home.
- Old Colony Builders, Barrington, IL

Responsible for 15 different homes valued up to $400,000 each.

- Ivanhoe Development, Mundelein, IL; three homes valued up to $500,000 each.
- Schwall Builders, Northbrook, IL; custom home valued at $650,000.
- Kelgor Construction Company, Barrington, IL; home valued at $600,000.
- Sauers Bros. Construction, Laguna Niguel, CA

One home valued at $1 million and five duplex homes:
- Carpenters, Inc., St. Charles, IL

## EDUCATION:

Washburne Trade School, Chicago, IL        1990

Completed Journeyman four-year program in three years.
High School Graduate

# ALBERT L. CALL

2145 Devon Avenue
Hanover Park, IL 60103                    Bertmail@call.com                    630-555-5882

## COMMERCIAL DIVER

**PROFILE:**

▶ Comprehensive experience in a wide range of technical functions including commercial diving and pipe fitting.

▶ Skilled in heavy-duty welding, brazing pipe leaks and penetration diving to 5000 feet coordinate and oversee complete ground operations.

▶ Proven ability to perform heavy duty work in difficult conditions. Handle equipment management responsibilities such as maintenance and light repair; CPR and First Aid Certified.

## EXPERIENCE:

Scott Diving Service, Palatine, IL                    6/06-Present
**Diving Submarine Contractor**
Perform all types of underwater operations including construction, debris removal, traveling screen repair and measurements.
Handle penetration work up to 5000 feet; video tape and inspect structures.
Document findings with verbal and written reports.
Perform contaminated diving as well as underwater burning to repair and rebuild traveling screens.

H. B. Fuller Tea Inc., Palatine, IL                    11/04-6/06
**Materials Handler**
Responsible for a wide range of materials management functions such as inventory control, stock organization and stock retrieval.
Handled forklift operations.
Assisted in the development and documentation of ISO 9000 procedures.
Performed quality assurance testing of tile grout to ensure compliance with product requirements.

▶ Created, documented and presented a plan to reorganize the inventory storage system. The adopted plan improved inventory accuracy, production line productivity and allowed for proper cycle of dated inventory.

The Tree Company of Barrington, Barrington. IL          10/03-11/04
**Ground Man**
Managed the setup, operation and maintenance of all ground equipment, including chippers and shredders, during tree trimming functions.

## TECHNICAL TRAINING:

International Commercial Diving Institute, Wilmington, DE
**Graduated: Certified Commercial Diver**          2006

**Certifications in CPR and First Aid**          2005

**DANIELLE GLOSSLEP**
2221 Morningside
Roselle, IL 60172
630/555-0715
Dani@mail.com

*COSMETOLOGY / TRAINER*

**PROFILE:**    ▶ Skilled in all aspects of cosmetology training for groups and individuals, including full program planning, seminars, classroom presentations and student performance reviews.

▶ Topics include hair coloring and pressing, skin care, makeup, platform work and aesthetics; well versed in Nexxus and all major cosmetic brands.

▶ Handle direct customer service and sales with personal communication skills; fluent in Italian and familiar with Spanish.

**EXPERIENCE:**

Gianni Cosmetics, Bloomingdale, IL                                        2005-2017

**Makeup Artist / Aesthetician**
Worked directly with all types of customers and applied cosmetics; trained customers in product lines and applications.

Ippolito School of Cosmetology, Chicago, IL                    Intermittent: 2005-2006
Planned and conducted courses in theory, (Milady textbook) as well as basic and advanced courses in permanent waving, color, hair cutting, braiding, air waving, curling iron, skin care, makeup, waxing and aromatherapy.
Trained a wide range of students in product lines and applications, primarily through practical demonstration and supervision of hands-on practice.

* Conducted clinics on sales presentations.
* Supervised all practical work done by students and provided feedback.
* Conducted a lecture and in-salon demonstrations for Nexxus' Aloxxi color, Chicago area, 2006.
* Supervised vocational education field trips and community involvement; prepared students for competitions.
* Prepared students for testing; supervised the mock state board exam; contacted judges and oversaw student competitions.

**ACTIVITIES:**    Administered classes for Capilustro, Inc.
Worked the Midwest Beauty Trade Show for this Florida wig company. Assisted in training for competition on student and professional levels. Set up and managed a skin care center, performing facials, makeup, aromatherapy and waxing.

**EDUCATION:**    Ippolito School of Cosmetology, Chicago, IL
Completed cosmetology and instructor training.                    2005

College of Lake County, Grayslake, IL                    2004
Completed courses in Basic Computing, Psychology and Spanish.

**MARIE R. DANCER**
512 Heath Court
Streamwood, IL 60107
630/555-9460
Swing@mail.com

## CRUISE SHIP ENTERTAINER

**PROFILE:**

▶ Comprehensive experience and training in dance including Modern, Lyrical, Pop, Ballet, Pointe and Jazz.

▶ Quickly learn new dance routines; skilled in modeling for various corporate accounts such as Margie's Bridal and House of Brides; experience in runway modeling.

▶ Willing to travel or relocate for the right opportunity; traveled nationwide for weeks at a time, especially on the east coast.

▶ Trained or danced with various professionals including: Waltamore Casey, Van Collins, Jason Myers, Ted Jackson and the Homer Bryant Dance Troupe.

**EXPERIENCE:**

The Chicago Honeybear Dancers, Chicago, IL                     2005-2007
**The Honeybears** - Director: Greg Schwartz
As member of the Chicago Honeybears, formerly the Chicago Bear Cheerleaders, performed at numerous shows and fulfilled dance and modeling contracts.

Ted Jackson: Midwest Jazz Troupe, Chicago, IL                     2005-2006
**Dancer**
Learned numerous routines and performed in various shows in the Midwest.

**TRAINING:**

Golden's School of Dance, Schaumburg, IL
**Master Classes: Dance Training**

Waltmore Casey, Director: Illinois Ballet Academy, Chicago, IL
**Dance Training**

Aragona Dance, Bartlett, IL
**Dance Training**

**EDUCATION:** Elgin Community College, Elgin, IL
**General Studies**                                                          2008

Streamwood High School, Streamwood, IL                     Graduated 2007
Completed college preparation courses
\* **Captain Senior Year: Varsity Pom-Poms**                     Member: 2004-2007

**PERSONAL:**  Height: 5'7"              Measurements: 34-24-34
                      Blue Eyes / Brown Hair      Weight: 120 lbs.
                      Size 3/5                        Born 7/11/89

# Diana M. Service

43138 Wasdale Avenue
Elk Grove Village, IL 60007                Diana@mail.com                                 847/555-1569

## *CUSTOMER SERVICE: AIRLINE INDUSTRY*

► Comprehensive experience in professional customer service, with a proven ability to identify and meet client needs and expectations.

► Completely fluent (verbal and written) in Spanish and English. Proficient in many major PC applications, including Windows 7, Excel and MS Word; utilize ACT! and update/maintain client information on proprietary software and systems.

## EXPERIENCE

Sloan Valve Company, Franklin Park, IL
**Assistant to the Manager**                                                           2006-2017
Promoted to this position to perform various customer service and administrative functions, including writing correspondence and file/ documentation maintenance.
Met client requests for information such as marketing materials and product specifications.
► Developed an Excel spreadsheet to track and calculate monthly sales commissions.

**Customer Service / Data Entry**                                          2004-2006
Responsible for entering correspondence in MS Word, creating invoices, maintaining accurate files and handling incoming phone calls. Provided product information to customers and entered sales orders into customized software package.

USA One National Credit Union, Bensenville, IL                       2001-2003
**Assistant Branch Supervisor**
Responsible for supervising the daily operations of this facility, including handled cash transactions and customer service.
Opened and closed checking and savings accounts; issued loan checks, money orders and travelers' checks; explained loan programs to customers.

Howard Johnson Hotel, Schiller Park, IL                              1998-2001
**Front Desk Supervisor**
Handled all aspects of customer check-in/out, reservations and staff supervision. Effectively identified and resolved problem situations in a professional manner.
Prepared weekly staff work schedules, and approved or denied all customer credits.

Holiday Inn, Des Plaines, IL                                           1996-1998
**Reservations Manager**
Assigned rooms to guests and managed space availability. Worked with major clients to negotiate and reserve blocks of rooms. Handled the billing for major accounts and Privilege Plus Members.

## EDUCATION

Harper College, Palatine, IL                        **Associate Degree in Business**
Successfully completed nearly two years of credit toward degree.
Relevant courses included Marketing, Management, French and Accounting.

# CATHERINE N. MYERS

| 287 Lewis Drive | Kate@mail.com | Salem, OR 67488 | 723/555-1730 |

**OBJECTIVE:**

DATA ENTRY / GENERAL OFFICE SUPPORT
A position where proven organizational skills would be utilized.

**PROFILE:**

* Experience in basic accounting including billing, inventory control and order entry on Windows systems; familiar with MS Word and Excel for spreadsheets.

* Assist in staff hiring, training and supervision with solid communication skills; handle customer complaints and problems with tact and professionalism.

**EMPLOYMENT:**

Alomo Canyon Hotel, Bloomingdale, VA          2000-2017
ASSISTANT SUPERVISOR
Responsible for training and supervising one assistant in order entry and billing for this high-volume resort with ski lodge, restaurant and hotel.
Worked directly with the clientele: booked reservations, distributed keys and delivered phone messages in the absence of regular front desk staff.
* Promoted to this position from Front Desk Clerk.
* Volume of positive customer response cards increased by 20 percent in the last two months at this position.

Speedy-Quick Shop, Richmond, VA          1998-2000
ORDER ENTRY ASSISTANT
Utilized an IBM PC for order expediting and the printing of customer invoices.
Packed and shipped hundreds of individual orders via the post office, UPS and various overnight carriers.

Blue Shirt Warehouse, Newton, VA          1995-1998
Promoted to three positions, most recent first:

ADMINISTRATIVE ASSISTANT
Responsible for order entry, stock transfers and price code updates.
Work directly with store managers to facilitate new openings.
Expedite stock procurement and the delivery of store fixtures.

MERCHANDISING REPRESENTATIVE
Acted as liaison between managers of six stores and corporate directors.

WAREHOUSE REPRESENTATIVE
Distributed bulk shipments to 54 stores nationwide.

**EDUCATION:**

Oakton Community College, Richmond, VA  5/95
Successful completion of courses in English, Algebra and Psychology

# MICHAEL TONKA

22637 Fairview Lane
Schaumburg, IL 60193                    Tonkmike@mail.com                    847-555-5987

## DRIVER: CONSTRUCTION EQUIPMENT

**EXPERIENCE:**

▶ CDL Class A License holder with accident-free record; skilled in driving a wide range of trucks including:

* Dump trailers          * Redi-mix
* Flatbeds               * Low boys

▶ Experience in the safe loading and unloading of construction materials.
▶ Update and maintain accurate records of shipments, routes and related costs.
▶ Additional skills in construction, general carpentry and contracting for remodeling, patios and decks.

**EMPLOYMENT:**

Mark Kennedy / WEN Enterprises, Batavia, IL                    4/02-Present

**Driver**
Responsible for the safe driving of various trucks, including flatbeds and dump trailers.
Assist in training new drivers in all company procedures, including updating of daily trip sheets and work orders.

* Duties include loading, delivery and unloading of large sewer pipe, including strapping and chaining.

Newton Construction, Schaumburg, IL Part-Time/Weekends     2002-Present
**Construction**
Perform general construction for room remodeling, concrete and wood patios and decks.

Harry W. Kuhn, West Chicago, IL                    199-2002
**Driver**
Handled daily driving of Redi-mix and dump trucks, delivering gravel and concrete.

**EDUCATION:** W.R. Harper College, Palatine, IL                    1986-1987

Successful completion of several classes in Culinary Arts and Restaurant Management.

J.B. Conant High School, Hoffman Estates, IL                    1984
**Graduate**

*STEVEN B. JOBBS*

1019 Woodside Drive
Roselle, IL 60172                                    Job@mail.com                                    630/555-3387

## ROAD WORKER / DRIVER

**PROFILE:**   ►   Proven abilities in road repair including patching with asphalt and concrete; work well with others at all levels of experience.

►   Experience in heavy lifting and the driving of equipment including Class "C" trucks (licensed), bobcat shovels, snowplows and small steamrollers.

## EXPERIENCE:

Illinois Department of Transportation (I.D.O.T), Schaumburg, IL 9/07-4/09
**Highway Maintainer**
Responsible for a wide variety of road service functions including road maintenance, damage repairs and snow removal.
Communicated with others in the field to coordinate activities and maintain high project quality.

Schneider National Carriers, Green Bay, WI                                    9/02-9/07
**Licensed Driver - CDL Class C**
Performed all aspects of product delivery and pickup including customer service, transportation and equipment maintenance. Served successfully in four divisions with unique responsibilities in each.

\*   Received special recognition for Exceptional Customer Service, Safety and Skills.

*Specialized Division:*
**Lead Driver** responsible for all equipment maintenance and repairs.
Worked directly with clients in a professional, personable manner to identify and meet client needs.
\*   Recognized as the top producer at Weyerhaeuser.

*Truck Rail Division:* Transported trailer loads within rail yards throughout Chicago.
Developed contacts and utilized communication skills to improve efficiency.

*Dedicated Division:* Delivered merchandise from a distribution center to area Target Department Stores.

►   Provided 100% on-time delivery service.

## EDUCATION:

International Truck Driving School, Northlake, IL            2002
Completed the Driver Training program.

William Rainey Harper College, Palatine, IL            2001
Successfully completed courses in Psychology and Social Studies.

# IZIO SITTARO

2294 Route 53
Addison, IL 60104
Sitt@mail.com
630/555-8062

## *SALES REPRESENTATIVE / ROUTE DRIVER*

**PROFILE:**
► Skilled in direct customer service, sales and delivery procedures, including cash collecting, account tracking and status reporting.

► Class "C" Driver with an excellent safety record; skilled in driving forklifts and stackers; handle basic data entry and retrieval on computer systems.

► Experience with credits, returns and UPS/FedEx shipments; assist in stocking, inventory control and all major warehousing operations.

► **Fluent in English, Italian and Spanish;** experience in training and supervising staff in customer service and business procedures.

## EXPERIENCE:

Calabrese Baking Company, Franklin Park, IL                     2005-Present
**Driver / Sales Representative**
Responsible for the prompt delivery of bread and baked goods to key accounts in the Chicagoland area, including Dominick's and Jewel Foods.
Service a variety of stores, restaurants and food stands.
Determine efficient routes and drive in a safe manner.
Work closely with customers and update and rotate products on store racks; accurately count and check all items.
Compile and issue customer invoices; handle product returns and credits as required.
Collect accurate payments from accounts.

► Developed a strong client base and constantly seek new accounts.

Turano Baking Company, Bloomingdale, IL                     2001-2005
**Driver / Production**
Duties included mixing and baking for items such as bread and cookies; filled cannoli shells and handled a wide range of production duties. Used kitchen equipment and performed route driving to retail accounts.

Ciao Café, Norridge, IL                     2002-2005
**Manager / Owner**
In charge of all operations at this coffee shop, including food purchasing, general accounting and sales.
Performed all staff hiring, training and supervision.

## EDUCATION:

Triton College, River Grove, IL
**State of Illinois Sanitation Certified**                     1999-2001

DeMarinis School, Bari, Italy                     2002
**Graduate: High School Equivalent**

# ILYA PATEL

671 Windmill Drive
Hanover Park, IL 60103          Patel@mail.com                    708/555-1858

**OBJECTIVE:** *ELECTRONICS: PROTOTYPE / MECHANICAL ASSEMBLY*
A position utilizing proven technical and training skills.

**EXPERIENCE:**

- Expert in building, testing and repairing electronic and mechanical components for telecommunications products.

- Proficient at interpreting and implementing blueprints, schematic drawings, engineering scratch diagrams and Macintosh drawings.

- Effectively work with engineers and managers to develop cost-effective electronic assembly procedures that meet established production deadlines.

**EMPLOYMENT:**

Teradyne Inc., Deerfield, IL                              2016-Present
**Mechanical Assembler**
Personally perform and train others in technical assembly of telecommunications components: remote measuring unit 2000; test system control units 400, 410, 710 and 720; Telzon block wire-wrapping; artificial lines and voice response systems 400 and 700.

* Selected to provide periodic training on these projects for other employees.
* Assist with troubleshooting and repair of machinery.
* Assist other employees with slide line production functions.

Tektronix, Portland, OR                              1990-2016
**Electronic Assembler**
Performed wire connection, wire wrapping, board stuffing, hand soldering, clipping and troubleshooting on circuit boards, capacitors, resistors, oscilloscopes and generators.

**EDUCATION:**

Sardar Patel University, Anand, India

**Completed courses in Physics (Electricity), Mathematics, English and Chemistry.**

# SAMUEL ROBERTS

2229 West North Avenue
#A Villa Park, IL 60181                    Rob@mail.com                    650/555-7124

## *JOURNEYMAN ELECTRICIAN*

**PROFILE:**  ▶  Comprehensive experience in the repair and maintenance of motors, control panels and major mechanical and electrical systems, including timers, circuit breakers, feeders, coils and relays.

▶  Experience in commercial and residential electrical wiring, repair and maintenance, as well as mechanical system troubleshooting,

▶  Effectively train staff in system repairs, operations and procedures; utilize multi-meters and
oscilloscopes; familiar with Windows for data entry and retrieval.

## EXPERIENCE:

Steiner Electric, Chicago, IL                                    2016-Present
**Journeyman Electrician**
Responsible for the repair and maintenance of AC, DC, single and 3-phase motors, including rewinding and clutch/brake repair.
Perform commercial/residential wiring, and mechanical repair of machine shop equipment.
Utilize troubleshooting skills for a broad range of electrical operations and equipment.

Advanced Electric, Addison, IL                                  1997-2016
**Electrician**
Utilized a variety of skills in the repair and installation of wiring, as well as winding for electrical motors, breakers and reducers.

New Super Laundry Machine Co., Chicago, IL
**Customer Service Manager**                                    1990-1997
Trained and supervised staff in diagnostic techniques and the repair of laundry equipment.
Repaired control panels and acted as company representative on the phone and in the field.
Updated inventories of parts and worked with vendors and suppliers.

*   Saved more than $200,000 in equipment costs.

## EDUCATION:

DeVry Institute of Technology, Chicago, IL
Received certificate for two-year program in Digital Electronics

Coyne American Institute of Technology, Chicago, IL
Electrical Maintenance Diploma
*   Dean's List; maintained a 95% GPA.

D.A.V. Inter College, Krakow, Poland
Certificate for courses in physics, chemistry and mathematics.

**LYLE W. POLI**
2285 Unit A College Drive
Bloomingdale, IL 60108
708/555-4529
Lyle@mail.com

---

## ELECTRICIAN / CONSTRUCTION

**EXPERIENCE:**

■  More than five years in electrical maintenance and construction for major commercial and residential projects, including wiring and panel installations.

■  Skilled in blueprint reading, troubleshooting and general construction for electrical systems to codes and customer specifications.

■  Assist in job planning and estimating; work well with foremen, engineers and all other tradesmen.

■  Knowledge of lighting and emergency systems, as well as all types of conduit, supplies and testing equipment.

**EMPLOYMENT:**

Day Electric, Inc., Hanover Park, IL                                          12/02-5/16
**Electrician**
Specialized in commercial and residential power distribution and the installation entire systems, primarily for strip malls.
Installed conduit, full service panels and all related wiring to final phase.
*   Involved in numerous projects for such customers as Sears Roebuck, Goodyear, Meineke Muffler and two major bakeries.

J.WP. Gibson Electric Co., Chicago, IL                                      1/00-11/02
**Electrician**
Responsible for the installation of wiring, conduit and lighting fixtures, as well as emergency systems.
*   Installed systems for the U.S. Post Office, One Schaumburg Place, Sears in Hoffman Estates, and O'Hare Terminal and Marshall Field's flood damage.

Hardt Electric, Chicago, IL                                                       1/98-1/00
**Apprentice Electrician**
Supervised up to two employees in various shop procedures. Ordered/purchased parts and materials from numerous vendors.

Electrical Association                                                             1998
**Certificate:** Topics included Electricity Theory and Magnetism.

**Successful completion of Wireman's Exam**                        1998

**EDUCATION:**

Glenbard North High School, Carol Stream, IL

# JOHN D. REVVING

22609 Deerfield
Streamwood, IL 60107       Blast@mail.com       630/555-2393

## ENGINE REBUILDING / AUTOMOTIVE MECHANIC

**EXPERIENCE:**

▶ Skilled in the total rebuilding and fabrication of custom and stock engines, rear-ends and gears, as well as blown gas and alcohol motors.

▶ Proficient in boring and honing blocks and heads; skilled in the use of lathes, mills, grinders and all general shop equipment.

▶ Utilize diagnostic equipment including dynamometers, Bridgeports, CV616 honing machines, Sunnen rod machines and line honing equipment

▶ Perform chassis fabrication and frame work; assemble roll cages and suspensions; proficient in arc, heliarc and gas welding.

▶ Worked on a wide range of custom vehicles including Blown gas hydro, 1982; Blown alcohol flat bottom, 1983; a modified production record car, 1982; Top Alcohol Dragster, 1982.

**EMPLOYMENT:**

<u>J & R Automotive,</u> Streamwood, IL       1/16-Present
**Mechanic**
Responsible for all aspects of engine rebuilding and repair, and extensive work on high-performance rear-ends and gears.
Rebuild and install manual transmissions for a wide range of classic and late-model cars.
Assist in training and supervising new mechanics.

\* Utilize an all-data computer for part tracking, as well as labor guides and engine specifications.
\* Perform valve jobs and install bronze walls and cylinder heads.

<u>Opel Engineering,</u> Elk Grove, IL
**Mechanic / Engine Specialist**       1994-1996

**Manager / Owner** (Prior to selling the company in 1994)       1986-1994
Rebuilt and/or repaired numerous high-performance engines.

**Prior Experience:**

<u>Chapman Automobile,</u> Chicago, IL
**Head Tune-Up Man**
Ran diagnostic tests and dynos; rebuilt stock and race engines.

**EDUCATION:**

<u>Maine West High School,</u> Des Plaines, IL       Graduate

**DAVID A. BERG**
224 Gold Circle
Hanover Park, IL 60103
630/555-7278
Berg@mail.com

## FACILITIES / EQUIPMENT MAINTENANCE

**PROFILE:**
► Extensive background in the design, production and installation of electronic panels and conveyer equipment, with a proven ability to troubleshoot and take corrective action on projects.
► Skilled in prevention maintenance activities, including job scheduling, inventory control and contractor supervision; read and interpret blueprints and schematics; specialized knowledge of electrical and electronic systems.

## EMPLOYMENT:

Filtran/Division of SPX Corporation, Des Plaines, IL          9/06-2/17
**Maintenance Technician**
Maintained injection molding equipment, high-speed steel presses and production presses.

Rollex Vinyl Siding, Elk Grove Village, IL          9/04-9/06
**Lead Electrician / Maintenance Technician**
Maintained and repaired all extrusion equipment and related gear, including computerized PowerTec DC power drives/motors, and American Mapland and Kraus-Maffi PCV extruders and chilled water systems.
Diagnosed and corrected problems accurately and promptly; interfaced with the plant manager, maintenance manager, equipment vendors and maintenance contractors.
► Visited the Michigan Roll Form plant to gain additional details about the operation and maintenance procedures for this company's equipment.
► Utilized various tools proficiently, including digital volt meters, air ratchets, AMP probes, thermo-test probes and dial caliber micrometers.

Process Control Technologies (PCT), Addison, IL          8/04-9/04
**Lead Electrician**
Developed and implemented electrical panels and conveyor equipment; supervised crews in the operation and installation of machinery with AC/DC motors of 120/220/24 volts.

Donepace, Arlington Heights, IL          1/00-1/04
**Lead Electrician**
Responsible for the design, development and implementation of electrical panels, including the set-up, maintenance, troubleshooting, reworking and installation of machinery; hired as an Electrician, 1/00; promoted to Lead Electrician, 1/01
► Key team member involved in the development of a prototype shuttle turntable.

U.S. Navy, Alameda, CA          1/97-1/00
**Electrician, Rank** E-5
Trained as an electrician for marine systems; supervised electrical tag-out and civilian workers on the overhaul of the USS Carl Vinson.
Awarded an Armed Forces Expeditionary medal.

**EDUCATION:** Southern Illinois University, Carbondale, IL          1995-1997
Received a full scholarship for Technical Theater coursework.

**REGINA ANGLE**
230 Wildwood Lane
Hanover Park, IL 60107
630/555-0622
Angled@mail.com

## FACILITY and EQUIPMENT MAINTENANCE

**PROFILE:**  ► Extensive background in all aspects of facility maintenance and operations management in manufacturing and warehouse environments, with full P&L responsibility.

► Skilled in machine setups, equipment repair, cost-effective purchasing, inventory scheduling and shipping/receiving, as well as capacity planning and production cycle control.

► Organize, coordinate and supervise crews in the maintenance of physical structures and mechanical equipment, including maintenance scheduling and on-site troubleshooting; expert in HVAC systems and a wide range of electrical and plumbing systems.

► Well-versed in production manual/automated machining and assembly equipment installation and operation; interpret blueprints/schematics; effectively work with engineering, quality and operations personnel; fluent in English, Polish and Russian.

**EXPERIENCE:**

All Star Food, Schaumburg, IL                                  12/04-Present
**Vice President, Production**
Manage the full production of packaged health cookies including mixing, baking, assembly, packaging and purchasing functions.
Determine production capacity and coordinate raw materials with vendors and suppliers.
Supervise facility maintenance; read and interpret blueprints and schematics.
► Reduced lead times/run cycles and increased finished goods pallets from 5 to 24 daily.

Harvest Valley Bakery, Spring Valley, IL                       8/00-12/03
**General Manager**
In charge of the setup and operation of this manufacturing plant for LifeStyle USA with outlets in Australia, Canada, England and Japan. Hired, trained and supervised 40 mixers, packers and machine operators in production, quality control and adherence to customer specifications.
► Promoted to this position from Maintenance Engineer/Supervisor, 8/00-1/02

All Star Food, Schaumburg, IL                                  10/05-8/00
**Maintenance Engineer / Supervisor**
Supervised crews in plant facility/equipment maintenance and machine setups.
► Promoted to this position from Mechanic, 12/95-8/97; and Mixer, 10/95-12/95.

**Additional Experience:**

Bednarz Meat and Deli, LaSalle, IL                             12/03-Present
**Manager**
Provide oversight management of this family-owned retail business; train and supervise employees in food preparation, cashiering and customer service.
► Select, install and maintain capital equipment and negotiate supplier contracts.

**EDUCATION:** National Education Corporation, Electrical Engineering      2003-Present

Illinois Valley Community College, Oglesby, IL                 2003

# DAVID KINSMAN
1222 Plaza Drive
Fort Wayne, IN 46806
219/555-2893
David@kinsmail.com

**OBJECTIVE:** A position utilizing skills in heavy equipment repair, machine shop procedures and staff management.

**EXPERIENCE:**

► Skilled in all aspects of equipment maintenance and repair, as well as inventory control, purchasing, shop procedures and general management.

► Familiar with parts fabrication and all major shop equipment including lathes, grinders, mills, drill presses and arc, mig and gas welders.

► Effectively train work crews in on-site and shop repair of cranes, (25-225 ton) backhoes, excavators, forklifts and boomtrucks.

► Skilled in reading blueprints and schematics, as well as magnet/general setups, shearing machines and sheet metal work.

► Experience in the complete overhaul of diesel and gas engines and hydraulic, electrical and mechanical systems; hands-on experience with all major brands and systems:

■ Link Belt: eight years of experience with LS, UC, HSP, LS48 and LS418 models.
■ Forklift models include Clark, Tow Motor and Yale. Electrical, commercial/household: 110, 220, 3-phase.
■ Automotive/construction: 12-24 volt and millivolt.

**EMPLOYMENT:**

B and W Equipment Company, Inc., Fort Wayne, IN                    2015-Present
**Shop Foreman / Service Technician**
Responsible for training, scheduling and supervising a team of eight employees in heavy equipment troubleshooting and maintenance.
Handle direct customer service and communications to quickly solve equipment problems.
Travel to major construction sites for repairs.

■ Management duties include inventory control, parts purchasing, warranty claim processing and invoicing.

**CERTIFICATES:**

Certified in Prentice Hydraulic Machines
Certified in Daewoo Hydraulic Excavators and the Mega 400 Loader
Certified for completion of Series 671 Diesel Overhaul Training.

**EDUCATION:**

Ivy Technical School, Fort Wayne, IN                                    Graduate: 2014

**MARK A. TORCH**
27W22 Sycamore Lane,
West Chicago, IL 60185
708/555-3877
Mark@mail.com

---

### *FIREFIGHTER*
A position as full-time or paid-on-call Firefighter where solid training and skills would be utilized.

## EXPERIENCE:

▶ **Certified EMT-A,** including hands-on experience in emergency situations; trained in basic life support and extrications.

▶ **Certified Fire Apparatus Engineer; Certificate** in Fire Ground Tactics and Fire Alarms and Systems.

▶ Trained in fire codes and regulations for buildings and sprinkler systems, and in fire science apparatus and fire spreading in various types of buildings.

▶ Knowledge of sprinkler installations and plumbing/building systems, including water connections and sewer systems.

## EMPLOYMENT:

Globe Plumbing, Inc., West Chicago, IL                              6/05-Present
**Plumber / Engineer**
Perform engineering and installation for piping in industrial, commercial, educational and correctional facilities.
Layouts include sewer, water, process and chemical piping.
Utilize a transit to survey grades as needed.

Pro-Care Ambulance Service, Roselle/Elgin, IL                    10/04-3/05
**Shift Supervisor**
Involved in a wide range of emergency situations including auto accidents, prompt medical care/patient stabilizing and transportation to hospitals.

## VOLUNTEER:

Lombard Fire Protection District, Lombard, IL
**Volunteer / Firefighter Trainee**
Assisted in ambulance calls and gained direct experience as EMT-A        1/04

## EDUCATION:

College of DuPage, Glen Ellyn, IL
Trained in subjects listed above, as well as fire prevention, protection techniques and equipment.
Trained in Hydraulics for FAE Certificate, 5/05.


Additional Education in Engineering and Calculus.
Courses included Fire Prevention II, Emergency Medical Technician, Building Construction, and Fire Science Apparatus.

# MICHAEL D. FLYER

6601 N. Cuyler 3rd Floor
Oak Park, IL 60302                    Fly@Mail.com                    708/555-8005

Seeking to channel my extensive customer service and communications skills
into a position as a **Flight Attendant.**

**PROFILE:**  ▶  Comprehensive experience in effective customer service and business administration, including communications and problem-solving with tact and professionalism.
▶  Familiar with human resource functions and staff development; plan and conduct meetings and staff training in professional customer relations, computer systems and full office support.
▶  Utilize and streamline computer systems using Windows 7, MS Word, Excel, Productivity Point and EMH networks for email.

## EMPLOYMENT:

Elmhurst Memorial Hospital, Elmhurst, IL
**Assistant Manager: Registration and Scheduling Services**        5/06-Present
Perform monthly staff meetings and implement new policies and procedures; constantly train and motivate staff regarding changes to systems and operations.
Update and process payroll on a bi-weekly basis.
Conduct staff performance reviews; draft memos and submit general notices.

* Computer functions include managing user codes, testing and upgrades.
* Developed and implemented an Accountlink optical imaging system.
* Created a new hire packet and developed a computer training guide, as well as a master binder outlining insurance benefits.
* Conducted training of numerous off-site staff personnel in patient registration and related procedures; attended Continuous Improvement Training.
* Act as United Way representative and the Infection Control Manager.
* Developed a strong team environment among all front-house staff.

**Registrar**                                                        5/05-5/06
Admitted all types of patients to the hospital; secured medical insurance documentation and verified coverage.
Registered patients for outpatient testing and the emergency room.
Acted as information/reception desk operator: greeted patients and provided directions and customer service.

Old Kent Bank, Lombard, IL                                           3/02-5/05
**Customer Service Representative / Teller**
Handled direct customer service and cash/non-cash transactions in a professional manner.
Assisted customers with CDs, checking/savings accounts and credit cards.
* Completed extensive training in directed customer service, telephone skills, sales, positive image and managing difficult situations.

## EDUCATION:

Elmhurst College, Elmhurst, IL
**B.S. Degree, Major: Health Management**
Minor: Sociology

# ANNA L. NIKI

4276 Raleigh Court #202
Glendale Heights, IL 60139                    Gads@mail.com                              708/555-9257

**OBJECTIVE:**     **Flight Attendant:** A position utilizing customer service and communication skills.

**EXPERIENCE:**    ■ Proven abilities as Flight Attendant, including food service and customer relations, waitressing, sanitation and the preparation of work stations.

                   ■ Trained in pre- and in-flight procedures and safety, including emergency evacuation procedures; fluent in Spanish.

**EMPLOYMENT:**    American Airlines/American Eagle, Chicago, IL          7/03-Present
                   **Flight Attendant**
                   Responsible for all aspects of customer service and in-flight safety.
                   Successful completion of four week's training in a wide range of safety procedures, including general first aid, emergency exit use, mouth-to-mouth resuscitation, the Heimlich maneuver and water, fire and hijacking emergencies.

                   Truffles Grove Restaurant, Itasca, IL          Part-Time, 11/02-Present
                   **Waitress**
                   Responsible for professional serving of food and liquor to a wide range of customers.
                   Communicate with customers and answer questions on menu items.
                   Handle a full range of side work and cleanup duties.

                   Dearborn Construction & Development, Roselle, IL          11/00-6/03
                   **Secretary / Bookkeeper**
                   Communicated daily with customers and provided information on account status, products and services.
                   Processed AP/AR, receipts and monthly/quarterly financial statements.

                   Indian Lakes Resort, Bloomingdale, IL          1/00-11/00
                   **Front Desk Clerk and Reservationist**
                   Performed daily check-in and check-out for customers; assigned rooms and solved problems in a professional manner.
                   Arranged transportation for customers and updated and maintained their accounts via computer terminal.

                   Carson Pirie Scott, Bloomingdale, IL          7/99-1/00
                   **Sales Representative**

**EDUCATION:**     Palm Beach Junior College, Lake Worth, FL
                   Successful completion of various Business Courses          1997-1999

                   Cardinal Gibbons High School, Ft. Lauderdale, FL          Graduated 1997

**PERSONAL:**      Excellent Health; Non-Smoker; Willing to Relocate.

# BETH A. WINEGLASS
226 Garden Circle Drive #6
Streamwood, IL 60107
708/555-3857
Beth@mail.com

**OBJECTIVE:  Food Service:** A position utilizing skills in food preparation and customer service.

## EXPERIENCE:

- More than nine years in food service operations including creative, specialty food preparation and personalized customer service.
- Assist in staff hiring, training and supervision; organize work schedules, purchasing, inventories and stock rotation.

## EMPLOYMENT:

Cub Foods, Naperville, IL                                                    1/98-Present
**Deli Clerk**                                                                          5/17-Present
Assist in supervising up to six employees in creative food preparation, assembly and presentation, as well as customer service and sales activities.
Update and maintain inventories of food, kitchen equipment and supplies; assist in timely, cost-effective stock ordering with vendors and suppliers.
Responsible for sales and answering customer questions related to food storage and preparation.
*        Ensure excellent sanitation of all equipment.

**Seafood Clerk** - Lombard Location                          1/98-5/02
Effectively hired, trained and supervised up to six employees in seafood preparation, sales and direct customer service.
*        Chosen to train for management positions.

Cee Bee's Finer Foods, Glen Ellyn, IL                  1/97-1/98
**Deli Manager** (smaller scale store)
Involved in cost-effective food and equipment purchasing with numerous vendors.
Hired, trained and supervised staff in all deli procedures; maintained inventories and assisted in ordering and inventory control.
*   Trained for management position.

Supreme Lobster, Palatine, IL                               1/95-1/97
**Chef's Assistant**
Hired and trained staff in inventory control and stock ordering.
*   Trained under chef's supervision in gourmet cooking with fish.

Cub Foods, Arlington Heights, IL                          8/94-1/95
**Seafood Manager**
Performed inventory control and maintained product freshness and presentation.
*   Ensured high standards of customer satisfaction and service.

## EDUCATION:

Buffalo Grove High School, Buffalo Grove, IL                    Graduate

**PHIL ZANE**
1228 Winder Lane
#6 Cordova, TN 38018
901/555-3229
Phil@mail.com

## *FORESTRY / TREE SCIENCE*

**PROFILE:** ► Comprehensive experience/education in a wide range of forestry applications including reforestation, cruising, marking, inventory and land management.

► Detailed knowledge of all regional tree species; proven ability to set and meet challenging objectives.

► Utilize personal communication, negotiation and interpersonal skills to coordinate activities and work effectively in a team environment.

## EXPERIENCE:

Spray-Tech. Inc. / Sears Home Improvement, Memphis, TN
**Outside / In-home Sales Representative**          2007-Present
Handle all sales and marketing functions, including presentations and needs assessment for home improvement products such as vinyl siding, patio doors and windows.
► Close 27% of prospective clients.

Pomeroy & McGowin Forestry Company, Monticello, AK
**Forestry Assistant / Forester**          2005-2006 and 2007
Responsible for all aspects of forestry including cruising, marking and reforestation.
Conducted inventory by species; identified and marked trees ready to cut and sell.
Surveyed lands to check for various natural problems such as defects and disease.

► Planned and prescribed controlled fires to manage lands; stimulate tree growth,    prevent wild fires and reduce timber litter.
► Coordinate controlled fire activities with other personnel in the field.
► Established, brushed, blazed and marked land lines.

University of Tennessee. Dendrology Department, Knoxville, TN
**Forestry Assistant / Work-Study**          2006-2007
Performed a wide range of tasks and projects designed by the department faculty for teaching entry-level forestry students.

Jack D. Branch. Jr. and Company, Consulting Foresters, Collierville, TN
**Forestry Assistant**          1999-2005
Cruised and marked trees for selective harvesting.

## EDUCATION:

University of Tennessee, Knoxville, TN
**Bachelor of Science Degree in Forestry**          2007

► Assembled a complete collection of bark samples from every tree species native to Tennessee, now in use as an instructional tool for forestry students.

# MAX HEADLIFT

22298 Meadow Lane
Carol Stream, IL 60188                MaxCat@mail.com                708/555-1786

## FORK LIFT DRIVER / WAREHOUSING

**EXPERIENCE:**
- Proven abilities in stocking, order-picking, shipping and receiving.

- Skilled in safe forklift driving and warehouse operations; handle order expediting of electronics and fragile equipment.

- Experience in worker training and supervision; knowledge of general bookkeeping and business administration; self-motivated and energetic.

**EMPLOYMENT:**

Apple Computer, Inc., Through ADIA Services, Itasca, IL          7/02-Present
**Permanent / Lead Warehouseman**
Responsible for safe forklift driving, order-picking and stocking of computer equipment at this major warehouse.
Perform loading/unloading of trucks on a daily basis.
Assist in cross-training employees in order-picking, stocking and packing for international shipment.

\* Recognized as Employee of the Month, 2/03, for prompt, safe work.

Max and Sons Foodservice, Addison, IL          2001-2002
**Manager / Owner**
Involved in the setup and operation of this company.
Assisted in the training and supervision of 15 employees in the delivery of fresh and frozen foods to restaurants and stores.
Handled all budgets and general bookkeeping.

Tower Contractors, Addison, IL          1999-2000
**Laborer**
Responsible for the custom application of aluminum siding.

**EDUCATION:**

Davea Career Center, Chicago, IL          2001-2002
Trained in computer repair and maintenance.

Austin High School, Chicago, IL          Graduated 2000

# DAVID A. MELTER

6N817 Longacre
St. Charles, IL 60175                          David@mail.com                          630/443-4092

## FOUNDRY OPERATIONS

**PROFILE:**

▶   Extensive background in foundry procedures and metallurgy, including experience in machining and assembly for a wide range of products.

▶   Assist in product development and post-sale customer service; familiar with hiring, training and scheduling work crews.

▶   Well-versed in manufacturing processes and equipment; read and interpret blueprints to comply with close-tolerance, industry and customer specifications; develop a strong rapport with customers for solid business relationships.

**EMPLOYMENT:**

Rice Lake Weighing, Rice Lake, WI                          8/04-Present
*A privately held manufacturer of replacement mechanical parts for industrial scales.*
**Casting Operator, Machining Operations**
Produce mill raw castings received from such foundries as Waupaca and Badger, in accordance with blueprint specifications and weights by industry.
Utilize, setup and maintain a variety of machining tools, including drill presses, lathes, hydraulic presses and Milwaukee Kearney Trecker single/dual spindle milling machines.
*   Train new employees in machining/assembly operations, product specifications, equipment maintenance and technical support.
*   *Crew member, construction project:* built rough deck platforms to hold the electronic equipment used to program machining specifications.

Carpet Town, Rice Lake, WI                          2004-2006
**Sales Associate, Part-time**

Davenport Agency/American Family Insurance Co.. Chetek, WI   1990-2004
**Manager / Insurance Agent**
Marketed and sold multiple-line commercial and residential insurance, with P&L responsibility for account acquisition and maintenance.
*   Earned an award for the highest life insurance sales nationally.

Sir Anthony James, Rice Lake, WI                          1985-1990
**General Manager / Owner**
Directed sales and office staff in marketing, sales and business operations of this franchise selling home fire alarm systems and appliances.

**MILITARY SERVICE:**

U.S. Navy, Norfolk, VA
**Musician / 3rd Class:** completed the U.S. Naval School of Music coursework.

**EDUCATION:**

University of Wisconsin Technical College, Rice Lake, WI
**A.A. Degree: Marketing**

# RETT MOWER

22816 Oriole Drive
Streamwood, IL 60107                    Rett@mail.com                    708/555-4226

**OBJECTIVE: Grounds Maintenance**

A position where grounds keeping, building maintenance and carpentry skills will be utilized.


**EXPERIENCE:**

► More than three years in grounds keeping and building maintenance, including all-season work; experience in complete lawn mowing/trimming and snow removal.

► More than eight years in carpentry work and building maintenance; experience in drywall, taping and painting.

► Skilled in use of Bobcat, grasshopper mower, John Deere tractor with snowblower and 4x4 truck with attached plow; knowledgeable in light plumbing and electrical work.


**EMPLOYMENT:**

Building By Beto, Inc., Bartlett, IL                    4/16-Present
**Carpenter**
Perform carpentry work including drywall, taping and painting.
Assist in plumbing and electrical work.
Maintained exterior of buildings including repair and painting.

Streamwood Park District, Streamwood, IL                    Winter, 2000-2005
**Snow Removal - Part Time**
On call for snow removal utilizing pickup trucks with 6-foot plow blades.

Jenson Windows, Elgin, IL                    4/01-9/01
**Carpenter**
Removed commercial windows and installed new windows.


**PERSONAL:**

Completed an OSHA Safety Course.
Member of Carpenter's Union Local 839 of Hoffman Estates.
Active member of the Streamwood Moose Lodge #2055.
Former Board Member and Coach of the Streamwood Little League.
Currently Umpire for the Streamwood Little League.


**EDUCATION:**

J.B. Conant High School, Hoffman Estates, IL
**Graduate**                    2000

**KATHY WALTERS**
7733 White Oak Drive
Roselle, IL 60172
708/555-6770
Kath@mail.com

**OBJECTIVE:** A position as Hostess, where professional, yet personal communication skills would be utilized.

**EXPERIENCE:**

- Proven abilities in customer service and staff training in fine dining and resort restaurants.

- Assist in record keeping, inventory control and general bookkeeping; experience with the Squirrel computer system, as well as Windows 7 and MS Office applications.

- Handle telephone communications, reservations and banquet coordination in a professional manner.

**EMPLOYMENT:**

Indian Lakes Resort, Bloomingdale, IL                          2016-Present
**Hostess**
Responsible for up to 20 servers at the Frontier Grill/Cafe and On-The- Pond, a fine dining restaurant, with a combined capacity of 340.
Perform monthly inventories of supplies and equipment, including glassware and wine.
Utilize the Squirrel system for bill processing.
Handle virtually all telephone reservations for large and small groups.

* Perform light typing and assist in payroll processing.
* Supervise the setup of daily buffets.

Jimmy's Cock and Bull Restaurant, West Chicago, IL          1999-2000
**Manager / Hostess**
Trained/supervised and scheduled up to 16 servers in customer relations and cashiering.
Handled extensive billing, check writing and accounts payable.

TPI Plumbing Co., Villa Park, IL                              1997-1999
**Administrative Assistant**
Duties included correspondence typing, bill processing and telephone communications with customers and suppliers.
Performed a wide range of customer service and general office functions.

Drake Hotel, Oak Brook, IL                                    1992-1997
**Reservationist / Corporate Relations**
Worked closely with hundreds of businesses to arrange VIP accommodations for executives and travelers.
Handled all communications in a professional, yet personalized manner.

**EDUCATION:**

Wright Jr. College, Chicago, IL
Successful completion of various business courses               High School Graduate

**PERRY VASQUEZ**
4249 Sebring Circle
Elgin, IL 60120
847/555-9314
Perry@mail.com

---

*HVAC REPAIR AND MAINTENANCE*

**PROFILE:**

► Hands-on training in HVAC system repair, troubleshooting and maintenance, covering heating systems, air conditioning, electronics and refrigeration.

► Diagnose and repair problems with oil, gas and high-efficiency furnaces.

► **Certified** by Rheem for 90+ efficiency furnaces and the True Blue furnace; **Certified** by the EPA to handle refrigerants.

► Experience in direct customer service, job scheduling and general bookkeeping; background in staff training, supervision and motivation.

**EDUCATION:**

ETI: Environmental Technical Institute, Itasca, IL
**HVAC Certificate**
Completed numerous classes and lab training, including:

* Basic Electricity
* Oil Heating Systems
* Hydronic Heating Systems
* House Wiring
* Electric Heating Systems
* Gas Heating and Steam Heating Systems
* Advanced Electricity & Low Voltage Wiring
* High Efficiency Heating Systems & Air Filtering Devices
* Sheet Metal & Associated Equipment
* Pipe Sizing, Cutting, Threading & Soldering/Brazing
* Air Conditioning & Refrigeration Systems

**EMPLOYMENT:**

Jewel Food Stores, Lisle, IL                                          10/16-Present
**Produce Manager**
Responsible for direct customer service and sales support, to determine and meet the customer's needs.
Update and maintain weekly job schedules and write daily orders for vendors and suppliers.
Process daily and weekly books.

► Consistently exceed all sales records and earnings in the department.
► Completed supervisory training levels 1, 2 and 3.
► Qualified to manage the entire store in absence of the Store Manager.

**WILLIAM M. SHIPPER**
22119 12th Avenue
Bartlett, IL 60103
708/555-7798
Will@mail.com

---

## *IMPORT / EXPORT and FREIGHT OPERATIONS*

**EXPERIENCE:**

■ Proven abilities in freight dispatching and routing, including full responsibility for import/export operations and fleet coordination.

■ Skilled in freight consolidation and air and ocean transport; strong knowledge of customs, tariffs, carriers, rates, services and routes.

■ Handle all NVOCC department functions, as well as data entry/ retrieval on computerized systems; file tariffs with the FMC.

**EMPLOYMENT:**

Nettles and Co., Inc., Elk Grove Village, IL                    5/16-Present
**Export Specialist**
In charge of all NVOCC operations and the coordination of fabric shipments via ocean carriers from the Southern and Northern U.S. Involved in all aspects of ocean export documentation and bookings. Organize container movement and LCL with co-loaders. Perform ocean consolidations and file tariffs with the FMC.

* Work extensively with Intertrans, Ltd, Barking, England.

WE.S.T. Forwarding Services, Elk Grove Village, IL           5/99-5/01
**Ocean Freight Consolidator**
Responsible for all phases of NVOCC and duties listed above.

A.C. Express, Elk Grove Village, IL                    Part time 7/98-1/99
**Supervisor**
Effectively trained and managed five drivers and four employees in office support. Organized trucking operations for virtually all types of outgoing domestic freight.

Expeditors International, Wood Dale, IL                       8/97-5/98
**International Export Documentation Agent**
Performed all aspects of export and professional customer service.

**EDUCATION:**

Manatee Junior College, Bradenton, FL

Hartford Airline Personnel School, CT
Successful completion of Two Year's Courses in Business

**ROBERT WOK**
2341 Custer Court
Fox Lake, IL 60022
708/555-4739
Cook@mail.com

---

## *KITCHEN MANAGEMENT / FOOD SERVICE*

- Experience as Sous Chef and Line Supervisor including menu pricing, continental cuisine and customer service; train and supervise staff for peak performance.
- Proven abilities in all kitchen operations, including food preparation, cooking and cost-effective purchasing and inventory control.
- Sanitation Certified, State of Illinois, 2001; background in catering, line cooking and banquet/kitchen coordination.

## EMPLOYMENT:

Key Colony Inn, Key Colony Beach, FL                    10/04-5/09
**Sous Chef**
Responsible for daily food preparation, line opening and sanitation at this restaurant rated #1 in the Middle Keys by The People's Choice Awards.
- ► Handled menu preparation, inventory, quality control and cleanup.
- ► Assisted in banquet preparation, specializing in pasta and sauces.
- ► Worked pantry and broiler stations.

Holiday Inn, Marathon, FL                    10/03-10/04
**Chef, Royal Pelican Restaurant**
Transferred by Embassy Suites; successfully brought hotel restaurant to a full-service facility providing breakfast, lunch and dinner.
Implemented new menu; hired, trained, scheduled and supervised staff.
Set up banquet operations and implemented procedures for purchasing, inventory and quality control; handled purveyor and vendor relations.

Embassy Suites Hotel, Schaumburg, IL                    5/03-10/03
**Sous Chef**
Prepared and coordinated banquets for up to 800 guests.
Supervised line staff and created daily specials; ensured excellent product quality.

Wyndham Hotel, Naperville, IL                    10/01-5/03
**Night Supervisor/Lead Cook**
Responsible for the supervision of four employees in evening kitchen operations.
- ► Achieved Wyndham's # 1 ranking for food quality.

College of DuPage, Glen Ellyn, IL                    1/02-5/02
Completion of courses towards A.S. Degree include Culinary Arts, Nutrition, Menu Design and Food Purchasing.

Cooking and Hospitality Institute of Chicago, Chicago, IL
**Certificate:** Professional Cooking, 2002

**MICHAEL J. SCAPER**
2285 Wildwood Drive
Streamwood, IL 60107
630/555-2097
Dig@mail.com

*PROFESSIONAL LANDSCAPING*

**OBJECTIVE:** A position where lawn/garden sales and landscaping field experience would be of value.

**PROFILE:**
▶ Experience and training in the decorative planting and maintenance of residential and commercial gardens and grounds.

▶ Train, supervise and evaluate new employees in lawn mowing, fertilizer application, soil testing, seeding, starter planting, pruning, weed control and disease/insect problem resolution.

**EMPLOYMENT:**

Trugreen / Chemlawn, Schaumburg, IL                                2016-Present
**Tree & Shrub Specialist**                                        3/01-Present
In charge of the Tree & Shrub Division, with responsibility for field operations in a suburban territory.
Handle difficult customer problems for all routes; resolve discrepancies and respond to inquiries about disease, insect and weed control for full customer satisfaction.

**Lawn Care Specialist**                                           3/96-3/01
Responsible for a daily residential lawn care route schedule, including fertilizer applications, weed/disease control, inspections and homeowner instruction.
Maintained a truck and all equipment in operating condition.
*        Completed workshops on diseases, insects and fertilization applications.

Kmart Corporation, Elk Grove Village, IL                           10/06-Present
**Sales Associate, Part-time**
Sell, promote and merchandise lawn and garden products to retail customers. Respond to customer product inquiries and assist in sales promotions, stock replenishment, in-store display setups and inventory control.

Wal-Mart, Streamwood, IL                                           10/01-4/06
**Sales Associate, Part-time**
Rotated among departments to replenish shelves, count inventories, set up displays and assist customers with inquiries; unloaded and received goods on the night shift.

**EDUCATION:**
William Rainey Harper College, Palatine, IL
**A.A. Degree: Computer Science**

St. Viator High School, Arlington Heights, IL

# DONALD H. TRAINMAN
2201 Pleasant Place
Streamwood, IL 60107
Res: 630/555-7954
Cell: 708/555-0079
Train@mail.com

## LOCOMOTIVE ENGINEER

**PROFILE:**
▶ Experience in virtually all aspects of road and yard operations; completed Conductor School; military service in Vietnam; knowledge of Lotus 1-2-3 for Windows 7; Illinois class "C" driver license.

▶ Proficient analytical, technical and mechanical skills gained from 25 years in the railroad industry; communicate effectively to identify and resolve problems.

▶ Recent experience at:

| Terminal | Zone |
|----------|------|
| Bensenville | F |
| Milwaukee | C |

**EMPLOYMENT:**

<u>Canadian Pacific Railway/SOO Line</u>, HQ, St. Paul, MN     l/16-Present
**Conductor,** Bensenville, IL
Operate thru-freight and way-freight trains on the Bensenville/Davenport line, in full compliance with operating rules, state/local regulations and interstate laws.
Document run statistics; prepare reports such as train delay and wheel reports.

*Tard Service experience includes hump operations / transfer jobs to other railroads*.
<u>Union Pacific Railroad</u>, Chicago, IL     2001-2006
(formerly <u>Chicago & Northwestern Railroad</u>)

**Supervisor, Timekeeping Department**     1993-2001
Responsible for all payroll and timekeeping functions for train and engine personnel. Trained and supervised 14 employees.

**Office Manager, Credit & Collections Department**     1991-1993
Supervised a staff of four in cash transactions, payables and aging receivables.
▶ Directly handled funds transfers between railroad companies for settlements.

**Commuter Services Representative**     1985-1991
Handled passenger inquiries and complaints accurately, promptly and tactfully; inspected commuter stations for adherence to safety, cleanliness, service operations and maintenance policies and standards. Worked closely with the Engineering Department to resolve problems.
▶ Promoted to this position from **Clerk** in 1985.

**MILITARY:**    <u>U.S. Marine Corps.</u>, Camp Pendleton, CA     1981-1985
**Rank: Corporal**

Numerous seminars/courses completed include: Accounting I&II and Tax Accounting, Northwestern University.

# ED GRINDER

2315 Norridge Lane  Hoffman Estates, IL 60194  Edmail@mail.com  847/555-3890

**OBJECTIVE:** A position as *MACHINIST,* utilizing skills in manual or CNC machining and programming.

**PROFILE:**
 ► Read and interpret blueprints to adhere with close-tolerance (.0002) machining; well-versed in metrics and QC/SPC; utilize precision hand tool and measuring equipment; fluent in English, Polish and Russian.

 ► Graduated from Business Industrial Resources Training Center; Mazak CNC Operations & Setup, Mazak CNC Part Programming, CNC Lathe & Mills Operations, Programming with Fanuc Control, Quality Control & Blueprint Reading and Principles of CAD/CAM classes.

 ► Thorough knowledge of manual/computerized machining equipment including Mazatrol and Fanuc Control machining & turning centers; fabricate tool and die molds to manufacture Mazatrol and Fanuc Control equipment.

**EMPLOYMENT:**

A. M. Precision Machining, Inc., Elk Grove, IL   2016-Present
**Machinist, Milling Department**
Responsible for the setup and programming of horizontal and vertical machining centers with 3 and 5 axis Fanuc control.

Smalley Steel Ring Company, Wheeling, IL   2001-2016
**Machinist, Seal Division**
Performed setups/teardowns, tolerance pre-sets, operator maintenance and troubleshooting for the machining of seal rings for this contractor to biomedical, aerospace and military accounts.

 ■ Worked extensively with mills, lathes and grinders.
 ■ Rotated between Seal Division and the Retaining and Wave Spring Department.

The Spin Smith Corporation, Wood Dale, IL   1999-2001
**Machinist, Tool Room**
Milled soft/hard steel, including aluminum and stainless, to manufacture parts for lighting OEMs, utilizing various types of mills, grinders and lathes.

**TRAINING:** Courses completed include:
Quality Control/SPC, Safety on the Job, Jewelry Design/Production, CNC Lathe & Mill Operations and Programming with Fanuc & Mazatrol Control.

**EDUCATION:** W.R. Harper College, Palatine, IL
Completed courses in manual machining and CNC setup/programming.

WSOWRIR Engineering Technology College, Poland   1990

# VAL RIPKEN

2263 Daisy Lane, Unit 1 IS
Roselle, IL 60172          Val@mail.com          630/555-1509

## *MACHINE SETUP / OPERATIONS*

**PROFILE:** ► Extensive background in all aspects of job shop machining, including setup, drilling, milling, laser cutting/marking and lapping/fine grinding.

► Read and interpret blueprints; machine within close tolerances to meet strict job and quality specifications.

► <u>Utilize and operate a variety of machines, equipment and tools, including:</u>

- Multiple spindle machines
- Davenport machines
- Surface grinders
- Lathes
- Rotary transfer machines
- Gauges /Micrometers
- Mechanical tools

► Accurately machine steel, aluminum and brass fittings for parts and components ordered by OEMs in electrical, automotive and construction industries; ability to process up to 500,000 parts per order.

► Fluent in English and Spanish; willing to relocate.

## EMPLOYMENT:

**Machine Setup Operator** at various locations:

| | |
|---|---|
| <u>L.D. Redmer Screw Products, Inc.,</u> Bensenville, IL | 3/01-Present |
| <u>Norton Plastic Performance,</u> Elk Grove Village, IL | 6/98-12/00 |
| <u>Avanti Engineering,</u> Bensenville, IL | 2/97-4/98 |
| <u>K.K. Screw Products,</u> Itasca, IL | 4/93-1/97 |

## EDUCATION:

<u>Washburne Trade School,</u> Chicago, IL
**Two-year Certificate,** received 1993

# MARVIN A. MAKER

2277 Ontarioville Road, #309D
Hanover Park, IL 60103                     Marv@mail.com                     708/555-7385

**OBJECTIVE:  Manufacturing / Engineering**
A position where solid technical skills would be utilized in thermoplastic tooling, design and injection molding.

**EXPERIENCE:** ■  Proven abilities in plastic injection troubleshooting, two-color molding, production setups, tool samples and capability studies.

■  Skilled in CNC machinery programming, microscopes, CMMs, CIMCAD, CADKEY and Design View; proficient in Excel, Lotus 1-2-3, MS Word, UNIX, Windows 7 and Macintosh systems.

■  Perform tool studies; trained in metallurgy, steel tooling, jigs /fixtures, production and project management.

**EMPLOYMENT:**
Armin Molding, South Elgin, IL                     1/01-Present
**Process / Quality Engineer**
Supervise and inspect production of medical and commercial injection molded plastic products.
Directly involved in production setups, tooling changes and production troubleshooting.
Supervise up to 12 employees in production and quality control procedures.

* Develop capability studies for sample injection molds.
* Perform quality audits on finished goods.
* Plan and conduct meetings on quality control and individual worker performance.
* Write procedures for production equipment and processes.

APEX/Division of Cooper Industries, Dayton, OH                     2000-2001
**Cooperative Education Student**
Worked extensively with metallurgists and machinists in quality control, inspection and product design.
Controlled surveys in salt bath heat treatment furnaces.

* Produced technical documentation from test data and maintained part gauging calibration for military aircraft universal joints.
* Developed cost-saving tooling improvement methods via state-of-the-art design changes and titanium nitride coatings.

**EDUCATION:** Ohio University, Athens, OH                     Graduated 11/02
**B.S. Degree: Industrial Technology**
Minor: Business Administration                     GPA: 3.1/4.0

* Four-Year Member: Society of Manufacturing Engineers.
* Self-funded 90% of college costs.
* Active in Weight Lifting Club and Habitat for Humanity.

# CUTTER SHARP

| | | |
|---|---|---|
| 1132 Cane Garden Circle | | Res: 708/555-6144 |
| Aurora, IL 60504 | Cutter@mail.com | Cell: 708/555-8544 |

## *MEAT PROCESSING / FOOD INDUSTRY*
Willing to Travel or Relocate

**PROFILE:**
▶ Extensive background in virtually all aspects of meat processing and purveyor operations, specializing in sausage preparation and formula innovation, in both retail and manufacturing environments.

▶ Skilled in merchandising, sales, competitor analysis, purchasing, inventory control, advertising/promotions and customer service; experience in facility layouts, equipment and maintenance.

▶ Well-versed in formulas, meat selection and production processes; supervise quality control and adherence to health regulations, including HASB; utilize smokehouses, ovens and steamers efficiently; winner of the national Grand Championship for three different items in 2005.

## EMPLOYMENT:

CUB Foods, Naperville, IL                               5/15-Present
**Sausage Maker**
In charge of the cooking, display and sale of prepared foods, including smoked ham, chicken, meat loaf and sausage, with responsibility for quality workmanship, formulas and departmental gross margins and revenues.

- ▶ Directly grind, spice and stuff a variety of sausages, and order materials as needed.
- ▶ Handle all counter displays, product demonstrations weekly ads and promotions.
- ▶ Member, American Cured Meat Association.

- \* Set up the meat sections for four store openings, in accordance with layouts; developed the merchandising program.
- \* Achieved revenues of over $200,000 in 2009, with expectations to exceed the 2009 sales goal.

Jewel Stores, Melrose Park, IL                               1/86-1/15
**Foreman / Meat Processor, Plant Operations**
Supervised 15 employees in a wide range of meat processing and prepared food manufacturing activities, including raw material handling, formulas and packaging, with special attention to health and sanitation regulations. Coordinated daily facility cleanup, setup and maintenance operations. Handled USDA inspections as Journeyman Meat Cutter.

## EDUCATION:

Triton Community College, River Forest, IL
Successful completion of courses toward an A.A. degree in mathematics.

Kelly High School, Chicago, IL                               Graduate

# HERALD A. THREAT

23762 Bluff Street, Apt. 204

Carol Stream, IL 60188               708/555-1702               Herald@mail.com

## *MECHANICAL MAINTENANCE / REPAIR*

**PROFILE:**
▶ Extensive background in all aspects of the maintenance/repair of aircraft and vehicles, with responsibility for inspection, problem determination and prompt corrective action in team environments.

▶ Knowledge of parts specifications and applications; well-versed in researching, identifying and pricing parts.

▶ Skilled in a wide range of maintenance processes and equipment, including:

Tolerance settings utilizing a torque wrench
Corrosion control and aircraft painting
Comprehensive modification of aircraft structures
Balancing of control surfaces and manufacture of control cables
Sheet metal repair and familiar with fiberglass /bonded honeycomb repair
Removal and replacement of skin panels and aircraft fasteners
TA-75/JG-75 tow tractors & NC-8A portable electrical trucks

**EMPLOYMENT:**

Toyota of Westmont, Westmont, IL                    7/15-Present
**Parts Specialist**
Respond to customer and mechanic requests for automotive parts information promptly and accurately for this dealership with 300 units on the lot and an average of up to 60 units sold monthly.
Retrieve data for over 4,000 parts from a microfiche system; utilize an online database system to look up pricing information.
Complete and submit customer service forms to assigned mechanics.

▶ Contribute to departmental average monthly sales of $10,000.

Lombard Toyota, Lombard, IL                    8/04-7/15
**Parts Specialist**
Performed the same functions utilizing a TDM/EDI network system for this dealership with 150 units on the lot and sales of 40 units per month.

Sewell Toyota, Odessa, TX                    7/03-7/04
**Parts Specialist**

**MILITARY:** U.S. Navy, San Diego, CA                    6/99-6/03
Electrician / Mechanical Equipment Repair, Grade E-3 Maintained and repaired S-3 Squadron air anti-submarine aircraft.

▶ Received required support equipment licenses issued by the Command.
▶ Inspected aircraft before/after flights as an Airman/Plane Captain, 1999-2000; performed walkarounds with pilots.
▶ Promoted to Corrosion Control-9, 2002-2003; detected, removed, treated and restored paint finishes on six S-3B aircraft.

**TRAINING:** Numerous schools and courses completed include:
■ Mathematics/Communications/Airwing Weapons Training (USS Nimitz), 2002
■ S-3 Connector Repair, 2001

# DIANA KOVITZ

2214 Roosevelt Road
Hanover Park, IL 60103        Diana@mail.com        650/555-6649

## *INJECTION MOLDING*

**PROFILE:**
► Comprehensive experience in job scheduling, workflow management, conflict resolution, team building, motivation and training.
► Skilled in the operation of a wide variety of injection molding equipment such as Mitsubishi, Cincinnati Milacron, Nissei and Van Dorn Presses; handle communications in a professional manner.
► Handle multiple aspects of shop operations, including maintenance, tool shop, materials handling and machine processing.

## EXPERIENCE:

American Flange Company, Carol Stream, IL      2017-Present
**Lead Technician**
Effectively manage shift operations including safety and quality assurance. Assist in training and supervising a staff of six operators in injection molding.

Fellows Manufacturing Co., Itasca, IL      2003-2017
**Cell Leader**      2005-2007
Responsible for all aspects of operations for the cell, including scheduling, quality assurance and machine equipment maintenance.
Trained and evaluated a staff of eight machine operators.
Scheduled and organized work through the cell to optimize efficiency and productivity.
► Ensured quality control through examination of product and training of operators.
► Assisted other cells in identifying and resolving specific problems.

**Shift Lead / Foreman**      1998-2005
Directed all shift operations such as assignment of duties, quality control, safety, scheduling and staffing.
Oversaw a team of up to 52 trained workers; hired, evaluated and developed team members and handled personnel issues as needed. Directed all machine set-ups and arranged for training on specific equipment.
► Maintained very high safety and quality standards.
► Effectively communicated with other shift managers and supervisors to update on status of operations.

**Process Technician**      1997-1998
Set up machines and solved a variety of equipment problems.

**Set-up Technician**      1995-1997
**Material Handler**      1993-1995

**TRAINING:** Successfully completed a variety of certification and training courses, including Paulson Interactive Training.

Nissei America, Inc., Supervision & Team Building and various in-house programs.
**Certified: Injection Molding;** Northern IL. Univ. Bus. & Ind. classes.

**SEND T. SPINNER**
671 Waterfall Lane
Hanover Park, IL 60103
630/555-3602
Send@mail.com

*ELECTRICAL / MOTOR REPAIR*

**PROFILE:** ▶ Skilled in all aspects of motor repair and maintenance procedures, including worker training and supervision in safety and all shop procedures.

▶ Highly self-motivated and energetic, with a sharp eye for detail and quality; utilize calipers, micrometers, metric and inch measurements.

▶ Fluent in written and spoken Vietnamese.

**EXPERIENCE:**

Dreisilker Electrical Motors, Glen Ellyn, IL                          7/86-10/17
**Shop Repair & Maintenance**
Responsible for training and supervising up to 4 in all shop procedures, including the complete teardown, repair assembly and test running of electrical motors.
Gained extensive skills with a wide range of equipment, including the troubleshooting and maintenance of:

▶ Sleeve and ball-bearing motors up to 5000 h.p.
▶ Medium and large: generators, slipring motors, vertical high-thrust motors.
▶ AC and DC motors up to 5000 h.p. -Medium and large induction synchronous motors, as well as eddy current clutch motors.
▶ Repair special grinder and hermetic motors, including removing stator and install medium and large vertical motor thrust pumps.
▶ Install and braze rotor bars and connect endrings.
▶ Strip and pull windings from stators; work with gear motors and handle all mechanical work.
▶ Inspect and measure shafts and bearing housings; produce status reports for management.

**EDUCATION:** High School Graduate / Equivalent

**MILITARY:** U.S. Green Berets, Iraq
**Lieutenant**
Repaired and maintained of a wide range of weapons and mechanical systems.

**PERSONAL:** Non-smoker, with a strong aptitude for learning electrical and mechanical systems.

**WERNER B. HOGAN**
234 Dover Drive
Elgin, IL 60120
847/555-4706
Werner@mail.com

*PARTS MANAGER / DEALERSHIP OPERATIONS*

**PROFILE:**    ► Experience in business operations and full sales support, including inventory control, computer system setup and troubleshooting.

► Assist in staff hiring, training and supervision in data compilation, report preparation, collections and customer service.

► Skilled in various ADP systems as well as Windows 7, Quicken and MS Works for spreadsheets, word processing and databases.

**EMPLOYMENT:**

Woodfield Ford, Schaumburg, IL                              2018-Present
**Assistant Manager, Parts Department**
In charge of all parts department activities including hiring, training and supervising six employees in counter operations, parts receiving/stocking and deliveries.
Responsible for all computer system maintenance, updates and tape backups.
Structure prices and assist in collections for past-due invoices.
Utilize ADP parts management and inventory control software; execute all price updates, wholesale incentives and DOES (Direct Order Entry System).
Calculate profit margins and determine costs.
Train all personnel in processing claims, shortages, damaged goods, back orders, overages and shortages.
*    Personally established all major department computer procedures.
*    Certified Ford Parts Specialist.

Heritage Lincoln Mercury, Elgin, IL                          1996-2018
**Parts Manager**
Effectively trained and supervised two employees in data entry, report generation and all department procedures.
*    Winner of Ford's Silver Medallion Award (1st year) and the Bronze Medallion (2nd year).

Packey Webb Ford, Wheaton, IL                              1994-1996
**Parts Counter**
Performed direct customer service and updated/maintained accurate parts inventories.
Worked closely with managers to process paperwork.
*    Implemented Ford's new DCS computer system.

**EDUCATION:** Elgin Community College: Basic Computer Skills
Control Data Company: Insight Training
Ford Motor Company: DCS/UCS Computer Training

**PERSONAL:**    Strong aptitude for computers and electronics; skilled in soldering and assembly.

# JOHN VAN GOGH

2310 W St. Charles Road #3
Villa Park, IL 60181                                    John@mail.com                                    708/555-7524

## *PROFESSIONAL PAINTER*

**EXPERIENCE:**    ■ Proven abilities in interior and exterior painting, including full responsibility for surface preparation and paint selection; Certified, Journeyman Painter.
■ Experience with all types of wall covering, enamel/latex paints, color mixing and coding.
■ Skilled in painting walls, floors, ceilings, doors, boiler rooms and exterior surfaces including signs.

**EMPLOYMENT:**    Oakbrook Terrace Tower, Oakbrook Terrace, IL          10/97-4/17
**Painter**
Responsible for interior and exterior painting using all skills listed above.
Performed accurate cost and time estimating for all jobs.
Ordered paints and supplies from vendors in a cost-effective manner.
Painted tenant offices, storage locations and boiler and utility rooms.

* Provided prompt, courteous service for all tenants and staff.

C.E.E Industries, Addison, IL          2/90-9/96
**Department Supervisor**
Trained and supervised two employees in the production of flexible shafts.
Inspected all work and ensured excellent product quality.

* Scheduled production and improved procedures, resulting in greater efficiency and productivity.
* Promoted to this position from Factory Worker.

Crafts Unlimited, Elk Grove Village, IL          6/84-12/89
**Working Supervisor**
Responsible for paint/color mixing for painting and finishing of industrial models, patterns and prototypes to customer specifications.

**EDUCATION:**    TrainYou, Inc., Lombard, IL          3/96-6/96
Trained in accounting, business math, records management, touch calculator, general office skills and human relations.

Industrial Management Institute, Westchester, IL          12/90-5/92
Certificates in Supervision, Industrial Management and Psychology.

Northern Illinois Painter's Apprentice School, Batavia, IL
**Certificate**          1990

Glenbard North High School, Carol Stream, IL          Graduated 1984

**DIANE BONES**
224N50 Kenwood Road
West Chicago, IL 60185
630/555-1607
Diane@mail.com

*PHYSICAL THERAPIST ASSISTANT*

**PROFILE:**

- Highly skilled in all aspects of physical therapy, including file updating, accurate documentation, physician liaison and extensive patient contact.

- Certified as a **Physical** Therapist **Assistant** in the State of Illinois; successfully completed clinicals in physical therapy in outpatient, acute care, nursing home and work environments at various Chicagoland healthcare institutions.

- Consistently recognized by management and patients for superior talents in troubleshooting and problem resolution in high-pressure situations.

**EMPLOYMENT:**  Alexian Brothers Medical Center, Elk Grove Village, IL    2002-Present
**Physical Therapist Assistant II**
Responsible for patient care, treatment plans, chart updating, weekly summary reports and communications with nurses and physicians.
Familiar with Geriatric, Orthopedics, Sports Medicine and Manual Therapy.
Gained experience in training and prevention programs.

- One of the few PTAs trained in Myofascial Release.
- Work part-time with pediatric clients at Rosewood Therapy Challenge in Libertyville, IL, from 2008-Present.
- Serve as a Clinical Instructor for PTA students.
- Work closely with volunteer aides in daily tasks.
- Promoted to this position from PTA I because of excellent work performance.

**EDUCATION:**  Oakton Community College, Des Plaines, IL    2002
**A.A.S. Degree** in Physical Therapy

Elgin Community College, Elgin, IL    2002
**A.S. Degree** in General Studies

**ADDITIONAL TRAINING:**

- Myofascial Release, Muscle Energy to Lumbar, Spine & Pelvis, Strain/ Counterstrain, Integrative Therapy for Low Back and Lower Quadrant, Building & Rebuilding the Complete Athlete and Preferred Roles of the PTA.

**DAVID E. WINGTIP**
2267 Thomas Drive
East Troy, WI 53120
Cell: 708/555-9368
Dave@mail.com

## CORPORATE PILOT

**FLIGHT RATINGS:**

Airline Transport Pilot: MEL
A.T.P. Type Rating in BE-1900, BE-300
Commercial Pilot: SEL; Instrument
Flight Instructor: Airplane SEL/MEL; Instrument
First Class Medical - No Restrictions No Accidents or Violations

**FLIGHT TIME:**

| | | |
|---|---|---|
| TOTAL TIME: | 3801 | |
| Multi-Engine: | 2981 | |
| Total P.I.C.: | 1500 | |
| Total S.I.C.: | 2108 | |
| Multi-Engine P.I.C.: | 807 | |
| Turbine: | 2198 | |
| Instructor Pilot: | 1240 | |
| Instrument: | 337 | |

**EDUCATION:** **B.S. Degree in Aeronautical Science (December 1997)**
Embry-Riddle Aeronautical University, Daytona Beach, FL
National Dean's List 1995-1997                    GPA: 3.39/4.00

**EXPERIENCE:**

5/07-4/10   **AIR WISCONSIN, INC.,** Appleton, WI
First Officer, deHavilland Dash 8, Part 121 Scheduled Airline

7/03-4/07   **BAR HARBOR AIRWAYS,** Miami, FL Captain, Beach 1900, Part 135 Scheduled Airline

5/99-6/03   **ATLANTIC SOUTHEAST AIRLINES,** Atlanta, GA
First Officer, Embraer 120 Brasilia, Part 135 Scheduled Airline

8/98-5/99   **AIRLINE TRANSPORT PROFESSIONALS,** Atlanta, GA
Flight Instructor, Light Twin Engine

## ROCCO PODGORNIAK
2212 First Avenue
Bartlett, IL 60103
630/555-2143
Roc@mail.com

## *PLANT MANAGEMENT / PRODUCT DEVELOPMENT*

**PROFILE:**
► Comprehensive experience in all aspects of plant operations, including project expediting, purchasing, equipment maintenance and inventory control.

► Skilled in product design, with a proven ability to conceptualize, draft and fabricate products.

► Proficient in a wide range of technical skills including electrical, pipe fitting, welding (arc, mig, tig, gas) hydraulics, pneumatics, steel fabrication, forklift operations and material handling.

**EXPERIENCE:** Flight Ways Corporation, Batavia, IL                    2007-2017
**General Manager / Senior Engineer**
Responsible for all aspects of product design including drawings, prototyping and production. Worked with other team members to fully develop concepts from concept stage to completion.
*        Calculated and reduced material costs through vendor negotiations.

Cutting Edge, Batavia, IL                    2004-2007
**Manager**
Handled employee management and training, job assignment and supervision of plant operations for this company employed in rebuilding used shredding equipment.

Shredd Pax Corporation, Wood Dale, IL                    2001-2004
**Shop Manager**
Responsible for all daily operations of the welding and assembly departments including staff supervision and work flow organization.
Planned and implemented production improvements in the fabrication department.

Sunrise Welding, Bartlett, IL                    1997-2001
**General Manager / Owner**
Directed all day-to-day activities including business development, customer relations, personnel and hands-on production.
Performed welding activities using various materials and appropriate techniques.

## EDUCATION:

Southeast Illinois College, Chicago, IL                    1997-2000

► Completed various industry training courses.

# Mitch Vice

2253 South Victoria Lane
Streamwood, IL 60107
630/555-4825
Mitch@mail.com

## *POLICE OFFICER*

**PROFILE:** ▶ Extensive training in police procedures including patrol duty, traffic stops, warrants, search procedures and apprehensions.

▶ Trained in a criminal justice theory and effective written and oral communications for law enforcement.

▶ Familiar with computer systems including Windows 7 and various programs for data entry and retrieval.

## EDUCATION:

College of DuPage, Glen Ellyn, IL                    2009-2011
**Criminal Justice Program**
Successful completion of courses in Police Operations and Procedures.

* Courses include training in all daily police procedures, including those listed above.
* Enrolled to attend courses in Criminal Justice and Composition in the Winter semester.

## EMPLOYMENT:

Batesville Casket Company, Glendale Heights, IL       12/03-Present
**Driver**
Responsible for extensive driving and prompt deliveries to businesses in the Northwest suburbs. Developed a strong knowledge of streets and highways. Communicate with customers to ensure accurate shipments.

* Maintained an excellent driving record.

Osman Construction Company, Arlington Heights, IL     1998-2001, 2002-2003
**Laborer**
Involved in a wide range of commercial construction projects.

Lisle Electric, Sycamore, IL                          2001-2002
**Apprentice Electrician**
Performed wiring of electrical systems for new homes.

# JOHN X ROLLER
2205 W Golden Drive
Glendale Heights, IL 60139
708/555-5844
John@mail.com

## *PRESS MAINTENANCE / MANAGEMENT*

**EXPERIENCE:**

- Skilled in pressroom operations including full responsibility for teardowns, rebuilds and maintenance.

- Comprehensive experience with various web presses: roll to fold, roll to roll and roll to sheet.

- Utilize dry and wet offset presses and Hamilton, Ashton and Harris equipment, as well as collators and PCMs.

- Effectively hire, train and supervise workers in all aspects of press setup, repair and hazardous waste handling and disposal.

**EMPLOYMENT:**

Distributor Stock Forms, Addison, IL                    12/16-Present

**Maintenance Manager**
Responsible for training and supervising three employees in the troubleshooting, repair and maintenance of printing presses and equipment at three locations.
Perform cost-effective purchasing of parts, maintenance supplies and material handling equipment.

\*    Oversee all aspects of hazardous waste disposal and building and press preventive maintenance.
\*    Work directly with building and fire inspectors with a strong knowledge of building and fire safety codes and standards.

CST Group, Wheeling, IL                    4/99-12/16
**Pressman / Maintenance**
Effectively operated and maintained Hamilton Presses, Collators and PCMs.
Handled all aspects of troubleshooting, repair and maintenance.
Repaired and operated material handling equipment.

\*    Supervised preventive maintenance procedures for the entire building.

**EDUCATION:**

The Hamilton School, Chicago, IL
Completed special training in press systems.

**PERSONAL:**    High aptitude for electrical and mechanical system troubleshooting.
Self-motivated, energetic and detail-minded.
Mature, team player and a strong motivator.

**NELSON A. COLOR**
2234 South Justine Street
Chicago, IL 60620
312/555-4749
Nelson@mail.com

## *PRE-PRESS OPERATIONS*

**PROFILE:**  ► Experience in virtually all aspects of pre-press operations in team environments; specializing in disk to output with strict attention to quality control.

► Skilled in camera-ready setup, file conversions, proofing, imaging, trapping, sizing and transferring files to output devices.

► Proficient in numerous systems and equipment:

Scitex PS/2, Iris 3024, Dolev, AGFA/Selectset 5000 and Eray image setters; Scitex imager; Cromalin proofing; Hell Chromograph CP3900 scanner; and Fuji ScanArt scanner; familiar with Macintosh, QuarkXpress, PhotoShop and Adobe Illustrator.

**EMPLOYMENT:**

Precision Color Imaging, Addison, IL                  2017-Present
**Macintosh Operator, 2nd Shift**
Perform pre-press responsibilities for this subsidiary of Fenton Press, specializing in commercial advertising including 1/2/4-color ads, newsletters and publications; clients include Women's Health Magazine, Celestine Journal and Cahners.
\*      Occasionally work on DuPont waterproofs and a Crossfield scanner.

Johns Byrne Company, Niles, IL                  1998-2017
**Macintosh Operator, 2nd Shift**
Reformatted images from customer files for output to film according to job ticket specifications for this printer specializing in baseball cards.
Trained in scanning files, color correction and page assembly.
Adjusted line screens, and D'Max and excurve images.
Sent files to the PS/2 and Dolev 400 image setters for output with trapping.
Checked film detail against customer boards or laser copy; submitted film for proofing.
Checked Dylux, Kodak signature and Cromalin proofs for discrepancies.
\*      Occasionally shot camera-ready copy.
\*      Retrieved, edited and reran archived files from DAT tapes.

Color Image, Long Beach, CA                  1991-1998
**Camera Man / Black & White Scanner Operator**
Sized B&W prints and 4-color transparencies; output film from Hell image setters.
Utilized the Fuji scanner to scan B&W prints to half-tones.
Contacted and proofed film for stripping; produced proofs of various types.

**EDUCATION:**

William Rainey Harper Community College, Palatine, IL          1990-1991
Coursework in Advanced Quark on a Macintosh system.

Chicago Graphic Arts Project, Chicago, IL          1989-1990
**Diploma in Offset Litho Production**

### *KEN DOLOTS*
8989 Andrene Lane
Itasca, IL 60143
708/555-0290
Ken@mail.com

## *PRODUCTION OPERATIONS / ASSEMBLY*

- More than nine years in production operations, including full responsibility for line setup, worker training and quality assurance.
- Work directly with engineers and managers in procedure planning, parts ordering, status reporting and efficiency.
- Skilled in computer system use for inventory tracking and bills of material.
- Hire, train and supervise staff in equipment use and maintenance, QA and plant safety.

## EXPERIENCE

Sunstar Laboratories, Inc., Bensenville, IL                    2010-Present
**Production Supervisor**

Responsible for the setup and management of various liquid fill and assembly lines for the packaging of fragrances, hand/body lotions, liquid/bar soaps, deodorants and antiperspirants.
Brand names include Jovan, Aspen, Adidas and Yardley.
Compile daily production reports and utilize Tandem and Sequel software; verify components and bills of material for inventory control and efficient, on-time production.

Work with department engineers for new item changes and updates.
Train, supervise and conduct performance reviews for up to 50 employees utilizing MRM vacuum fillers, U.S. Bottler vacuum fillers, J&G fillers, Horix fillers, Elgin Sextet, Cavella Fillers, National Fill-A-Matic Fillers, Resina Cappers, Pro+ spin cappers, J.G. Crimpers and labelers by Avery, Precision, Patton and New Jersey.

* Efficiency at this plant is up 20% plantwide, 1996-present.
* Department rejects have dropped at a record rate, 1997-present.
* Maintain excellent productivity rates and product quality standards.
* Perform quality assurance checks on a regular basis.

## EDUCATION

Elmhurst College, Elmhurst, IL
**B.S. Degree - Business Major**

College of DuPage, Glen Ellyn, IL
Completed several business and general courses.

**Alan A. Pipeline**
2344 Springvalley Lane
Streamwood, IL 60107
630/555-7562
Alan@mail.com

## *PUBLIC WORKS / MAINTENANCE OPERATIONS*

### PROFILE:

► Comprehensive experience in all aspects of public works and building maintenance, including snow/ice control, water meter service/ installation, street cleaning and sewerage.

► Skilled a variety of functions such as forklift repair, arc welding, electrical, plumbing, snow removal, fire hydrant repair, valves and service lines.

► Operate end loaders, street sweepers, sewer flushers, back hoe, dump trucks and other small equipment. CDL trained and licensed, including tankers.

### EXPERIENCE:

Village of Itasca, Itasca, IL                                                      1999-2010
**Public Works**
Handled all aspects of providing public works services, including staffing, organizing work, performing all functions, budgeting and supervision.
Installed, repaired and read water meters.
Repaired water main breaks; installed and repaired fire hydrants and water main valves.
Performed snow removal and street cleaning.
Operated various equipment/machinery in performing duties, including sewer flushers, end loaders, 2 1/2 ton dump trucks, backhoes and black top rollers.

* Directed the activities of five departments; served as Superintendent.
* Completed a range of training programs.

F.W Woolworth Co., Chicago, IL                                             1995-1999
**Building Maintenance**
Performed a wide range of maintenance work such as electrical, plumbing and equipment repair.
Maintained and repaired a completely automated conveyor system, low pressure boilers and forklift trucks.
Programmed route sorters and assisted in snow removal.

### TRAINING:

Completed a variety of applicable seminars and training including:

| | |
|---|---|
| Business Management | Safety in the Workplace |
| Confined Space Entry | Snow and Ice Control |
| Blood Borne Pathogens | First Aid and CPR |
| Trench Safety | Disaster Control and Response |
| Defensive Driving | Equipment Repair and Maintenance |

### EDUCATION: Downers Grove Community High School,
Downers Grove, IL (GED)

# GOTTA B. PERFECT

2556 Marcie Court, #9
Addison, IL 60101                    Gotta@mail.com                    708/555-3224

## QUALITY CONTROL INSPECTOR
A position utilizing proven skills in electrical and mechanical applications.

**EXPERIENCE:**

- Skilled in the use of precision measuring instruments, including micrometers and multimeters.
- More than six years in drafting and CAD operations, including responsibility for a wide range of product and system designs.
- Proficient in AUTOCAD and Microstation/Intergraph.
- Skilled in blueprint and schematic reading, interpretation and development.
- Work directly with engineers and technical staff in configurations and upgrades; solid background in trigonometry, geometry and algebra.

**EMPLOYMENT:**

Sterling Technical Consulting, Inc., Westchester, IL    1/01-12/11
**CAD Designer**
Responsible for updating and computerization of manually drafted mechanical drawings using AUTOCAD versions 10 and 11.
Involved in re-draw work of blueprints for Commonwealth Edison residential and commercial power configurations.

Circuit Systems, Inc., Elk Grove Village, IL                5/99-1/01
**Quality Control Inspector**
Checked quality of printed circuit boards utilizing a micrometer, vernier and diameter gauge.

Elicon Company, VV Nagar, India                9/96-5/99
**Draftsman**
Worked directly with engineers and updated product sketches to strict quality control standards. Utilized precision measurement equipment for inspections of final products.

\* Currently employed at Prudential Insurance Co. as a Sales Representative.

**EDUCATION:**

**B.S. Degree Equivalent: Mechanical Engineering**    1997
S.R University, West Nagar, India

**Certificate: Microstation/Intergraph**                1994
College of DuPage, Glen Ellyn, IL

**Certificate: Mechanical Drafting and Design**        1991-1993
College of DuPage, Glen Ellyn, IL

# Steven M. Checkout

2258 Beech Court Carol
Stream, IL 60188                    Check@mail.com                    630/555-1371

**OBJECTIVE:**    *Seeking an opportunity to utilize my experience and skills in Quality Control.*

**PROFILE:**    ► Comprehensive experience in a wide range of business operations including quality assurance/control, staff scheduling, inventory control, freight forwarding, shipping and receiving.

► Background includes general accounting and status reporting using Windows 7, MS Word and Excel.

**EXPERIENCE:**    Mechanical Electrical Automation, Elk Grove Village, IL          1/02-Present
**Quality Control Manager**
Responsible for ensuring that all machined parts meet or exceed production standards.
Accurately read blueprints to determine part specifications.
Inspect parts for accuracy and approve for release to final assembly or reject.
Receive and process incoming materials; handle data entry and account updating.

Celadon Jacky Maeder, Bensenville, IL                    2/00-12/01
**Operations**
Handled the shipping and receiving of product for this air and ocean freight forwarder.
Performed cost analysis of international shipments and maintained files.

John's Garage Restaurant and Lucky's Diner, Schaumburg, IL          2/93-1/00
Served in various positions including Restaurant Manager, Bar Manager and Bartender for both of these high-volume restaurants under one ownership.
Performed all aspects of inventory control, accounts payable/receivable, pricing, ordering, cash management, staff scheduling, training and customer service.

**EDUCATION:**

College of DuPage, Glen Ellyn, IL and Harper College, Palatine, IL

► Successfully completed several computer and business related courses, such as Windows 7 and MS Office, as well as the core English requirements.

Elk Grove High School, Elk Grove Village, IL
**Graduate**

**TRAINING:**    Completed training in Metalworking Skills I and Measuring for Quality Control.

**INTERESTS:**    Actively involved in sports, reading and gardening.

# JERRY D. RAIL
220 Cedar Street, Apt. lA
Glendale Heights, IL 60139
Res: 630/555-8121
Cell: 312/555-8099
Rail@mail.com

## YARDMASTER / RAILROAD OPERATIONS
*A position where communication, organizational, problem-solving and technical skills would be utilized.*

**PROFILE:**   ▶   Experience in all aspects of field and office operations; plan, organize and conduct training sessions in on-track safety, track buckling, high-rail operations and maintenance of way; assist in safety training examinations.

▶   Utilize MS Word and Lotus Notes for Windows 7; authorized to retrieve, track and update a wide range of confidential information; Illinois Commercial Drivers License (CDL); current Brotherhood of Maintenance of Way member.

**EMPLOYMENT:**

Union Pacific Railroad, HQ, Omaha, NE                    2001-Present
(formerly Chicago & Northwestern Railroad)
**Machine Operator / Special Projects**                  1/06-Present

Execute a wide range of special projects for this thru-freight and way-freight railroad company in its Illinois/Wisconsin territory, in full compliance with operating rules, state/local regulations and interstate laws.

*Key Responsibilities:*
▶   *Track Maintenance and Repair:*
Organize, schedule and coordinate contractors in a building demolition project and asbestos abatement, including contractor selection.
▶   *Field Office Liaison:* coordinate information between corporate and branch offices.
▶   *Vehicle Licensing:* review licensing notices and renew/request licenses as needed; recommend vehicular retirement.
▶   *Territory Mapping:* prepare charts detailing tracks for use by such staff as inspectors, managers, conductors and locomotive engineers.
▶   *Safety Training Classes:* work with Safety Coordinators to administer rules examinations, including participant registration, class scheduling, classroom arrangements and examination grading/evaluation; plan and conduct training in specific topics such as on-track safety.
▶   *Safety Captain:* update employees on general orders issued by the Safety Engineering Department; inspect vehicles, observe the work of gangs, check for personal protection equipment and advise on techniques, procedures and policies.

**Foreman**                    1/02-1/06
Managed crews on rotational assignments:
■   **Surfacing Gang.** Organized and supervised machine operators in track surfacing and alignment. Processed timesheets, monitored schedules and controlled crew performance.
■   **Section Gang.** Supervised four machine operators/laborers in general track maintenance, including rail /tie inspection, broken rail repair, installation of ties and crossings reparation.

**Machine Operator, Surfacing Gang**                    8/01-1/02

**EDUCATION:** Sterling High School, Sterling, IL
Completed the building trades program at Pike Vocational Training Center.

**VENICE RAFT**
7875 Gross Point Road
Evanston, IL 60201
708/555-4656
Venice@mail.com

## *REAL ESTATE APPRAISER*

► Trained in full property assessment including measuring, picture-taking and analysis of comparable properties; compile and present final reports.

► Extensive knowledge of layouts, building materials and codes with experience in the construction industry; handle customer service, negotiations and communications in a professional manner.

► Licensed Real Estate Appraiser from the Appraisal Institute, 1995; Licensed Real Estate Sales Representative since 1988; willing to travel.

**EDUCATION:**

The Appraisal Institute, Chicago, IL                     Licensed 4/05
**Licensed Real Estate Appraiser**
Courses included training in all aspects of residential real estate appraisal, from 1 to 4 units.

**Real Estate Sales License Holder**
Attended additional training every two years to present.

Northern Illinois University, DeKalb, IL
**B.S. Degree:** Accounting                               Graduated 1998
Overall GPA: 3.3/4.0

**EMPLOYMENT:**

Sharp Garage Company, Chicago, IL          1993-Present
**Manager**
Responsible for all account prospecting, customer service and project management for this builder of custom garages.
Perform marketing and advertising, sales presentations, purchasing and accounting functions. Supervise sales and office support, as well as independent contractors. Negotiate contracts and determine/meet customer's specific needs for garages, room additions and remodeling work, including designs and materials.

   *     Developed sales from zero to $1.5 million annually through extensive travel and strong self-motivation.

Danley Lumber Company, Westchester, IL          1989-1993
**Sale Representative**
Worked closely with all types of customers to interpret their needs and design/build custom garages.

   ►     Ranked #1 in sales of 25 representatives.
   ►     Developed an extensive referral business by carefully listening to the customer and providing prompt, quality service.

# JUDY A. DUNA
22 Lime Lane, #2B
Schaumburg, IL 60193                     Judy@food.net                          847/555-7812

## RESTAURANT / FOOD SERVICE MANAGEMENT

**PROFILE:**

➢ Extensive background in all aspects of restaurant and food service management, including menu planning, food presentation and customer relations, with P&L responsibility for sales growth and business operations.

➢ Hire, train and supervise staff to achieve customer satisfaction and business goals; skilled in marketing, budgeting, purchasing, inventory control and facilities maintenance; proficient in front-house and kitchen operations.

➢ Cook County Board of Health certified in sanitation; Illinois certified and licensed in bartending; knowledge of computerized payroll and POS systems.

**EMPLOYMENT:**

Walker Enterprises, Softown, IL                                              8/15-Present
**Restaurant Manager**
Direct the daily planning, administration and operations of this full-service restaurant, with 65 employees working two shifts, in front and back house activities. Forecast sales, track inventories, maintain facilities/equipment; determine capital purchases; monitor budget variance and prepare financial statements. Negotiate contracts with purveyors including Sexton, Pedi Brothers and Sysco Foods.
→ Completed the 14-week Dale Carnegie Advanced Management Course.
→ Launched an evening dinner service; introduced and designed customer preference dinner menus.
→ Increased weekly sales from $26,000 to over $35,000 within one year.

Portillo's Food Group, HQ, Oak Brook, IL                                     2000-2015
**Manager, Barnelli's,** Schaumburg, IL                                      8/04-8/05
Accepted this lateral move to expand sales and business operations for this new food service line focused on restaurant style operations.

**Manager, Portillo's,** Schaumburg, IL                                      7/03-8/04
Responsible for the daily front/back house operations for this fast-food style restaurant, including opening/closing, cash receipts, payroll and inventory of equipment, food and uniforms; hired, trained and supervised 86 employees.
Performed weekly sales forecasting and scheduled employees accordingly.
→ Consistently met and exceeded the weekly $60,000 sales quota.

**Crew Chief/Inspector, Portillo's,** Streamwood, IL                         8/00-7/03
Gained experience in food service operations; trained, scheduled and supervised 27 employees in cashiering, food station maintenance and customer relations.

Polk Brothers, Melrose Park, IL                                              8/96-8/00
**Credit Department Manager**
Supervised 22 employees in consumer application credit checks and collections.

**EDUCATION:**

W.R. Harper College, Palatine, IL                                            1992-1994
**A.A. degree in occupational therapy**

*NICK J. ROUTER*
1224 Swift Commons, #501
Addison, IL 60101

Nick@mail.com
708/555-8731

## *ROUTE SALES / ACCOUNT MANAGEMENT*

- Proven organizational and interpersonal communication skills to build rapport and positive relationships with customers, clients and the public.
- Familiar with retail food product route sales, delivery, order fulfillment and processing, as well as warehousing.
- Effectively train, supervise and motivate subordinates and peers to meet organizational goals.
- Extensive background in motor vehicle and aircraft parts customer service in support of maintenance, repair and fabrications.

## EMPLOYMENT:

Frito-Lay, Itasca, IL                               2017-Present
**Warehouse Team**
Performed order filing, processing, stocking and shipping functions for retail food packaged products.

Brownberry Ovens, Glen Ellyn, IL                    2005-2017
**Order Processor**
Handled order fulfillment, delivery and troubleshooting on retail food product routes to Chicago-area supermarkets.

Acorn Radiator Supply, Rosemont, IL                 2002-2005
Managed an automotive and aircraft radiator supply and repair shop, including supervision and training of five technicians.
Performed fabricating of tools and equipment used in the radiator maintenance field.

Don's Radiator Service, Carol Stream, IL            2001-2002
**Shop Supervisor/Maintenance Technician**
Performed all shop operations, including staff scheduling, supply ordering, and liaison with wholesale and distributor accounts.

Other recent employment: One year as a vehicle repair technician and part-time work as a deejay/musical coordinator for social and entertainment events.

## EDUCATION:

College of DuPage, Glen Ellyn, IL                   2000
**Completed various courses in Electronics**

## JULIE A. FINDER
2229 S. Troy
Posen, IL 60469
708/555-4586
Julie@mail.com

### *SAFETY / LOSS PREVENTION*
A position where skills in loss control and/or government safety standards would be utilized.

► Experience in property evaluations and the planning/implementation of safety and loss control programs, including full OSHA compliance.

► Train and supervise staff in on-the-job safety and loss prevention, including surveillance and apprehensions.

► Develop and analyze claims and medical reports; proven ability to determine and reduce dollar reserves and create light-duty, return-to-work programs.

**EMPLOYMENT:**

**Loss Prevention Manager**
*Montgomery Ward, Inc.,* Chicago, IL                   11/12-Present
In charge of all loss control, security and safety procedures at this facility with 120 employees, including internal investigations and compliance to all OSHA standards.
Perform safety audits and evaluations to determine and solve chronic problems; conduct staff training in fire safety, first aid and overall worker safety.
Produce incident/medical reports for public liability and worker's compensation; work with doctor's offices and insurance companies.

► Ranked #2 in internal investigations, 2010.
► Interview injured persons and witnesses.
► Promoted from Lombard and Bloomingdale locations.
► Implement OSHA standards and plan/conduct safety training and evaluations for various departments.
► Handle extensive group and individual training in all safety and loss control issues, and the latest OSHA standards; assist in staff hiring and supervision.

**Graduate Assistant / Head Resident**
*Southern Illinois University,* Carbondale, IL               8/06-5/12
Managed a drug/alcohol and crisis intervention program.
Supervised 16 staff and emergency procedures for university housing.

**EDUCATION:**     Southern Illinois University, Carbondale, IL
                 **Bachelor Degree: Criminal Justice / Criminal Science**

**MEMBERSHIPS:**     American Society for Industrial Security, American Red Cross
                 American Red Cross: Certified First Aid Instructor

**CONSTANT SIGHT**
3478 Regal Court
Roselle, IL 60172
708/555-0786
Connie@mail.com

*SECURITY / LAW ENFORCEMENT*

**PROFILE:**    ▶    Skilled in general law enforcement procedures including patrol duty, surveillance and crowd/traffic control.

▶    Security Certified and trained in arrests and apprehensions, as well as firearms, the PR24 and incident reporting; conversant in Spanish.

## EMPLOYMENT:

Rosemont Police Department / Special Services, Rosemont, IL
**Auxiliary Police Officer**                                                    2000-Present
Responsible for basic law enforcement at Rosemont Stadium and the Expo center, including crowd surveillance and control.
Perform visual and ID checks of minors attempting to purchase or use alcohol, during foot and vehicle patrols.
Ensure adherence to local village ordinances; utilize radios and all police equipment.
Assist the general public with various logistic and legal matters.

▶    Compile and submit daily accident/incident reports.
▶    Assist in the training and orientation of new officers.

Hyatt Regency O'Hare, Rosemont, IL
**Security Officer**                                                    On Call, 2001-2003
Conducted foot patrols throughout this hotel to protect against vandalism and theft.
Checked IDs of persons leaving and entering the building.
Responded to reports of disturbances.
Issued keys to personnel in housekeeping, supplies and custodial engineering,

Paul Worth Company, Chicago, IL
**Electrical Apprentice**                                                    1995-2001
Responsible for assembly and maintenance of electrical systems including circuit breakers, vacuum break panels and plug fuse panels.

Illinois Protection Plant, Melrose Park, IL
**Security Officer**                                                    1993-1995

## EDUCATION:

Triton College, River Grove, IL
**Earned two certificates** for completion of 20- and 40- hour credit programs in Security and Fine Arms, 1997 and 2000.

Special Services Office, Rosemont, IL                                2000
Extensive training in police procedures.

# Steve Earl
155 Coldspring Terrace
Coldspring, TX 77331
409/555-5696
earlectron@aol.com

## *SERVICE TECHNICIAN: ELECTRONICS*

► Comprehensive experience in all aspects of machine maintenance and service, including troubleshooting, component installation and circuit repair

► Proven ability to identify problem areas, determine methods to correct and execute repairs quickly and accurately.

► Skilled in circuit board service; change clips, solder components, replace board tracers and perform diagnostic testing.

► Extensive background training others in over-the-road driving as well as machine repair.

## EXPERIENCE:

**DDS Aggregates**, Humble, TX                    12/17-Present
**Driver**
Operate large vehicles for hauling sand and rock to freeway construction sites.

**DuPre Transport**, Camden, TX                    3/07-11/17
Provided logistics services to Champion Paper Company.
► Qualified as a driver trainer.
► Top 3 in revenue production for the 1st and 2nd quarters of 2007.

**Stevens Transport**, Dallas, TX                    12/04-2/07
Performed professional driving and logistics operations for clients throughout 48 states.
► Trained students in all aspects of over-the-road driving.
► Named Driver of the Month April 2006 and December 2006.

**Circus-Circus / Slots-A-Fun Casino**, Las Vegas, NV    7/95-11/04
**Service Technician**
Responsible for all aspects of maintaining and servicing electronic and electro-mechanical gaming devices.
Performed troubleshooting of failed equipment. Identified and implemented repair methods including circuit and component replacement.

► Functioned as the swing shift Lead Mechanic. Coordinated and distributed all work assignments and supervised maintenance activities.

## EDUCATION:

Jesse Jones High School, Schaumburg, IL          **Graduate**
International Gaming Technology, *Fortune I Video Service*
International Union of Operating Engineers, *Electronics Competency*
Stevens Transport, *Phase I - VDriver Trainer Program*

# MIGUEL PACKAGE

22181 Betty Court
Bartlett, IL 60103           Mig@mail.com           708/555-1922

**OBJECTIVE:**    *SHIPPING / RECEIVING / WAREHOUSE OPERATIONS*
A position where self-motivation would be utilized.

**EXPERIENCE:**
- Skilled in driving forklifts and cherry pickers for stocking and truck loading and unloading.
- Operate automated wrappers and machines, including Insta-Pak equipment; skilled in the repair of automotive systems; strong mechanical aptitude.
- Coordinate the shipping and receiving of emergency orders.

**EMPLOYMENT:**

<u>Picker International Parts Organization,</u> Wood Dale, IL      5/01-5/18
**Parts Warehouseman**
Responsible for prompt, accurate stocking of medical equipment and parts.
Assisted in assembling shelves and organizing the entire warehouse.
Provided customer service to service engineers and updated/maintained accurate inventories.

► Implemented "Quality Driven Leadership" programs.
► Completed company-sponsored seminars in: Quality Driven Leadership, Problem     Solving Processes, Automated Inventory Systems and Customer Service.

<u>Edward Don Company,</u> North Riverside, IL      5/00-1/01
**Warehouseman**
Ensured proper picking and shipping of restaurant supplies. Assisted staff in the shipping and receiving department.

► Completed two month's training in efficiency, to meet company quality standards.

<u>Glassman Glass,</u> Chicago, IL      1/98-12/99
**Installer**
Ordered and installed auto and storefront glass to customer's specifications.
Provided customers with estimates and assisted in all shopwork and deliveries.

► Completed company training in customer service.

**EDUCATION:**

<u>Chicago School of Auto Mechanics,</u> Chicago, IL, Certificate: 5/97

<u>Benito Juarez High School,</u> Chicago, IL, Graduated: 5/95

# Jeffrey W. Batter

2228 Unit Court
Hanover Park, IL 60103                    Jeff@mail.com                    630/555-7281

## *SPORTS OPERATIONS / MANAGEMENT*

► Experience in the promotion of sporting events and programs, including community relations, advertising and general PR for the Kane County Cougars.

► Background in creative design and development for promotional items, such as displays, handouts, posters and other promotional items.

► Skilled in marketing, sales, customer service and new business development, including account management and vendor relations.

**EXPERIENCE:** (Most relevant first):

Kane County Cougars, Geneva, IL                              Summer, 2009
**Intern**
Responsible for a wide range of promotional and game-day duties for this highly successful, minor league baseball team.
Involved in creating and developing promotional materials, such as booklets and pocket schedules, aimed at Chicago-area merchants and the general public.
Set up displays and oversaw contests, games and giveaways with major supermarkets to promote and increase attendance among children and families.
Assisted in general box office and ticketing sales.
Conducted door-to-door promotional visits to local area businesses.

* Attendance doubled from 3,000 to 6,000 during this time.
* Effectively trained and monitored all vendors and employees in food preparation and sales techniques.
* Selected as one of a five-member team to maintain the playing field for game day.

Town & Country Distributors, Itasca, IL                      7/07-5/08
**Merchandiser**
Performed sales, direct customer service and merchandising of beverages, including creating, developing and using retail displays for all products.

Euclid Beverage, Inc., St. Charles, IL                       5/08-Present
**Sales Supervisor,** promoted from **Merchandiser**
Oversee drivers and merchandisers in the delivery and sale of beverages to major independent and chain retailers.
Manage promotions, contests and games, including giveaways to increase sales.
Ensure prompt, accurate product deliveries, as well as product rotation.

**EDUCATION:**

Western Illinois University, Macomb, IL

**Bachelor of Arts Degree:** Individual Studies
Concentration: Sports Management                             Graduated 5/07

# DONALD S. STOCKER

22317 Ridgewood
Bensenville, IL 60106      Don@mail.com      708/555-1577

**OBJECTIVE:**    A clerical position where proven organizational skills would be utilized.

**EXPERIENCE:** ►   Skilled in stocking, inventory control and parts expediting, including responsibility for order pulling and distribution.

►   Experience with computer databases for tracking and ordering parts and supplies; handle phone communications in a professional manner.

►   Assist in training and supervising staff in warehousing and order expediting; skilled in forklift driving and loading/unloading heavy equipment.

**EMPLOYMENT:**

Northwest Airlines, Chicago/O'Hare, IL      12/03-Present
**Stocking / Inventory Control**
Work closely with mechanics and quickly meet their needs for parts and systems used in aircraft repair.
Track and order parts through the company computer system and deliver them to hangers and job sites.
Drive forklifts and load/unload engines and parts quickly and safely.
Handle all aspects of stocking and inventory control.
►   Promoted to this position from a part-time Equipment Service employee.
►   Communicate with vendors, suppliers and technicians in a professional manner.

Stickler Premium Ostriches, Bensenville, IL      2003
**Sales Representative**
Conducted sales presentations to farmers and ranchers.

River Valley Cemetery, West Dundee, IL      2002-2003
Mt. Emblem Cemetery, Elmhurst, IL      1997-2001

**Foreman / Groundskeeper**
Trained and supervised three employees in all groundskeeping functions. Operated backhoes, lawn mowers and snowplows.

Murphy's Installation, Bensenville, IL      1995-1997
**Installer**
Performed expert installation of cedar siding, including training and supervising up to 15 employees in various work crews.
Scheduled jobs and purchased material; worked with customers for high product quality.

Wilson Pet Supply, Wood Dale, IL      1990-1995
**Dock Foreman**
Supervised order picking, forklift driving and efficient warehouse operations.

**EDUCATION:**    Fenton High School, Bensenville, IL      **Graduate**

**Frank J. Steel**
320 N. Harvard #E
Villa Park, IL 60181
630/555-1710
Frank@mail.com

## *STEEL PRODUCTION / SUPERVISION*

- Skilled in production, manufacturing and shop work, including equipment repair, job scheduling and quality control.
- Hands-on experience in the operation and maintenance of machinery such as die cutters, sewing machines, band saws and packaging equipment.
- Fluent in Spanish and English; strong aptitude for learning new procedures quickly and accurately, with a sharp eye on safety; **Certified Forklift Driver.**

**EXPERIENCE:**    Sea Converters Co., Addison, IL                    2017-Present
**Operations / Supervisor**
Supervise a wide range of production operations for the manufacture of protective covers for industrial equipment, using metal, plastic, foam and paper materials.
Operate various manufacturing equipment and measure products for custom designs.
Process payroll and update/maintain accurate inventories.
Determine prices and select freight carriers; assisted in shipping and receiving.

   * Schedule jobs and oversee quality control and product pricing.
   * Ship samples to customers and solve problems with products and billing.

Fore Supply, Addison, IL                    2000-2016
**Warehouse Operations / Driver**
Responsible for the safe, prompt delivery of supplies to approximately 20 golf clubs and health facilities per day.
Updated and maintained records on all deliveries throughout Chicago and the suburbs.
Assisted in training new drivers in all procedures.

   * Involved in all major warehouse operations including stocking, stacking, packaging and inventory control.

Snuzzo's Enterprise, Gary, IN                    1999-2000
**Bartender / Customer Service**
Duties included scheduling, inventory control and counting/balancing cash receipts.
Erdelac's Service Station, Merr, IN.

**EDUCATION:**    Portage High School, Portage, IN                    Graduate: 1996

# ROBERT P. SHOPMAN

2225 McKool Avenue
Streamwood, IL 60107                    Kool@mail.com                    708/555-9358

## *MOLDER / SHOP OPERATIONS*

**PROFILE:**

- Comprehensive experience in production, supervision and quality control from setup to finish; thorough knowledge of plastic injection molding processes including close-tolerance molding.
- Skilled in a variety of injection materials and equipment including engineering grade plastics, hot stampers, sonic welders, and Van Dorn, Kawaguchi, New Britton, HPM and Toshiba 45-1,000 ton plastic injection molding machines; familiar with robotics.
- Interpret blueprints and work with technical, quality assurance and operations personnel at all levels for high-performance teamwork; proficient in conversational Spanish.

**EMPLOYMENT:**    Suncast Corporation, Batavia, IL                    2004-Present
**Supervisor, 2nd Shift**
Responsible for 2nd shift plastic injection molding activities in the manufacture of lawn and garden products.
Schedule and monitor the performance of 70 machine operators, material handlers and foremen; submit daily production reports.
Provide on-the-job training in pulling raw materials, machine setup, maintaining run cycles, and problem identification.
Process payrolls and coordinate disciplinary actions with the union steward and plant manager.

* Promoted from Foreman, 1/04-8/05.
* Attended TQM training and participated on a Quest Team project.
* Completed Paulsen injection molding training.

Various Manufacturers, Chicago, IL                    2002-2004
**Production Foreman**
Accepted temporary assignments in production operations.

Basic Plastic Products, Bensenville, IL                    1993-2002
**General Foreman**
Monitored and controlled run cycles, production-line changeovers, idle time, bottlenecks and lot sizes.
Programmed machine startup times, speed, heat and pressure settings.
Interfaced with customers and quality assurance staff to correct design flaws.
Tested and evaluate prototypes; assisted mold makers and quality control staff in developing new mold specifications.

* Promoted from 1st and 3rd Shift Foreman, and Machine Operator.
* Major customers included Motorola, Xerox, IBM and AT&T.

**EDUCATION:**    Lane Technical High School, Chicago, IL                    Graduated 1992

PAMELA ANSWER

2277 College Green Drive
Elgin, IL 60123                      Pam@mail.com                      847/555-4545

OBJECTIVE:   **Switchboard / Customer Service**
A position utilizing proven abilities in administration, organization and customer service.

EXPERIENCE:

■ Comprehensive experience in all aspects of customer service, sales support and general office functions.

■ Handle customer inquiries and complaints, order processing, file maintenance and data entry/retrieval.

■ Conduct customer presentations in a professional manner; skilled at troubleshooting in high-pressure situations.

EMPLOYMENT:

Crawford & Company, Schaumburg, IL                      2004-2017
**Receptionist / Switchboard**
Greeted customers and answered questions on claims for worker's compensation; scheduled conferences and answered phone calls. Performed data entry and assigned new work to adjusters. Assisted in insurance billing and processing.

Locke Rental, Marianna, FL                      1998-2004
**Rental Agent**
Responsible for a full range of sales and office duties, including lease documentation, collections, cash deposit transactions, tenant relations, typing and problem resolution.

• Planned and conducted numerous customer tours of rental facilities.
• Coordinated the repair and maintenance of all rental facilities.

EDUCATION:

Unimax, Inc., Schaumburg, IL                      1997-1998
**Customer Service Representative**
Handled sales, order processing and telephone communications, as well as data entry/retrieval and customer relations.
Trained new personnel in all company procedures.
Participated in many industry conventions as a salesperson and company representative; conducted many presentations.

Elgin Community College, Elgin, IL                      1997-Present
Attending Paralegal and liberal arts courses on a part-time basis.

Marianna High School, Marianna, FL                      1995
**Graduate**
Volunteer: local community program for Downs Syndrome adults and children.

# WILLIE P. WHEELER

2235 Elk Trail
Carol Stream, IL 60188          Wil@mail.com          708/555-7655

*A **Technical** position where proven analytical skills would be utilized.*

**PROFILE:**

▶ Skilled in the repair and maintenance of Bantec and Opex systems, including the 5700 imaging system, 90690 reader/sorter with encoder, encoders and ink jet cartridges.

▶ Experience in computer repair and troubleshooting; utilize Windows 7, MS Word, Lotus and Excel for professional correspondence, graphs, charts and spreadsheets.

▶ Perform data entry and retrieval with speed and accuracy; communicate with staff and customers in a professional manner.

**EXPERIENCE:**    GE Capital Credit Services, Addison, IL        2/16-Present
**Expeditor**
Responsible for batch processing of checks through equipment listed above.
Perform key-in and stamping of checks for Ameritech; load MICR tapes, open envelopes and bundle checks for processing in a Bantec machine.

ABT Associates, Chicago, IL        2/05-12/15
**Field Interviewer**
Personally interviewed subjects in a government survey on drug use, including collection of laboratory test samples.
Performed beta testing of computer software and systems.
Coordinated job sites with government agencies for a drug study program.
Compiled and entered data on a computer system for modem transmission.
Assisted in public relations and staff training.

Radio Shack / Tandy Company, Norridge. IL        1/04-12/04
**Sales Representative**
Conducted sales presentations for a wide range of electronics. Provided customer service and handled cash transactions. Updated and maintained inventories on all product lines.

The Blueprint Shoppe, Chicago, IL        2/01-12/03
**Distribution / Driver**

**Prior experience** as **A/V Technician** and **Set Designer.**

**EDUCATION:**    DeVry Institute of Technology, Chicago, IL
Extensive training toward Associate Degree in Applied Electronics Science

Carl Schurz High School, Chicago, IL        Graduated 1999

# LINDA BOTHERS

2230 Fresno Court, Unit D
Hanover Park, IL 60103          Linda@mail.com                    630/555-2475

## TELEPHONE MARKETING

**PROFILE:**  ▶ Comprehensive experience in customer service, inter-department communications, telephone operations and inventory control gained during long-term employment with United Airlines and Dobbs International.

▶ Proven ability to meet customer needs, handle multiple priorities and perform effectively with co-workers.

**EXPERIENCE:** Alta Villa Banquet Hall, Roselle, IL
**Server**                                              Part-time, 2009-Present
Provide complete customer service to guests attending banquet functions.
Work with up to 30 customers at a time.
Serve food and beverages and ensure all needs are met in a timely, professional manner.

▶ Winner of Server of the Month award for outstanding performance.

Dobbs International, Schaumburg, IL                    2004-2008
**Interior Dispatcher**
Responsible for a wide range of service functions for this company providing catering to United Airlines.
Handled several phone lines and updated passenger information, including meal requests, on the computer system.
Coordinated meal needs of last-minute passengers; worked with the reservations department on last-minute requests.

▶ Distributed weekly payroll.

United Airlines, Elk Grove Village, IL                 1995-2004
**Load Flight Checker**
Handled customer service and inventory control activities for United flights.
Responded to phone inquiries from customers.
Checked flight inventory for meals, beverages, desserts and related items; restocked inventory as needed.

▶ Wrote employee work schedules for the following day.

**EDUCATION:** J.B. Conant High School, Hoffman Estates, IL          Graduate

# KENNETH GEARS

224 Freeman Road
Streamwood, IL 60107                    Ken@mail.com                    708/555-0390

**OBJECTIVE:**     A position in the Tool and Die industry where proven, hands-on skills in
Wire EDM programming, setup and operation will be utilized.

**EXPERIENCE:**
- ▶ Full project management abilities include programming, production scheduling and reading/interpreting blueprints.
- ▶ Skilled in the operation of Charmilles-Andrew, Agie and Sodick machines; operate lathes, grinders, drill presses and milling machines.
- ▶ Handle a wide variety of dies including extrusion, progressive, and compound, as well as gears, molds, jigs and fixtures.
- ▶ Proficient in close tolerance work; specialize in "A" work; accurately convert metric measurements.

**EMPLOYMENT:**     Sharp Metal Products, Elk Grove Village, IL                    8/02-Present
**Wire EDM Programmer / Operator**
Program and operate up to five wire machines, some of which are handling a full workload 24-hours per day, for this contract tool and die company.
Responsible for troubleshooting and all maintenance work.
Double-check blueprints for accuracy and make corrections as necessary Able to program in 3-D and Advanced Conies.

- ▶ Work with a wide range of dies and wire cutting projects within tight timeframes and budgets.

Richco Plastics, Chicago, IL                    2/97-8/02
**Tool Room Machinist**
Learned to set up and operate wire machines with this extrusion die maker.

**EDUCATION:**     William Rainey Harper College, Palatine, IL                    2000
**Completed Introduction to CNC Setup and Operation**

Maine West High School, Des Plaines, IL                    1990-1992
**Apprenticeship Program**

Prosser High School, Chicago, IL
**Machine Shop**                                                                    Graduated 1989

# RALPH R DENSON

229 Ivy Court
South Elgin, IL 60177                    Ralph@mail.com                    847/555-0774

## *TOOL AND DIE MAKER / PRODUCTION OPERATIONS*

**PROFILE:**
▶ Extensive background in virtually all aspects of production line functions, with full responsibility for supervision of tool and die machining activities.
▶ Skilled in machining and assembly work for specialty jobs; interpret blueprints/schematics, and fabricate tools and dies in accordance with customer specifications; proficient in close tolerance work.
▶ Train and supervise shop personnel in parts production and modification, routine maintenance and daily cleanups; provide specific training in a wide range of dies including progressive and compound.

**TECHNICAL:**
■ *Milling/Grinding Machines:* vertical/digital readout Bridgeport machines; 516 Van Norman; six-twelve deluxe Boyar Schultz FSG-612 Chevalier Surface Grinder; Okamoto Automatic Feed Wet-Grinder (12x18) Table; Norton 10x18 Wet Grinder; familiar with the Moore Jig grinder.
■ *Lathes:* 15x41 Tuda lathe; Hardinge Collet lathe.
■ *Drill Presses:* American Radial w/automatic feed; Fosdick 3'x4" press; PowerMatic 4'x5' press.

**EMPLOYMENT:**

DEC Tool Corporation, Bensenville, IL                    9/17-Present
**Tool and Die Maker / Lead Journeyman**
Supervise two apprentices in a wide range of shop procedures and fabrication of tool and die parts/components.
Provide on-the job training in equipment utilization, prevention maintenance and area cleanup; assign jobs and prepare status reports.
Visit customer sites to verify product fit; resolve problems promptly.
Order and inventory stock *of* all screws, dolls, nuts and bolts bi-monthly.
Maintain the tool crib and monitor tool/supply checkouts.
Perform routine repairs and regularly inspect tools for reconditioning.
* Set up tryout dies in a 30-ton punch press with an automatic air feed and direct refinishing jobs.
* In charge of all dies in absence of the plant manager.

Louisville Golf Club Company, Louisville, KY                    5/91-8/17
**Lead Assembler**
Mill cut wood heads for insert, with quality responsibility for the production line from first task to finished product, with output up to 900 clubs per day.
* Key corporate clients included Wilson and Austads Golf, and individual clients such as Eddie Mudd, Jodie Mudd and Andy North.

Smith & Silliaman, Louisville, KY                    5/90-5/91
**Laborer/Construction Crew**

**EDUCATION:**    College of DuPage, Glen Ellyn, IL
**Diploma, Apprentice School, Tooling Manufacturing Association**

# DEBORAH A. TRAFFIC

2219 Circle Drive                                                    Ofc: 847/555-5949
Roselle, IL 60172                    Deb@mail.com                     Res: 847/555-2508

## *TRAFFIC COORDINATION*

**PROFILE:**
- ► Extensive background in distribution, shipping/receiving and warehouse logistics, with attention to detail in fast-paced environments.
- ► Skilled in customer service, inventory tracking, expediting shipments and documentation; coordinate troubleshooting with carriers, distributors and sales personnel in a professional manner.
- ► Knowledge of various database and inventory control systems including AmCom, Walker and MB; proficient in Lotus 1-2-3; pursuing a course in ISO 9002.

## EMPLOYMENT:

**AM Multigraphics, Inc.,** Mt. Prospect, IL                          1995-Present
*A manufacturer/distributor, with $204 million in annual worldwide sales.*

**Traffic Coordinator**                                               4/95-Present
Responsible for the inbound/outbound logistics of shipping machines to customers, and receiving parts from suppliers and vendors. Select truck lines, routes and rates according to purchase order requirements. Interact with carriers to resolve problems including AAA, CCX and NW Trace and confirm shipments; prepare and analyze the weekly Transit Report to monitor actual time to deliver shipments. Process documentation promptly including bills of lading and order confirmations. Utilize Lotus to prepare and distribute numerous activity, control and billing reports.

- ► Created a Lotus 1-2-3 table of machine weights by model and part number.
- ► In charge of logistics for expediting heavy machines for display at trade shows including the Graph Expo '95 show at McCormick Place.

**Data Control Clerk**                                                2/95-4/95
Processed confirmation for shipments and open-order paperwork, including accurate and rapid data entry and report generation; identified and resolved discrepancies.

**Picker Intn'l Medical Equipment & Supplies,** Wood Dale, IL   8/94-2/95
**Customer Service Clerk**
Filled and processed telephone purchase orders including parts identification, stock availability and shipping/merchandise problems, working with the Purchase Department.

- ► Attended an Illinois Bell seminar on customer service.

**AM Multigraphics, Inc.,** Elk Grove Village, IL
**Group Leader, Inventory Control**                                   1984-11/93
Trained and supervised up to five CRT operators in accurately processing an average of 1,000 work orders daily; trained on the Cullinet System; maintained the equipment.

- ► Promoted to this position from Data Control Clerk in 1988.

**EDUCATION:**  Driscoll Catholic High School, Addison, IL        Graduated 1984

# RICHARD NETTER

2206 Beverly Lane
Streamwood, IL 60107                    Net@mail.net                    708/555-0339

**Transportation Operations:** A position where proven skills would be utilized.

## EXPERIENCE:

- More than seven years in freight routing and distribution, including full responsibility for LTLs, truckloads and ocean shipments.
- Handle claims processing and negotiate rates and contracts in a cost-effective manner with major carriers; plan and implement policies, procedures and special projects.
- Utilize Windows 7, Lotus Spreadsheet 2.3, Officewriter, Q&A Database, ProComm and QuickBooks for general accounting, freight accruals, chargebacks correspondence and reports.

## EMPLOYMENT:

Boise Cascade Office Products, Itasca, IL                    5/96-Present
**Administrative Technician**                    9/01-Present
A wide range of duties include policy/procedure planning, claims processing and transportation analysis for inbound and outbound freight. Negotiate rates for LTL, truckload and small package carriers.
Create and maintain database files for contracts and insurance certificates.

*    Familiar with hazardous material regulations (HAZMAT).

**Administrative Analyst** I                    7/00-8/01
Managed the entire freight consolidation program, including monthly freight accruals, routing and accounting statements.
Trained and supervised two employees in customer service, freight coding and claims processing.
Controlled line haul activity into 33 distribution centers.
Audited freight bills and negotiated rates.

*    Controlled up to $4.7 million annually in inbound freight expense; approximate tonnage: 7 million pounds.
*    Automated the billing process using Lotus and controlled a computerized freight chargeback program.
*    Controlled up to 40 truckloads per week, as well as annual catalog distribution.

**Administrative Specialist IV**                    5/96-6/00
Performed manual rating of bills of lading for the chargeback program.

**Prior Experience** with:
Kraft Foods Accounting Center as Credit Specialist and Data Entry Clerk.

## EDUCATION:

Completed extensive training in freight claims processing and quality control through Boise Cascade. High school graduate.

# RENCE M. USIK

283 E. Fairfield Court
Lombard, IL 60148                    Rence@mail.com                    630/555-8689

### *TRANSPORTATION / DELIVERY SERVICES:* Distribution Operations

**PROFILE:**    ► Experience in shipping/receiving and parcel/freight expediting activities, including unloading/loading, load balancing, productivity troubleshooting and problem resolution, with supervisory responsibilities.

## EMPLOYMENT:

RPS / Caliber System, Inc., Bedford Park, IL                    7/06-Present
**Package Sort Coordinator** Rotate between two assignments on a regular basis:
*Control Room Coordinator* Perform dock/yard troubleshooting activities and control throughput productivity, including load balancing, pace determination and sorter downtime, utilizing an AS/400 system and TV monitors.
   ► Direct the flow between unload/destination areas by radio and telephone.
   ► Contact maintenance personnel to resolve electrical and equipment problems.

*Unload Coordinator*
Train and supervise up to 20 package handlers per shift in daily shipping/receiving activities, including sort prioritization.

*Key Accomplishments*
   ► Certified in first aid by the American Red Cross.
   ► Set company Hub records for largest volume per hour throughput.

United Parcel Service, Hodgkins, IL                    2005-2006
**Yard Control Clerk**                                 12/05-3/06
Coordinated all international parcel mailing/delivery service activities, with responsibility for 30-35 loads, dispatching requests to outbounds and balancing optimal usage of equipment. Handled the stripping/respotting of trailers on primary/outbound location.
   ► Set up for next shift sort and dispatched hot cut-offs to the rail yard.

**Dispatch Clerk**                                     9/05-12/05
Dispatched inbound/outbound trailers and assigned loads to drivers. Called other UPS distribution locations to expedite shipments and check the availability/location of equipment.
   ► Logged arrival times for shipments during the Sunrise Sort shift.

Global Intelligence, Itasca, IL                        6/05-8/05
**Research Analyst**
Identified up to 30 applicants per available position, for client recruiters.

## EDUCATION:
Western Illinois University, Macomb, IL                 Graduated 5/05
**B.A. Degree in Public Communication and Human Relations**

College of DuPage, Glen Ellyn, IL                      Graduated 6/03
**A.A.S. Degree: Associate Applied Science**

## SONIA SPINNER

2213 Nautilus
Hanover Park, IL 60103                    Sonia@mail.com                    708/555-6681

## *THE TRAVEL INDUSTRY*
A position with an agency or tour operator, where professional skills would be utilized.

**PROFILE:**

► Proven abilities in all agency operations including ticketing, itinerary planning, bookings and effective customer service.

► Utilize Apollo and Sabre; handle price quotes and domestic/ international bookings with a strong knowledge of routes, rates and carriers.

► Professionally handle customer communications; familiar with German.

**EMPLOYMENT:**

United Express, O'Hare Airport, Chicago, IL          9/96-9/03 and 4/04-1/18
**Operations Agent**
Responsible for various airport and ramp operations, including updating passenger flight information, on the APOLLO system. Involved in determining aircraft weights and balances.

**Ramp Agent:** Loaded and unloaded planes with both cargo and passengers. Interlined baggage and worked in the bag room.

Travel Technology, Wheaton, IL          2/04-4/04
**Corporate Travel Agent**

Kwality Travel, Bloomingdale, IL          9/03-1/04
**Travel Agent**
Performed price quoting, ticketing and customer service on the SABRE system.

Midstate Airlines, Stevens Point, WI          6/84-8/86
**State / Ticket Agent, Gate & Operations Agent**
Utilized SABRE and tracked lost luggage; handled bag room and ramp agent duties.

**EDUCATION:**     Southeastern Academy, Kissimmee, FL
**Diploma**          1993
Trained in travel industry operations including OAG (domestic and international), domestic tariffs, ticketing, tours, cruises, hotel/motel booking, car rental, travel markets, programmed airline reservations systems and salesmanship.

College of DuPage, Glen Ellyn, IL          9/91-5/93
Studied travel, speech, English, composition, data processing, management, auto maintenance and German.

Addison Trail High School, Addison, IL
Graduated 1981

# MELVIN BURNER

225 Elm Court #8
Hanover Park, IL 60103                    Mel@mail.com                    630/555-9447

## WELDER / FABRICATOR

### EXPERIENCE:
Skilled in all types of welding including mig, tig, gas, stick and plasma for custom fixtures and finished products.

▶ Natural talent for innovation and fixture design; maintain strict quality standards, as well as shop safety and cleanliness.

▶ Trained in lathes, mills, drills and polishers; personally own more than $2,500 worth of hand tools.

▶ Communicate well with management, co-workers and customers as needed; assist in worker training in welding procedures.

## EMPLOYMENT:

**WELDER / FABRICATOR** at the following locations:

Flex-Weld, Bartlett, IL                                             6/06-Present
Responsible for all types of fixture welding including mig-tig welding of stainless to carbon steel.
Work within strict tolerances; perform welding of metal .005 to ¼ inches.
Involved in the fabrication of precision bellows (with EPEJ's and EJ's) for HVAC applications.
Maintain excellent cleanliness and safety of work areas.

Colony Display, Hanover Park, IL                          2005-2006 and 2003-2004
Performed all types of welding for a wide range of products.
Utilized customer's blueprints and assembled display racks and fixtures for such accounts as Wal-Mart, Home Depot and Eveready.

Precision Quincy, Woodstock, IL                          2004-2005
Responsible for precision welding of industrial ovens and dryers.

Lake Process, Barrington, IL and AEC, Inc., Wood Dale, IL    2002-2004
Welded cooling tanks used in plastic injection molding.
Assembled stainless steel equipment, often using purge/tig, free-hand and out-of-position welding.

**EDUCATION:**  Elgin Community College, Elgin, IL          Present
Completed 39 of 60 credits towards **Associate Degree** in Welding.

Dundee Crown High School, Carpentersville, IL          GED: 2001

**PERSONAL:**  Highly self-motivated, reliable and quality-conscious.

# DARRELL N. BLAZER

2252 Winding Glen Drive
Carol Stream, IL 60188                Darrell@mail.com                708/555-5192

**OBJECTIVE:**    **Maintenance Welder**
A position where self-motivation and professional skills would be utilized.

**EXPERIENCE:**    ■  Proficient in all types of welding including MIG, TIG, ARC, Flux-core and Acetylene.

■  Skilled in fabricating industrial and commercial products, using stainless steel, aluminum and brass.

■  Train and supervise shop personnel in a wide range of operations; handle spot welding, press brakes, punch presses and sheet metal rollers.

**EMPLOYMENT:**

Custom Enclosures, Elmhurst, IL                3/03-Present
**Welder**
Responsible for all duties listed above as well as shipping and receiving at this custom sheet metal fabrication shop.
Weld enclosures, steel columns and soundproof panels.
Perform electrostatic spray painting and track time requirements for specific projects.

Diamond Automation, Farmington Hills, MI                7/99-3/03
**Welder / Fabricator**
Welded and assembled specialty packing equipment using MIG, TIG & Gas welders.
Responsible for a wide range of maintenance welding throughout the plant.

Perimeter Security, Miami, FL                1/97-7/99
**Manager / Owner**
Hired, trained and supervised up to 4 employees in the welding, assembly and installation of gates and aluminum fences.
Involved in budget planning, payroll and direct customer service.

York Corrugating, York, PA                5/88-1/87
**Welder / Fabricator**
Performed a wide range of production work for Mack and Peterbilt trucks.

Rockland Manufacturing, Inc., Bedford, PA                2/86-5/88
**Welder / Fabricator and Supervisor**
Trained and supervised up to 7 employees in field repair, welding and maintenance of equipment including bulldozer blades and buckets.

**EDUCATION:**    High School Graduate
Successful completion of welding classes.

# ANDREW CLAMPER

1054 West Irving Park Rd.
Bensenville, IL 60106                     Andy@mail.com                                    708/555-3670

**OBJECTIVE:**     A position where skills in Warehousing and/or Plant operations would be utilized.

**EXPERIENCE:**  ■     More than seven years in shipping, receiving and distribution, including forklift driving, order picking and stocking.

- ■     Experience in computerized order tracking and form preparation, labeling and the packing of rail cars and semi-trailers.

- ■     Operate factory equipment including clamp trucks and boom lifts.

**EMPLOYMENT:**

Nexxus Distributors, Schaumburg, IL                     1999-2018
**Warehouse Clamp Operator**
Responsible for safely driving a clamp truck to load/unload large paper rolls, zinc ingots and pallets on semi-trailers and rail cars.
Supervise two employees in shipping/receiving and the writing of order forms on the computer system.
- Handled stocking, order pulling and warehouse maintenance at this major facility.

Cincinnati Steel, Elk Grove Village, IL                     1998-1999
**Shop Labor**
Performed shipping, receiving and routing; wrote and filled orders. Operated a bandsaw and ensured quality of material dimensions, paint color and color codes.

Carson Pirie Scott & Co., Elk Grove Village, IL                     1997-1998
**Warehouseman**
Operated a carpet boom/forklift for the pulling and stocking of large rolls of carpet.
- Responsible for product labeling, wrapping and stocking.

**MILITARY:**     U.S. Army, **Combat Engineer**                     1987-1991

Davea Center, Addison, IL                     1986-1987
Certificate: Construction and Electrical Wiring.

Fenton High School, Palatine, IL                     Graduated 1987

# DARYL MAKER

227 Altgeld
Glendale Heights, IL 60139          Daryl@mail.com                    630/555-5472

## *WAREHOUSING / PRODUCTION*

- Comprehensive experience in a wide range of steel production and warehouse functions including crane operations, loading, machining and torch cutting.

- Trained in hem saw operations to cut steel within tight tolerances.

- Proficient with a variety of tools such as saws, air guns, power tools and scales.

- Licensed and highly skilled forklift driver; operate electric, gas and propane powered lifts including stand-ups and high-lifts. Proficient crane operator.

## EXPERIENCE:

Triple S Steel, Houston, TX                          1/07-1/09
**Warehouseman**
Responsible for all aspects of stock movement, inventory control and truck loading.
Operated cranes to handle the movement and loading of steel products.

▶ Performed torch cutting and hem saw operations; cut steel products to customer specifications.

Compaq Computers, Houston, TX                        5/06-11/06
**Material Handler**
Operated a forklift to pull stock from inventory and deliver to production and assembly lines.
Unloaded trucks and restocked inventory.

Nippon Express, Wood Dale, IL                        2/00-4/06
**Forklift Operator**
Unloaded trucks, loaded 20- and 40-foot containers for sea shipment and restocked inventory.
Utilized various power tools, saws and air guns; worked with the crating department.

Express Fasteners, Glendale Heights, IL              4/97-1/00
**Plater**
Entered material movements in the computer. Operated forklifts and used scales for various warehouse functions.

## EDUCATION:

Glenbard North High School, Carol Stream, IL
Graduate

# GEORGE X. RAYMOND

123 N. Addison Road
Addison, IL 60101                    George@mail.com                    708/555-3916

**OBJECTIVE:**     **X-Ray Technician / Radiology**
A position requiring skills in patient diagnosis and personalized care.

**EXPERIENCE:**     ■ Comprehensive experience in radiology and clinical care, including mammography; utilize C-arm, GE, OEC and Siemens equipment, as well as mobile units.
■ Proficient in general diagnostics including fluoroscopy, UGI and LGI, osteopathic and T-Tube cholangiography, tamography-axial and appendicular; experience in trauma cases.

**EMPLOYMENT:**     Northlake Hospital, Melrose Park, IL                    1/00-4/10
**Staff Technologist**
Responsible for a full range of general radiology and direct patient care, including the majority of procedures listed above.
This 280-bed hospital includes an extensive outpatient facility.
Worked effectively with physicians, nurses and technical staff at all levels.
*    Utilized a CRT and conducted patient reception/scheduling in a personalized, yet professional manner.
*    Experienced with portable traumas, pacemakers, angiograms and line placements.

Mercy Center, Aurora, IL                    1993-1999
**Pharmacy Technologist**
Accurately filled prescriptions; gained a strong knowledge of drugs and interactions. Conducted pharmacy inventories and verified/maintained orders and patient records.

**ACCREDITATION:**     American Registry of Radiologic Technologists  Registered:    11/99-11/02
Illinois Department of Nuclear Safety              License:        10/99-10/03

**CERTIFICATIONS:**     **Certified** in CPR; **Certified** Pharmacy Technician

**EDUCATION:**     College of DuPage, Glen Ellyn, IL                    1999
**A.A.S. Degree**                    Graduated with High Honors: 3.9/4.0
*  Continuing Education Points: 35, including 14 in Mammography.

Hines VA Hospital, Chicago, IL
Trained in Special Procedures and clinical applications.

Delnor Community Hospital, Geneva and St. Charles, IL
**Clinical Experience**

**MEMBERSHIPS:**     American Association of Radiologists and Technologists Illinois Society of Radiologic Technologists, 1999

Resumes Examples for:
Office,
Business,
Supervisory
and
Technical Positions

# BERNICE PAYER

9422 South Broad Street
Scottsboro, AL 35768                     Bernie@mail.com                          847/555-9877

## *ACCOUNTS PAYABLE / BOOKKEEPING*

**PROFILE:**    ▶  Skilled in AP/AR, journal entries, general ledger maintenance, payroll processing, quarterly tax returns and financial statement preparation.

**EMPLOYMENT:**

Marriott Hotel Corporation, Elmhurst, IL                         8/95-6/99
**Night Auditor / Front Desk Clerk**
Greeted customers, verified reservations, assigned rooms and handled problems.
Performed all aspects of daily audit procedures, including the reconciliation of food/beverage and guest statistic accounts.
Forecasted daily, weekly and monthly occupancy rates.

- Reviewed, updated and adjusted budgets; produced the monthly and fiscal year-end budget variance reports.

West Suburban Currency Exchange, Wood Dale, IL           4/06-9/06
**Cashier / Part-time**
Accepted and handled a wide range of state-authorized financial transactions, including check cashing, money orders, vehicle plate, sticker and title issuance, food stamps and Western Union telegrams/moneygrams.
Opened/closed the cash drawer, reconciled deposits and deposited receipts daily.

Affordable Closet, Roselle, IL                               3/88-8/96
**Bookkeeper**
Responsible for prompt, accurate processing of all billing, payroll and quarterly tax returns for this designer of custom shelving systems; handled AP/AR matters.
Scheduled appointments and quoted prices to customers in a professional manner.

- Produced profit/loss statements and reconciled bank accounts.

**PRIOR**
**EXPERIENCE:**  A&P Tea Company, Chicago, IL
**Store Managers' Trainer / Head Cashier**
Trained and assisted store managers throughout Chicagoland in general accounting, bank deposit procedures and cash flow analysis; analyzed cash flow and compiled/presented weekly status reports to headquarters.

**EDUCATION:**  Northwestern University, Evanston, IL
Completed a two-year program in accounting.

# ROZ HALIBURTON

8789 Limerick Lane
Schaumburg, IL 60193                Roz@mail.com                                847/555-9158

**OBJECTIVE:**    A position where office administration, communication and computer skills would be utilized.

**PROFILE:**    ▶ Comprehensive skills in office administration including operations, scheduling and customer relations.
▶ Proficient in Windows 7 and MS Word 2007; familiar with Lotus 1-2-3; utilize various office equipment efficiently including copiers, facsimile machines, calculators and computers.
▶ Skilled in accounts payable, payroll, writing correspondence, switchboard operations, data entry/retrieval and communications.

## EMPLOYMENT:

Century 21 All Professionals, Glen Ellyn, IL                1/04-3/17
**Administrative Assistant**
Provide administrative support to various companies in the metropolitan Chicago area.
▶ Write correspondence utilizing MS Word, and presentations in PowerPoint.
▶ Handle telecommunications and greet clients.
▶ Update and prepare scheduled/on-demand reports.

Homemaker                                                        11/02-12/04

Dutkovich Properties, Hoffman Estates, IL                1/01-1/02
**Administrative Assistant**
Performed various office duties for this property management company including record keeping, customer service, correspondence and credit checks.
▶ Scheduled a maintenance crew of up to six members; distributed payment checks.
▶ Greeted renters and resolved complaints.

Olsten Temporary Services, Schaumburg, IL                5/98-10/99
**Secretary / Accounts Payable Clerk**
Provided a wide range of services including accounts payable, data entry/retrieval, word processing and office administration.

Motorola, Inc., Schaumburg, IL                                7/94-5/98
**Payroll Clerk**
Compiled and maintained current payroll records; entered and retrieved data on computer. Verified payroll codes/hours and distributed weekly paychecks.

**EDUCATION:**    College of DuPage, DuPage, IL
**Microsoft Office for Windows 7**

District 211 Continuing Education Program
**Completed Lotus 1-2-3**

# LARRY CAPP

2441 Player Lane
North Beach, CA 34560        Lar@mail.com        212/555-5892

## BUSINESS ADMINISTRATION

**PROFILE:**
- Skilled in human relations, staff training and motivation; well-versed in group dynamics and processes.

- Conduct written and oral presentations in a professional manner; organize meetings, programs and events.

- Hands-on experience in vendor relations, customer service and sales; write and distribute correspondence; coordinate budgets and business operations.

- Proficient in Windows 7 and the full MS Office suite for presentations and status reports.

**EDUCATION:**

University of Illinois, Urbana-Champaign, IL
**Bachelor's Degree, Major: Psychology**        Graduated 5/17
* Pledge class Social Chairman: Delta Upsilon Fraternity.

Elgin Community College, Elgin, IL
Activities required extensive human relation, motivation and organizational skills:

* Elected to ECCs College Community Council, representing the student body among various community groups and the general public.
* Represented ECC at various conferences: NACA, ACUI and ICCSAA.
* Served as coordinating Vice President for the Student Senate. Co-founder of first Phi Alpha Delta pre-law fraternity at any Junior College.
* Awarded Leadership Scholarship for two consecutive years. Attended numerous leadership seminars.

**EMPLOYMENT:**

The Gap, Elgin, IL        12/16-Present
**Sales Associate**
Handled direct customer service, sales and inventory control.
* Ranked #3 in sales of 26 Associates in the first month.

The Sealmen, Bartlett. IL        Summer, 2015
**Co-Owner**
Hired, trained, motivated and supervised four employees.
Responsible for marketing, sales promotions and professional customer relations.
* Trained and supervised several employees in sales and all store operations.

# DON JORDAN

2345 Whispering Oak
Drive Palatine, IL 60074                   Act@mail.com                        847/555-8658

## *ADMINISTRATION / CUSTOMER SERVICE LEADERSHIP*

**PROFILE:**    ► Extensive experience in customer service, sales and general office activities, including cash management and procedure development.

► Effectively train, motivate and supervise staff to meet established goals; plan and conduct training sessions.

► Skilled in inventory control and in-store merchandising; familiar with MS Word, WordPerfect, Lotus and Excel for data analysis and report preparation.

**EXPERIENCE:** Best Buy Stores Inc., Schaumburg, IL                      2004-Present
**Customer Service Lead**                                               2005-Present
Responsible for all daily activities in the Customer Service department of this high-volume retailer of computers and all major consumer electronics.
Train staff in departmental operations including total customer satisfaction, procedures and the in-house computer system. Submit and record credit application; document and manage files for all repair work.
Track and control parts inventory through the entire supply chain; follow up with customers.

* Improved parts order collection rate from 40% to 90%, providing annual savings of $30,000; researched, documented and trained staff on correct procedures.
* Twice earned the "Hero" award for outstanding customer service.

**Retail Sales Associate**                                             2004-2005
Worked with customers to identify and meet their individual needs and expectations for consumer electronics.
Acquired a detailed knowledge of product features and benefits.

Schaumburg Park District, Schaumburg, IL                      2000-2004
**Pool Manager**                                                       2002-2004
Managed daily operations of the recreational facility.
Responsible for scheduling employees and lifeguard post rotations to ensure proper coverage.
Planned and presented daily training sessions on topics such as emergency procedures, CPR, First Aid and lifesaving.

**Life Guard**                                                  2000-2002 (Summers)
Provided for the safety of facility patrons.
Coached several junior swim teams and gave swim instruction.

**EDUCATION:** Roosevelt University, Chicago, IL

**B.S. in Actuarial Science** in progress; extensive coursework in mathematics and statistics.
GPA: 3.4/4.0.

*HAROLD RINGER*

1776 Norwood #G-8
Itasca, IL 60143                          Ring@mail.com                          708/555-7933

## ALARM TECHNICIAN

**EXPERIENCE:**

■ Skilled in the installation and wiring of residential and commercial alarms, control panels and keypads by Digital Control Systems, as well as a full range of motion detectors.

■ Experience with virtually all types of accessories; skills applicable to new products and business environments.

■ Current License, Department of Professional Regulation, expires 9/1/12.

**EMPLOYMENT:**

Emergency Networks, Inc., Alarm Company, Itasca, IL       3/97-Present
**Lead Technician**
Responsible for prompt, effective installations of residential and commercial alarm systems listed above.

Lock-Up Storage, Evanston, IL                          6/94-8/94
**Elevator Operator**

**MILITARY:**   U.S. Army, Fort Drum, NY                  10/94-7/96
**Infantry**

* Honorable Discharge
* Army Service Ribbon
* Rifle Expert Badge
* Completed basic training at AIT, Fort Benning, GA. Served 13 Weeks.

**EDUCATION:**

Professional Truck Driving School. Chicago, IL       8/96-11/96
**CDL License**

Major High School, Chicago, IL
**Graduate**

# SIMON MAKER

3412 N. Ash
Wood Dale, IL 60191        Simon@mail.com        708/555-1982

## *ASSEMBLER / PROGRAMMER*

**EXPERIENCE:**
- Proven abilities in equipment assembly and the programming of PROMS, chips, bits and disks.
- Skilled in soldering and the use of power hand tools for building PC power units and NC/robotic systems to blueprints and specifications.
- Fluent in English and German; self-motivated and energetic, with a sharp eye for detail and quality.

## EMPLOYMENT:

Siemens, Erlangen, Germany          9/99-12/17
**Assembler**
Responsible for the prompt, accurate assembly of power units for PCs and NC and robotic devices to job specifications.
Handled extensive soldering and board swapping, as well as mounting and setup of machine tool controls.
Conducted accurate programming of PROMS, bits, disks and chips; numeric power units include the 810, 820, 840, 850 and 880.
Utilized all types of power tools; soldered PC boards for bridge connections.

* Performed final assembly and packaging of Simo drive systems.
* Updated notes on job orders for high-quality work.

Quelle, Erlangen, Germany          1997-1999
**Order Processor**
Duties included order picking, sorting and shipping for this catalog sales warehouse.

Vad & Fry, Erlangen, Germany          1995-1997
**Assembler**
Involved in high-quality clothing production.
Assisted in training one employee in pattern placement on fixating machinery.

Ramada/Renaissance Hotel, Aurora, CO          1995
**Housekeeper**

* Awarded Certificate for Most Conscientious Worker.

Army & Air Force Exchange Service, Aurora, CO          1992-1995
**Sales Representative**
Performed retail sales and direct customer service in a professional manner.

* Certified for completing a course in Human Relations.

## EDUCATION:

High School Graduate Degree / Equivalent
West Germany

# ROSA CLERKMAN

2227 Hesterman Drive
Glendale Heights, IL 60139   Clerkit@Rose.com     708/555-7778

**OBJECTIVE:** **A Clerical** position where proven analytical skills and attention to detail will be utilized.

**PROFILE:**
- ► More than three years in various business environments, including office support and the research/reconciliation of reports for purchasing and inventory control.
- ► Perform data entry/retrieval and balance cash transactions with speed and accuracy.
- ► Proficient in Windows 7 and MS Office, as well as Paradox and PageMaker.

**EMPLOYMENT:**

Tri Star Metals, Inc., Carol Stream, IL       4/04-Present
**Office Clerk**
Provide a wide range of office services in a professional manner, including data entry/retrieval of purchase orders utilizing Paradox. Analyze and update monthly purchase order and inventory reports.

- Perform proofreading, verification and distribution of invoices.
- Conduct research to resolve discrepancies.
- Compile documentation for freight bills.

Footlocker, Bloomingdale, IL        5/02-4/04
**Cashier**
Responsible for customer service and sales transactions for this high volume shoe retail outlet. Accurately handled large amounts of cash.

- Operated a computerized register system.
- Trained a new employee in professional customer service, store procedures, product lines and register operations.

Phar-Mor, Inc., Bloomingdale, IL       8/00-5/02
**Cashier**
Duties similar to those at Footlocker including training, customer service and computerized register transactions.

**EDUCATION:**

College of DuPage, Glen Ellyn, IL
**Associates Degree in Arts**        Graduate: 2009

Glenbard North High School, Carol Stream, IL    Graduate: 2006

**SUSAN B. SASSY**
23180 S. Waters Edge Drive #102
Glendale Heights, IL 60139                    Suzy@mail.com                    630/555-1402

*AUDIO / VISUAL PRODUCTION*

**PROFILE:**    Skilled in all aspects of sound production and technical direction for radio,
special events and the theater, including recording, dubbing, editing and final mix.

- Radio Disc Jockey experience includes voice-overs, commercials, public service
announcements (PSAs) and news writing/reporting.
- Background in the setup of 8- and 12-channel soundboards, amplifiers, microphones,
loudspeakers and related equipment.
- Familiar with Windows 7, MS Word and Excel.

## PRODUCTION EXPERIENCE:

Village Theatre Guild, Glen Ellyn, IL                    2001-Present
**Technical Director: Sound *and*Member** (Volunteer)
In charge of all sound setups for numerous theatrical productions.
Function as Stage Manager and oversee lighting, sound design and set decoration.
- Chairman: House Supplies, 2004-2005
- Chairman: Membership, 2002-2003
- Chairman: Vending Concessions, 2004-Present
- Realized a 1000% profit

Audio Visual Techniques, Elk Grove Village, IL                    2000-2001
**Audio Visual Technician:** Set up and maintained A.V equipment for meetings and special events
at Oak Brook and O'Hare Marriott locations.

The Green Hotel, Naperville, IL                    1995-1999
**Convention Setup:** Assembled stages, chairs, tables and audio/visual equipment.

## Prior Experience:

Good Samaritan Hospital, Downers Grove, IL
**Senior Supply Services Clerk**
Responsible for a staff of 10 and a medical product inventory of $500,000.
\*        Twice awarded the Good Samaritan "That's the Spirit" award.

**Disk Jockey / Announcer** experience at:
WKKD AM/FM, Aurora, IL, Adult Contemporary Music
WRAJ AM/FM, Cicero, IL, Adult Contemporary

## EDUCATION:

Southern Illinois University, Carbondale, IL
**B.S. Degree, Studied Radio-Television Broadcasting and Communications**

*NANCI TALKER*
225 Santa Clara Street
Vallejo, CA 94590                        Nan@mail.com                        707/555-7050

## *COUNSELING / RECOVERY*

**PROFILE:**  ▶ Extensive experience in case management, group/individual counseling and facilitation, including positive parenting and full responsibility for curriculum planning.
▶ Skilled in teaching 12-step recovery concepts; Certified to teach informational anti-smoking programs covering sociological trends, advertising and chemical dependency.
▶ Background in behavior modification, re-entry work and client sponsoring, as well as documentation and the design of custom treatment plans for individual clients, physicians and court cases; CPR and First Aid qualification.
▶ Personally establish rapport with people of all ages and philosophies, with a long-standing commitment to recovery; prioritize, motivate and delegate people in team settings; skilled in documentation, research and detailed report writing.

**EXPERIENCE:**  Our Family Inc., Napa, CA                        2005-Present
**On-Call, Counselor**
Responsible for personal counseling and supervision of up to 10 adults with various addictions, from screening and intake interviews to long-term treatment.
Coordinate 12-step orientation and act as the client's liaison to judicial, job training and social service agencies for comprehensive treatment. Compile and present extensive written and oral reports, including case narratives for supervisors, social services, families and judicial systems. Perform group facilitation for parenting, processes and therapeutic community activities.

*   Personally established the 12-step curriculum, including all training of recovering, non-recovering and on-call staff.
*   Founded the first positive parenting support program for the adult population.
*   Formerly in charge of up to 15 adult clients and 7 juvenile clients.

**VOLUNTEER:**  Solano Alano Club, Vallejo, CA                        1993-2005
**Director.** Involved in financial and operational decisions; assisted in record keeping, inventory and advertising.

Solano Partnership Health Plan, Vallejo, CA                        1992
**Consumer Advocate.** Served on an informational board that assisted the State of California in the reconstruction of the MediCal benefit program

Southern Solano Alcohol - S.S.A.C.,                        1989-1992
**Staff Assistant.** Adhered to policies and procedures, codes of ethics and laws regarding confidentiality. Performed crisis intervention and community referrals and collection of statistical data; assisted clinical staff.

**EDUCATION:**  Napa Valley College, Napa, CA
**Correctional Officer Certification**

# STEPHEN A. SAVER

2456 Randall Ridge Drive
Elgin, IL 60123                          Saver@mail.com                          847/555-6072

**OBJECTIVE:**   A position utilizing EMT skills, such as medical assistant, phlebotomist or EKG, respiratory or emergency room technician.

**PROFILE:**

▶ Comprehensive skills as Paramedic and EMT, including emergency care such as defibrillation, IV therapy (venipuncture & phlebotomy), CPR and First Aid.

▶ Operate all major life support equipment and interpret EKG strips; perform triage and work closely with doctors, nurses and medical staff at all levels of experience.

▶ **Certified Paramedic and Firefighter II;** additional training in Biology, Chemistry, Anatomy and Physiology.

**EMPLOYMENT:**

Hanover Park Fire Protection District, Hanover Park, IL      9/07-Present
**Paramedic / Firefighter**
Perform all aspects of emergency care in high-pressure, fast-paced situations, including patient defibrillation, bandaging and stabilization.
Administer CPR as required and provide all essential life support services, prior to and during patient transport to various hospitals.

Pro-Care Ambulance Service, **EMT-B (Emergency Medical Technician)**
Superior Ambulance Service, and
American Medical Response/AMR, **EMT-B**

Located in Elgin, Elmhurst and Glendale Heights, IL      5/06-2/08
Ameritech, Inc., Elgin, IL      8/04-7/05

**Telephone Technician**
Communicated with customers on a daily basis and repaired/installed service through switches and the Ameritech infrastructure.

**EDUCATION:**   John A. Logan Community College, Carterville, IL
**Major: EMT-B**

Southern Illinois University, Carbondale, IL
**Major: Biology**

St. Francis Hospital, Evanston, IL
**Paramedic Program**

**MILITARY:**   U.S. Navy, San Diego, CA (Two years)
**Rate-Sonar Technician**
Trained personnel in office procedures and operated various electronics.

# LISA A. NERF

27 Bay View Point
Schaumburg, IL 60194

847-555-0796
LNerf@hotmail.com

## EXECUTIVE ASSISTANT

**PROFILE:**

- Comprehensive experience in the support of top corporate management, including all aspects of scheduling, calendar management, travel/program planning, personal client relations and the expert writing of correspondence for internal staff, managers and customers.
- Skilled in sales development and contract interpretation/negotiation, as well as creative theme development for promotions, special events, meetings and projects, with a sharp eye for detail.
- Self-motivated and energetic, with a strong aptitude for learning new systems and procedures; utilize MS Word, Excel, PowerPoint, Outlook and Lotus Notes for communications, spreadsheets and documentation.

**EXPERIENCE:**

**Manhattan Bank, Chicago, IL**                                                                              2003-2005
Meeting Manager
Trusted to consult directly with key internal clients to execute custom financial programs for all levels and lines of business, with a very high level of autonomy.

- Performed extensive project management including total logistics coordination, DMC hiring and oversight, facility and staffing management, contract administration and budget analysis.
- Wrote high-impact materials for invitations, websites and management promotions.

Total Event Resources, Inverness, IL                                                                         2001-2003
**Event Producer**
Acquired accounts within corporate and association markets, and developed new business opportunities.
Acted as primary client contact on a variety of events hosted in the U.S., including various executive programs, product launches, award ceremonies, holiday parties, dinners and spouse activities.

- Negotiated contracts and all aspects of executive transportation, creative theme development, venue research and selection, entertainment, audio visual support, décor design and installation, as well as invitation and attendance monitoring.
- Established operating budget based on client requirements; provided end-of-project reconciliation.

The Pampered Chef, Ltd., Addison, IL                                                                         1999-2001
**Meeting Coordinator**
Played a key role in planning annual National and Leadership Conferences in the U.S., U.K., Canada and Germany, including stage production, award ceremonies, special events, transportation, housing, registration, workshops and A/V support.

- Established program requirements; selected sites, negotiated contracts and directed events.
- Researched sites, coordinated logistics; oversaw on-site execution for annual executive meetings.
- Drafted and reconciled budgets for international programs; arranged travel for attendees.

First Health Corp., Downers Grove, IL                                                                        1994-1999
**Project Coordinator / National Travel Coordinator**
Planned Executive Committee and Sr. Management Meetings.
Managed all aspects of two National Conferences; organized seven Continuing Education Seminars; executed two summer and three holiday employee celebrations; arranged bi-annual, on-site luncheons for 650 colleagues.

- Monitored corporate travel policies and compliance; advised support staff on meeting planning issues; supervised five travel agents in two offices.

**EDUCATION:**
Loyola University of Chicago, IL  **B.A. Degree**  - Major: Organizational and Interpersonal Communication

**CONNI M. FILMER**
220 West Roscoe #2B
Chicago, IL 60657                           Film@mail.com                              312/555-5669

## *FILM / TELEVISION PRODUCTION ASSISTANT*

**EXPERIENCE:**

- Proven abilities as assistant to executives in production, home video and business administration.
- Experience with such companies as Warner Bros., Hanna-Barbera and Twentieth Century Fox.
- Skilled in office operations and department activities; knowledge of WordPerfect and Lotus 1-2-3.
- Plan and conduct written and oral presentations in a professional.

**EMPLOYMENT:**

Hanna Barbera Productions, Hollywood, CA                                     8/01-Present
**Assistant to the Executive Producer**
Planned and coordinated numerous aspects of production, including synopsis preparation and manuscript reading.
Coordinated writers, editors and producers of an animated TV series in collaboration with the Executive Producer.
\* Provided additional support as needed to the Senior Vice President.

Twentieth Century Fox Film Corporation, Century City, CA
Temp. Assignment                                                              6/01-7/01
**Assistant to V.R and General Counsel**
See description of 4/99-5/00, below.

Warner Bros., Burbank, CA                                                    5/00-5/01
**Assistant to V.R and General Counsel**
(Warner Home Video)
Managed an entire Home Video Department in direct collaboration with the General Counsel. Researched, prepared and drafted all agreements related to domestic and international home video distribution.
\* Directed and organized virtually all office support functions.

Twentieth Century Fox Film Corporation, Century City, CA        4/99-5/00
**Executive Assistant / Contract Administrator to the V.R and Deputy Counsel**
Drafted contracts for talent and production staff, as well as option notice reports and contract status reports.
\* Designed and improved administrative and office management procedures for the department.

**EDUCATION:**    Glen Oaks Community College, Glen Oaks, CA             1988-1989
            **English Major**

Becker G. Stylish

2247 Wentworth Lane
Bartlett, IL 60103                    Beck@mail.com                    708/555-2348

## EXPERIENCE:

### Graphic Designer                                    2/02-Present
Associated Stationers, Itasca, IL
Responsible for the layout, design and production of consumer office product catalogs and various promotional materials from concept through press proof.
Proficient in QuarkXpress; familiar with Adobe Illustrator, Adobe Photoshop, Windows 7 and Microsoft Word.
▶   Design corporate signage for branch locations.
▶   Conceptualize, lay out and art direct catalog covers.

### Graphic Design Specialist                           1/98-1/02
Boise Cascade Office Products, Itasca, IL
Developed page layouts for wholesale consumer product catalogs.
Worked with pressroom staff on four-color projects.
Coordinated product photography.
Designed and art directed numerous dealer catalog covers.
▶   Developed and produced an eight-page catalog insert for recycled products, 2002.
▶   Produced the top selling and standard covers for wholesale and consumer catalogs in 2001.
▶   Achieved continuous cost savings: initiated a change in film size.

### Staff Artist                                        4/96-1/98
Acme Wiley Corporation, Signs and Systems, Elk Grove, IL
Designed architectural signage to meet specific client needs; utilized building and zoning codes, as well as color and budgetary guidelines.
Produced signage brochures for custom signage programs. Developed a company promotional brochure of signage options.
Created architectural and mechanical drawings, marker rendering presentations and scale models for client programs.

### Assistant Advertising Manager                       4/95-1/96
Blue M, A unit of General Signal, Blue Island, IL
Planned, developed and distributed product brochures, catalogs and informational pieces throughout the organization.
Placed advertisements in major trade publications and updated/maintained customer mailing lists.

## EDUCATION:

### Bachelor of Fine Arts, Graphic Design
Ball State University, Muncie, IN
Formal Macintosh training through Black Dot Graphics, Crystal Lake, IL

# RANDIE SLEEPER

1105 Orchard Avenue
Schaumburg, IL 60193                    Easy@mail.com                    847/555-3678

## *HOSPITALITY MANAGEMENT / OPERATIONS*

**EXPERIENCE:**

► Skilled in new business development for bar and kitchen operations, including full responsibility for staffing, sales and business administration.

► Coordinate budgets, inventories, purchasing and quality control for food, beverages and supplies; manage creative advertising, promotions and marketing, as well as entertainment services.

► Effectively hire, train, supervise and motivate staff and management in all bar procedures, food service activities and personal customer relations.

**EMPLOYMENT:**

Ramada O'Hare / Marriott, Rosemont, IL                    10/96-Present
**Department Manager / Supervisor**
In charge of virtually all operations in the sports bar and grill of this 723-room hotel, including training, scheduling and supervising a team of 12 in food/cocktail serving and bartending.
Constantly expand the customer base through creative planning and execution of promotions, PR and advertising, including special events, booking of disk jockeys, karaoke setups and contests.
Create and promote food and drink specials on a regular basis.
Work closely with vendors and suppliers and handle cost-effective purchasing, forecasting, budget control, payroll processing, bank deposits and purchase requests.
Utilize DTS and Remaco computer systems, and the DSS satellite system; familiar with Windows 7 and MS Word.
TIPS Certified for alcohol intervention procedures.

► Organize and/or design buffets, menus and in-house decorations.
► Develop job descriptions and assign duties to appropriate staff.
► Advanced from Server and Bartender to this position.
► **Training through Marriott:** Completed and taught Marriott's Gold Standard Training; completed numerous courses in management, hospitality, motivation and communications, discipline and documentation.

Jimmy's Bar & Grill, Elmwood Park, IL
**Manager**                    1994-2001
Effectively hired, trained and supervised a team of eight in direct customer service, upselling and the serving of food and beverages.

**Bartender / Kitchen Crew**                    1992-1994
Responsible for all bartender duties including mixing drinks, working with customers, problem solving and maintaining sanitation.

# VERONICA L. CHANDLER

2242 East Bryn
Mawr Avenue
Roselle, IL 60172                           Veron@mail.com                           630/555-3791

**OBJECTIVE:**  *INTERNSHIP*
A spring/summer internship where skills in communications, creative arts and environmental studies will be of value.

**PROFILE:**
- Skilled in photography, writing and editing, radio production and newspaper reporting.
- Trained in psychological and sociological issues, processes and techniques.

**EDUCATION:**  Beloit College, Beloit, WI                           2006-Present
**Bachelor of Arts Degree Candidate**
Major: Sociology                           Minor: Environmental Studies
Award: WC Hooker Scholarship                           AP Credit: Psychology

*Courses:*
Calculus
Elementary Japanese I & II
Introduction to Sociology
20th Century American Literature
Geological Hazards & Environmental Geology

*Extracurricular Activities:*
- WBCR weekly radio show D.J.
- BelSAC Floor Representative
- Intra-mural Soccer Team Player
- Bible Study Group Member
- Ballroom Dance Club Member
- Fall Ball Steering Committee

*Work-Study:* Physical Plant Worker/Recycling
*Volunteer Service:* Rockford Animal Shelter

Lake Park High School, Roselle, IL                           Graduated 2006
GPA: 4.14/5.0

*AP Classes:* Psychology, Biology and World Literature and Composition Participated in numerous activities including photography, newspaper reporter, Earth Club, Creative Arts Club, Marching Band Color Guard, Youth & Government, Psychology Club and Class Council.
*Public Service:* Proposed the establishment of a Teen Museum in Roselle and organized a poetry reading at the La Dolce Vita Cafe.

**PART-TIME:**  **Cashier,** Pik-Kwik Foods, Roselle, IL                           9/05-8/06
                           **Sales Associate/Cashier,** Wild Pair, Bloomingdale, IL                           1/05-7/05

# LYNDA V. MICROPHONE

2205 Washington Street
Oak Park, IL 60302
Cell: 708/555-5753
Res: 708/555-8077
Lyn@mail.com

## INTERNSHIP: RADIO BROADCASTING
A position where proven communication and technical skills would be utilized.

- Comprehensive experience in program production, including interviewing, mixing, editing, and final presentation.
- Background in weather and traffic reporting; coordinate talent and create introductions, sound bites, PSAs, and professional formats.
- Hands-on experience as traffic/news reporter and talk show host for numerous programs.

**EXPERIENCE:**     TCI of Illinois, Inc., Mt. Prospect, IL                    2003-Present
**Community Public Access TV Producer / Playback Operator**
Responsible for all aspects of development for local programs, including story origination, writing, interviews, camera operation, floor direction, sound setup and final editing.
Coordinate schedules; operate a variety of cameras, soundboards, and editors.
Manage programs from concept to completion; subjects include local artists, authors and community services.

- \* Test marketed TCFs Intelligent Television project for audience control of pay-per-view movies and commercial programs.
- \* Completed numerous TCI training programs in broadcasting and production.

Walden Apartments. Schaumburg, IL                    1999-2003
**Marketing Director / Leasing Consultant**
Manage all aspects of leasing for 619 residential units, including marketing, promotions, and sales presentations.
Handle public relations and written/oral communications in a professional manner.
Coordinate special events and create advertisements.
Assist in training and supervising three employees in creative sales, resident retention/renewal, and special promotions.

- \* Earned national award for Top Sales and Customer Support.

Draper & Kramer, Inc., Chicago, IL
**Leasing Consultant**                    1997-1999

**EDUCATION:**     **B.A. Degree: Mass Communications**                    Graduate: 1996
Rust College, Holly Springs, MS

- \* Employed as **Announcer** / **DJ** on a local radio station.
- \* Earned various awards for producing and hosting a variety of talk show programs and weather, traffic and news reports.

# CHERYL CROWLEY

2044 Easton Court
Hanover Park, IL 60103                    Cher@mail.com                              630/555-4760

## *MANAGEMENT TRAINEE*

**PROFILE:**    ► Proven abilities in supervision and training of associates, team development, cash management and customer service.

► Experienced in research, organization and presentation of data; skilled in Windows 7 and the entire MS Office suite.

**EDUCATION:**   University of Iowa, Iowa City, IA
**Bachelor of Arts, History:** Minor equivalency in Mathematics, Political Science and Chemistry.
Researched, compiled and organized data for several large-scale reports.
Tutored other students in French, Math, Chemistry and History.

► Awarded a scholarship for studies during freshman year.
► Served as Building Coordinator and Member of Residence Hall Government; coordinated several dance, sporting and fund-raising events.

**EXPERIENCE:**   Northwest Mosquito Abatement District, Elk Grove, IL          Summer, 2006-2017
**Inspector**
Worked in a team environment to identify mosquito populations. Documented stages of larvae development. Safely handled equipment and various chemicals.

Warner / Electric / Atlantic, Bensenville, IL          Summer, 2003 and 2005
Responsible for general warehousing duties including inventory control, receiving and re-stocking.
Operated materials handling equipment.

Radio Shack, Bloomingdale, IL          Summer, 2004
**Retail Sales**
Worked with customers to identify needs; discussed product features and benefits.
Responded to customer inquiries and accepted orders.
Processed and submitted credit card and cell phone applications.

► Professionally handled cash transactions, prepared bank deposits and closed store for daily business.

Santa's Village, East Dundee, IL          Summer, 2000-2002
**Lead Game Operator**
Trained new employees on game operations, and set daily work/relief schedules.
Handled customer relations and cash transactions in a professional manner.

# ANITA PASTUKH

2290 Darby Lane
Roselle, IL 60172                     Ani@mail.com                          630/555-5138

**OBJECTIVE:**   *OFFICE ADMINISTRATION / MANUFACTURING OPERATIONS*

**PROFILE:**
► Experience in office administration and production scheduling activities, including updating of daily work order changes, workloads and job assignments.

► Hire, train and supervise employees in job procedures and adherence to quality; familiar with MS Word and Lotus 1-2-3 for Windows 7; bilingual in Polish/English and proficient in Russian.

**EMPLOYMENT:**

Sweet Pea's Cleaning, Inc., Lombard, IL                     2001-Present
**Supervisor**
Organize, coordinate and supervise multiple cleaning crews for this residential cleaning service, including job and route assignments, with responsibility for customer relations.
Hire, train and review the performance of new employees; maintain payroll records. Schedule daily appointments, with attention to special client instructions and work order changes. Identify procedures to streamline operations and contain costs.

► Changed service delivery from an all-route, single van-operation to an owner-operator operation, whereby each employee drives to assigned clients directly.
► Accepted this position soon after relocating to the United States in 2000.

Juvenile Detention Home/Center, Bielsko-Biala, Poland                     1996-2000
**Teacher / Counselor**
Instructed problematic and learning disabled children of ages 7 to 18, placed in this juvenile detention home by the Court.

► Counseled minors on substance abuse problems; organized a summer camp, with daily recreational activities.
► Worked with LBD children on academic lessons and individualized therapeutic treatment plan goals for improvement.

Urzad Skarbowy, Bielsko-Biala, Poland                     1994-1995
**Accountant**
Responsible for the processing and collection of tax payments from business owners.
Researched financial histories, *to* review for payments due.
Reconciled individual taxpayer monthly balances and prepared closing statements.

► Set up and maintained accounting records.

**EDUCATION:**   College of DuPage, Glen Ellyn, IL
Attend English and English as a Second Language courses.                     2007-Present

Slaski University, Katowice, Poland                     1995-1999
Completed four years of a five-year undergraduate degree program in Social Work/Counseling, with a focus on youth development.

GRACE STYLE

2217 Devon
Roselle, IL 60172                    GraceMarie@mail.com                    630/555-2263

*PATIENT REGISTRATION / OFFICE ADMINISTRATION*

**PROFILE:**    ▶    Comprehensive experience in a wide range of administrative functions, including patient registration, switchboard operations and data entry.

              ▶    Superior communication skills used to coordinate between various departments and provide patients with excellent service. Fluent in English and Italian; familiar with Spanish.

**EXPERIENCE:**

Alexian Brothers Hospital, Elk Grove Village, IL
**Patient Registration / Float Person**                    2008-Present
Responsible for all aspects of patient registration, including the entry of insurance information into a mainframe computer system.
Work in ER, Out-Patient and In-Patient registration areas.
Order blood and urine tests and register patients for various tests and procedures.
Coordinate with floor staff for bed assignments.
Take calls from physicians to reserve bed space and procedures for patients.

**Switchboard / Admitting**                    2005-2008
Handled and routed all incoming calls to the hospital.
Wrote messages and paged doctors; relayed information from patients.
Updated codes in the computer system as required.

Parkway Bank and Trust, Elk Grove Village, IL                    2003-2005
**Universal Teller**
Promoted to this position after three months.
Responsible for the main vault with over $200,000.
Handled all aspects of teller services including customer relations and cash management.

Home Federal Savings, Roselle, IL                    1999-2003
**Bank Teller**
Provided customer service and handled cash and financial transactions.

Jorgensen Steel Company, Schaumburg, IL                    1997-1998
**File Clerk** (Temporary)
Responsible for various office functions including data entry and file management.

Nitram Metal, Elk Grove Village, IL                    1997
**General Office** (Part-time)
Performed a wide range of office work such as file maintenance, data entry and reception.

**EDUCATION:**    **Graduate:** Lake View High School

# MATTHEW PICTURE

2215 Lincoln
Glendale Heights, IL 60139        Mat@mail.com        708/555-7187

## *PIC SUPERVISOR*

**EXPERIENCE:**

- More than nine years in production operations including responsibility for line setup, management and quality control.
- Skilled in strategic planning, MRP, budgets and forecasting; coordinate purchasing, JIT, cost-effective inventory control and cycle counts.
- Strong background in A.P.I.C.S. requirements and safety/housekeeping inspections.
- Hire, train, supervise and motivate production teams and foremen in procedures and operations; fluent in Spanish and English.

**EMPLOYMENT:**

Suncast Corporation, Batavia, IL
**PIC Supervisor**        2001-Present
Responsible for all aspects of production and inventory control in the manufacture of various lawn and garden supplies.
Effectively hire, train and supervise five foremen on three shifts; indirectly responsible for 15 line workers; currently on 24-hour call.
Plan and schedule jobs for molding and assembly in a cost-effective manner.
Involved in molding and assembly operations with more than 35 mold presses.
Coordinate MRP and update/maintain accurate inventories on PRAXA software on a VAX/VMS system; supervise WIP inventories on a regular basis.

- \* Developed a strong team atmosphere among virtually all personnel.
- \* Maintain excellent product quality through communication with the customer service department.
- \* Coordinate/purchase projects through outside manufacturers and vendors.
- \* Work directly with engineers; organize shipping and receiving for parts and product lines.

| | |
|---|---|
| **Materials Control Foreman** | 2000-2001 |
| **Leadman** Chosen as Employee of the Month | 1998-1999 |
| **Furniture Production Foreman** | 1994-1997 |
| **Assistant Foreman, Furniture Department** | 1992-1994 |
| **Machine Operator** | 1991-1992 |

| | | |
|---|---|---|
| **EDUCATION:** | Waubonsee Community College, Sugar Grove, IL<br>Attending courses in APICS Standards. | 1/02-Present |
| | Aurora College, Aurora, IL    **Supervisory Management Certificate** | 1991 |
| | College of DuPage, Glen Ellyn, IL | 1994-1998 |

Completed various courses including Business.

**CAINE LAIT**
225 Berry Lane
Streamwood, IL 60107
630/555-2330
Milk@mail.com

## *PRODUCTION OPERATIONS / MATERIAL ANALYST*

**PROFILE:**
► Comprehensive experience in manufacturing and procedure documentation, as well as staff training in product assembly and troubleshooting.
► Communicate with customers and suppliers on product updates; work closely with staff, management and suppliers for status reporting and in-process changes.
► Experience with Windows 7, MS Excel, Word and PowerPoint for inventory control, data entry, spreadsheet updating and correspondence.

**EXPERIENCE:** <u>Motorola, Inc.</u>, Schaumburg, IL                    11/08-Present
**Material Analyst and Instructor / Trainer**
Responsible for in-plant transfers of production materials, including posting, receiving and resolving a wide range of issues related to circuit board production.
Perform group and individual training of new hires, including documentation of progress, liaison between supervisors and the training department.

► Directly involved in writing and updating Manufacturing Process Standards (MPS) for postwave, mechanical assembly, board test and repair, with detailed, step-by-step procedures for each area.
► As **Team Leader,** tracked daily production versus production goals, requiring constant involvement with customers and suppliers.
► Involved in initiating the cellular educational training program, with an emphasis on problem solving.

**Motorola Training includes:**
APD Safety Fundamentals, The Ownership Spirit, Windows 7, Diversity Awareness, Wingz 1.1, Framemaker 4.0, MPC, Factory Control System (APD), Surface Mount Technology, Individual Dignity Entitlement for Employees; Lotus 1-2-3, Introduction to POPI, Effective Team Leadership, Problem Solving, Right to Know, CMO Performance Review Training, New Job Skill Training, Beginning Symphony and Interaction for Manufacturing Employees.

**CERTIFICATIONS and DUTIES:**

Soldering, Testing, Assembly and Repair, Team Trainer, Material Handling, including posting, receiving, pick requests and troubleshooting for Location 77.

| | |
|---|---|
| <u>Sealed Power Corporation,</u> Des Plaines, IL | 1991-1998 |
| <u>Zenith Corporation,</u> Chicago, IL | 1986-1988 |

**EDUCATION:** <u>Malcolm X City College,</u> Major: Accounting

<u>Elgin Community College,</u> Attending courses in English, Writing and Typing.

# RACHELLE MEMO

2348 Hesterman Drive
Glendale Heights, IL 60139                    Memo@mail.com                    708/555-7778

## *RECEPTIONIST*
A position where proven communication skills and attention to detail would be utilized.

**PROFILE:**    ▶    More than three years in various business environments, including customer service, office support and the reconciliation of reports for purchasing and inventory control.

▶    Handle telephone communications in a professional manner, as well as message taking and data entry/retrieval; balance cash transactions with speed and accuracy.

▶    Proficient in Windows 7, Paradox and MS Word, as well as PowerPoint.

## EMPLOYMENT:

Tri Star Metals, Inc., Carol Stream, IL                    4/04-Present
**Office Clerk**
Provide a wide range of office services in a professional manner, including data entry/retrieval of purchase orders utilizing Paradox.
Analyze and update monthly purchase order and inventory reports.

- Perform proofreading, verification and distribution of invoices.
- Conduct research to resolve discrepancies.
- Compile documentation for freight bills.

Footlocker, Bloomingdale, IL                    5/02-4/04
**Cashier**
Responsible for customer service and sales transactions for this high-volume shoe retail outlet. Accurately handled large amounts of cash.

- Operated a computerized register system.
- Trained a new employee in professional customer service, store procedures, product lines and register operations.
- Processed returns and exchanges on a daily basis.

Phar-Mor, Inc., Bloomingdale, IL                    8/01-5/02
Duties similar to those at Footlocker including training, customer service and computerized register transactions.

- Balanced daily register receipts.

**EDUCATION:**    College of DuPage, Glen Ellyn, IL                    Attending part-time
**Associates Degree** in Arts expected May, 2010

Glenbard North High School, Carol Stream, IL                    Graduate

# KAREN R. HEADSET

671 Rodenburg Road #304

Roselle, IL 60172        Kar@email.com        708/555-3201

## *RECEPTIONIST / OFFICE SUPPORT*

Skilled in general reception, switchboard operation and customer service,
as well as personal communications in fast-paced environments.

**PROFILE:**
- Familiar with Windows 7, MS Word and Excel for customer correspondence, spreadsheets and status reports.

**EXPERIENCE:**

Sunbeam Household Products, Schaumburg, IL        11/05-2/06
**Receptionist**
Responsible for switchboard operation and telephone answering for 90 extensions.
Communicate with customers, answer questions, and expedite messages.
Compile and print purchase orders and requisitions; handle incoming and outgoing faxes, copying and filing.

* Coordinate travel plans and schedules for staff and managers.

Centennial Executive Suites, Schaumburg, IL        2003-2005
**Switchboard Operator**
Answered hundreds of calls daily for up to 43 companies in shared executive suites.
Greeted visitors, notified clients of appointments and delivered mail.

ERA Abbott Real Estate, Schaumburg, IL        2002-2003
**Secretary**
Duties included reception and switchboard operation for up to 60 agents.

Remcor Products Company, Glendale Heights, IL        2000-2001
**Receptionist**
Operated a switchboard for up to 200 employees.
Performed data entry/retrieval of credit memos and processed accounts receivable for the company register.

Builders Plumbing Supply, Addison, IL        1999-2000
**Receptionist**
Handled four telephone lines for 300 employees; greeted customers and sorted, prepared and distributed daily mail.

Suburban Computer Services, Palatine, IL
**Receptionist**        1997-1999

**EDUCATION:**    College of DuPage, Glen Ellyn, IL
**A.A. Degree: Office Management**        Graduated 1997

# OLIVIA K. WRECKTEAM

2247 Georgetown Drive
Carol Stream, IL 50188
Olive@mail.com                                                   Res: 630/555-4343

## COMMUNITY SERVICE: *RECREATION SUPERVISOR*

- Plan and implement programs, projects and special activities for large organizations; serve as liaison with companies and their employees.
- Experience in youth development, childcare and parenting functions, with full responsibility for daily recreational, educational and social activities in family, childcare center and social agency environments.
- Skilled in motor skill and social interaction development, especially with behavioral learning and developmentally disabled children; handle multiple priorities and communicate sensitive issues to children, parents and staff with tact and professionalism.
- B.S. Degree in park and recreation studies, with a minor in law enforcement; formerly certified in CPR and First Aid; volunteer youth counselor/teacher,

## EMPLOYMENT:

Chicago Title & Trust, Carol Stream, IL                     11/17-Present
**Searcher, Special Search Department**
Conduct computerized tract searches, including extensive communication with attorneys, property owners and utility companies seeking information recorded on or against subject properties.

- ► Launched the company's first coed softball team.
- ► Instituted a blood drive through Heartland.

Central DuPage Hospital, Winfield, IL                      2/02-11/17
**Shift Supervisor, Surgical Department**
Hired, trained and evaluated department personnel and acted as employee liaison to management; organized, directed and reviewed work.

**Sterilization Tech II, Surgical Department**
- ► Hospital representative for the United Way campaign.

Faith Covenant Church, Wheaton, IL
- Counselor, Church High League Winter Retreat.
- Youth Counselor, ages 8-9, Pioneer Club Sunday School Teacher, Preschool, ages 4-5.

## EDUCATION:

College of DuPage, Glen Ellyn, IL                          Present
**Certification program:** Elementary Education

Western Illinois University, Macomb, IL                    2006
**B.S. Degree in Parks and Recreation**
Minor: Law Enforcement *Twelve-week Internship:* Cunningham Children's Home, Urbana, IL
*Volunteer, Macomb Rehabilitation Center,* improved children's motor skills.

# STEVEN B. TIRED

2653 Catalpa Lane
Bartlett, MI 40103

Steve@mail.com

673/555-0798

**OBJECTIVE:**

*SOLID / HAZARDOUS WASTE MANAGEMENT*
A position where hands-on training would be utilized.

**PROFILE:**

Proven abilities in research and material/cost estimating; trained in biomonitoring system design and analysis; familiar with RCRA and CERCLA legislation.

Handle written & oral communications in a professional manner; strong aptitude for learning technical systems and procedures.

Familiar with Lotus 1-2-3 and Quattro for spreadsheets, as well as Windows 7 and the full MS Office suite.

**EMPLOYMENT:**

Village of Bartlett, Bartlett, MI                    Summer, 2016
**Internship**
Assisted in material and cost estimating for several village projects.
Responsible for collecting measurements of sidewalks and streets and updating all documentation.
Involved in setting slopes at construction sites.

- Collected data and handled plan reviews, as well as a variety of fieldwork.
- Communicated with city residents and resolved problems and complaints.

American Flange, Carol Stream, MI                    Summers, 2006-2009
**Materials Handler**

Home Depot and Walgreens, Bartlett, MI                    Summers, 2001-2003
**Cashier / Customer Service Representative**

**EDUCATION:**

University of Illinois, Urbana-Champaign, IL
**Bachelor of Science Degree**                    May, 2012

**Major: Civil Engineering**
**Concentration: Environmental Engineering**

* Major GPA: 4.3/5.0; self-funded 100 percent of college costs.

* Class projects included extensive research and the writing of a 20-page report on surface drainage of an urban creek.

* Key courses included:
Wastewater Management, Air & Water Quality Control
Solid and Hazardous Waste Management and Biomonitoring

# STEVEN G. BOSS

221 West Wrigley
Schaumburg, IL 60613                    wowboss@aol.com                    847/555-4235

**PROFILE:**

➢ Proven abilities in inside/outside sales, including account prospecting & acquisition, cold calling, and market penetration.

➢ Plan and conduct sales presentations for senior-level clients; design sales proposals and price quotes; assist in new product introduction and full client development.

➢ Skilled in MS Windows systems including Lotus, Word and Excel for account tracking and updating; analyze spreadsheets and assist in forecasting.

**EMPLOYMENT:**

PMI: Professional Marketers, Inc., Villa Park, IL                    4/02-Present
**Territory Representative**
Perform sales and account development in a Northwest suburban territory for this major supplier of gas/arc welders and supplies to industrial clientele.
Handle cold calling and sales presentations; review and update client activity via spreadsheets and process orders.
* Create sales proposals and negotiate deals with key decision makers.
* Travel throughout the territory and provide customer feedback on products for senior-level management.
* Chosen as the first outside sales representative at this company in 12 years.
* Promoted to this position from:

GMI: Greatest Marketers, Inc., Lombard, IL                    5/01-4/02
**Category Manager**
Responsible for product merchandising and promotions implementation.
Conducted full product resets to new planograms and increased sales volume.
* Winner of $2k in contest money from various principles.
* Placed 3rd in quarterly contests; sold Brach's product line in 90% of territory.

**Inside Sales Representative**                    12/00-5/01
Worked closely with customers and processed up to 350 orders/month via telephone.
* Achieved the highest volume of orders for a one-month period.
* Wrote more than $200k in sales.

Dependable Cleaning, Inc., Elmhurst, IL                    Summers, 1989-1999
**Assistant Manager**
Hired, trained, scheduled and supervised up to 20 employees in office cleaning and maintenance operations.
Involved in sales and direct customer service; purchased supplies and equipment.
* Personally acquired two major accounts valued at more than $10k.

**EDUCATION:**

Indiana University, Bloomington, IN                    1987-1991

**B.C.S. Degree: General Studies**        Emphasis on Business, Psychology and History.

*MICHAEL SCANNER*

11227 N. Overhill
Chicago, IL 60631                     Mike@mail.com                          773/555-1576

*SCANNER / MAC OPERATOR*

**EXPERIENCE:**

- More than nine years in lithography including full responsibility for Macintosh assembly and plotting.
- Specialize in advanced film output and color separations; handle color correction, enlargements, reductions & stretches.
- Utilize Macintosh, Windows 7, Scitex and Rampage systems, the 340 Hell Scanner and 2-color silkscreen presses.
- Working knowledge of QuarkXpress and Illustrator; familiar with PhotoShop, FreeHand and PageMaker.

**EMPLOYMENT:**     Compo Graphics, Chicago, IL                              4/08-Present
**Mac Operator**
Responsible for preflight, assembly and output of four to six color files.
Perform plotting on the Dolev 4-press.
Ensure high quality of films and proofs.

Electronic Prepress Services, Arlington Heights, IL     10/03-4/08
**Mac Operator**
Responsible for preflight, assembly and output of four to six color files.
Handled plotting on Dolev 400 and 800 output devices.
*    Promoted to this position from Plotter Operator.

The Color Company, Elk Grove Village, IL                8/99-6/03
**Apprentice Scanner Operator**
Performed prompt, accurate scanning of transparencies and reflective art for Conde Nast publications including House & Garden, Glamour, Vogue and Mademoiselle magazines. Trained one employee in proofing, vertical camera work, the 340 Hell and the Crossfield system.
*    Matched and/or improved subjects; handled all aspects of enlargements, reductions and stretches.

TCR Graphics, Streamwood, IL
**Proofer / Camera Operator**

**EDUCATION:**     Triton College, River Grove, IL
Successful completion of a course in Offset Printing.
*    Awarded Apprenticeship for Journeyman Status.

Harper College, Palatine, IL
Completed a course in QuarkXpress

Hoffman Estates High School, Hoffman Estates, IL          Graduate

# YVETTE M. SPEAKER

2200 Lacy Avenue
Streamwood, IL 60107                     Speak@mail.com                          630/555-3949

*TEACHERS AIDE:* Elementary and Middle School Levels

**PROFILE:**     ▶   Skilled in problem identification and resolution with attention to detail; proven ability to focus on the learning needs of children and obtain appropriate assistance, materials and resources.

▶   Work well with groups and individuals from diverse backgrounds; actively participate in school and neighborhood meetings, programs and events; strong work ethic and desire to nurture students to achieve their potential.

## RELATED EXPERIENCE:

Heritage Elementary School, Streamwood, IL                    10/06-Present
**Volunteer Parent**
■  *Book Fair.* Set up and disassemble the exhibit area, display books and advise children on their book selections.
■  *Lunch Supervisor:* serve parents and students lunches and monitor activities.

*Involved in numerous parent-child and neighborhood activities:*
■  Christmas drama productions.
■  Walk-a-thon for Kid's Play.
■  Roger's Park Neighborhood Police Department public service meetings on gangs, drugs and youth development issues.

## EMPLOYMENT:

Standard Parking, Inc., Chicago, IL                    1998-9/06
**Cashier, Prudential Plaza Garage**
Handled individual cash and automatic card parking ticket transactions daily. Answered telephone calls and responded to inquiries about rates and hours.
Resolved fee and service discrepancies accurately, promptly and tactfully.
Worked closely with security and the senior manager to resolve customer problems and emergencies dealing with such matters as lost keys, broken door locks, tire changes and dead batteries.
Reconciled cash receipts and prepared a Cashier Report for the senior manager.

U.S. Post Office, Chicago, IL **Casual Employee**                    Seasonal, 1997-1998

## EDUCATION:

Harry S Truman College, Chicago, IL                    1996-1998
**Completed A.A. Degree-level coursework** in Child Development.

John E Kennedy High School, Chicago, IL                    Graduated 1996

*KAREN CLICKER*

22549 South Beth
Lombard, IL 60148                    Kclick@mail.com                    630/555-4596

## OFFICE SUPPORT / ADMINISTRATION

**PROFILE:**    ▶    Detailed experience with proprietary software for data entry and retrieval; update
and maintain customer data; familiar with general office equipment including copiers, fax
machines and 10-key calculators.

▶    Skilled in customer service and telephone operations; handle customer inquiries and
phone presentations in a professional manner.

▶    Trained in various emergency situations as telephone operator; identify problems
and coordinate emergency response.

▶    Utilize Windows 7 and the full MS Office suite for professional correspondence,
graphs, charts and status reports.

**EXPERIENCE:**

The Signature Group, Elmhurst, IL                    2005-2016

**Phone Service Representative**
Handled both dial-in and dial-out phone contacts with tact and professionalism.
Utilized proprietary software for entering customer information into a computerized
database.

- Performed phone interviews and sales presentations for major clients including
Montgomery Wards, CitiBank, Mobile Oil and Fleet.

Ameritech, Lombard, IL                    1998-2005
**Information Operator**
Effectively handled customer inquiries for the information center. Retrieved phone numbers and
addresses from the company database. Traveled to other company sites to assist with special
projects.

- Provided critical information to emergency service departments as part of 911 operations.
- Alertly identified and reported emergency situations; calmly talked with victims while
coordinating emergency response.

**EDUCATION:**

Conant High School, Hoffman Estates, IL                    **Graduate**

**EDWARD X. PLANTMAN**
22751 Sunnyside Road
Roselle, IL 60172
630/555-5055
Ed@mail.com

## *OPERATIONS / PLANT MANAGEMENT*
Industrial Manufacturing & Distribution

► Extensive background in virtually all warehouse service and industrial manufacturing operations, with hands-on production supervisory responsibilities in customer-driven, ISO 9002 certified, team environments.

► Skilled in troubleshooting and problem resolution; train and supervise machine operators in quality, adherence to work order specifications and equipment maintenance on Chicago 60", 48" Monarch stamco and 12"-18" slitters, Dahlstrom 48" cut-to-length machines and 18"-20" edgers; **Certified Internal Quality Auditor.**

## EXPERIENCE

<u>Precision Steel Warehouse,</u> Franklin Park, IL
*A privately held service steel warehouse set up to cut metals for job shops; part of Precision Steel with two other branches in North Carolina and Illinois.*

**Slitting Supervisor**                                                      6/12-Present
Responsible for all slitting operations, including setups/teardowns, basic equipment maintenance, work order completion and adherence to quality control standards.
Train and supervise 26 employees on four 12" to 60" slitters to cut coils to specified widths.
Program gauges on the digital Chicago slitter; check and adjust tolerance limits.
Inspect coils for defects before production startup.
Order warehouse supplies and submit orders for equipment/tools such as grinding slitting knives, lumber and packaging paper products.
Hold monthly safety meetings to review accident rates and prevention measures;
C.P.R. and Basic First Aid certified.

► Key customers include Allen Bradley, Square D, Eaton and Acco International.
► Part of ISO 9002 certification team; drafted job descriptions.
► Utilize a PC system to process staff bonuses based on piecework per hour.
► Contributed to a 30% reduction in rejections over the prior four years.

**Cut-length Supervisor**                                                      6/98-6/12
Supervised up to 17 people on seven machines to cut/edge steel coils.
Produced a master production staffing schedule, including overtime and vacations.
Promoted to this position from Operator,4/92-8/98; hired as a **Coil Handler, Packaging,** 4/89-4/92.

► Managed the UPS Department.

## EDUCATION / TRAINING

<u>MIMA Management Institute,</u> Chicago, IL
Completed courses in Supervision, Key Link to Productivity I & II, Advanced Supervisory Techniques I & II, Communication in the Real World, Training the Employee on the Job and Principles and Practices of Management I & II.

# Resume Examples For:

# Veterans Returning to the Workforce

# DENNIS E. CLOUD
2291 Ashley Drive
Granger, IN 46530
219/555-4841
Cloud@mail.com

**Private Pilot:** A position utilizing skills as Flight Crew member.

- Proven abilities as pilot, first officer and mechanic, including full flight management responsibilities.
- Flight Time: PIC 3000, SIC 4400, MEL 6300, SEL 1100, CFI 363.
- Total Flight Time: 7500; SIC Turbo Prop 4200, SIC Turbo Jet 182, Instrument 800, Cross Country 6500, Night 1400.
- Certificates: ATP MEL/SEL; CFI SEL FEW/Passed; A&P Certificate.

## EXPERIENCE:

Atlantic Coast Airlines, Washington/Dulles Airport, Herdon, VA
**Captain:** DHC-8, BAe J-4100                                          9/13-Present

Air Wisconsin, Inc., Outgamie Airport, Appleton, WI
**First Officer**                                                        5/99-9/13
Responsible for numerous flights in the F-27 Fokker, SD3-60 and Bae ATP.

Northwest Airlines, Inc., Hartsfield Intnl. Airport, Atlanta, GA
**A&P Mechanic**                                                         7/98-5/99
Handled troubleshooting and maintenance of C-CKs, DC-9s and B-727s.

Aerospec, Inc., Falcon Field, Peachtree City, GA
**Pilot / A&P Mechanic**                                                 5/98-7/98

Eastern Metro Express, Hartsfield International Airport, Atlanta, GA
**First Officer - Jetstream 31**                                         5/97-3/98
Part 135 - 121 Regional Carrier.

Eastern Airlines, Inc., Hartsfield, International Airport, Atlanta, GA
**A&P Mechanic**                                                         8/96-5/97

Responsible for phase check for the B-727, B-757, DC-9, A-300, L-1011, D-Check, B-727, DC-9, L-1011 and the A-300.

**EDUCATION:** Embry-Riddle Aeronautical University, Daytona Beach, FL      1994-1996
**Studies in Aeronautical Science and Airport Management.**

Spartan School of Aeronautics, Tulsa, OK                                 1992-1993
**Airframe and Power Plant License**

**MILITARY:** U.S. Army, **Flight Engineer on Turbine Powered Aircraft**      1990-1992
Completed U.S. Army Turbine/Airframe Repair Training.
Completed more than 2000 hours of flight time.

**CARIA A. STEELBAG**
7736 Cypress Drive
Streamwood, IL 60107
630/555-0916
Car@mail.com

*RAMP SERVICE / AIRLINE INDUSTRY*
A position where problem-solving and team skills will be of value.

**PROFILE:** ▶ Hands-on experience in construction, warehouse and receiving/shipping functions; proven ability to organize crews, prioritize tasks, meet deadlines and adhere to quality for customer satisfaction.
▶ Numerous classes attended toward a private pilot license; completed 57/60 flight hours; maintain current in industry trends at EAA/FAA forums and conventions; member: Experimental Aircraft Association (EAA) since 1991.

**EMPLOYMENT:**

Lakeview Lumber Construction, Lake Barrington, IL          10/15-Present
**Apprentice Carpenter**
Remodel kitchens, bathrooms and basements, including siding/roofing installation and room additions, for multiple and single-family residential construction projects.

JWK Painting, Algonquin, IL          7/05-10/15
**Painter**
Contracted to paint interior/exterior surfaces of commercial and residential properties.

Classic Contract Cleaning Company, Rolling Meadows, IL          12/04-6/05
**Crew Supervisor**
Organized, scheduled and supervised crews at multiple locations in cleaning commercial properties, including inventory tracking and equipment maintenance.
*          Responded to customer inquiries and resolved complaints.

Artlow Systems, Addison, IL          11/01-2/02 and
**Laborer**          6/89-8/99
Performed structural jobs, including paint/sealant removal, joint restoration, mud jacking and floor system seeding.

*Prior Experience Includes:*
**Part-time Loader,** Overnight Transportation Company; **Stocker,** F&M Distributors
**Loader,** Roadway Packaging Systems; **Sales Associate, Part-time,** Sportmart, Inc.

**MILITARY SERVICE:**

U.S. Army, Ft. Leonard Wood, MO and Ft. Lewis, WA
**Bco. 864th Engineer Bn / Motortransport Operator / Carpenter**
**Certifications:** Bus driver, 44 passengers; vehicle inspection; 64C Motortransport.
Passed the U.S. Army physical readiness test.

**EDUCATION:** William Rainey Harper College, Palatine, IL
Streamwood High School, Streamwood, IL

**JOHN P. WRENCH**
3400 Conway Bay
Roselle, IL 60172
630/555-0869
Wrench@mail.com


*MAINTENANCE MECHANIC*

**PROFILE:** Perform cost-cutting modifications that improve safety and boost machine productivity. Troubleshoot systems accurately and repair breakdowns quickly to maintain operating efficiency.
Completed the advanced, two-day Omron PLC Programming course.
Proven abilities in a wide range of technical skills, including Blueprint reading Mig, Arc and Gas Welding.

| | |
|---|---|
| Hydraulics | 3-phase electric motors |
| Sheet metal layout, fabrication | 480 V AC-24V DC |
| Air compressors | AC & DC drives |

## EXPERIENCE:

Knight Plastics, Arlington Heights, IL                    2/08-Present
**Maintenance Mechanic**
Responsible for all aspects of troubleshooting and repair of a wide range of machines such as Injection Molders, Decorating Machines, Vacuum Loaders and Assembly Machines.
Planned and implemented alterations for added safety, to improve operator ergonomics and increase machine productivity.

SPX Filtran, Des Plaines, IL                    2007-2008
**Maintenance Mechanic** (Third Shift)
Performed maintenance and repair of semi-automated equipment, PLC controlled assembly lines, and handled all duties similar to those listed above under Knight Plastics.

American Flange & Mfg. Company, Carol Stream, IL                    2006-2007
**Maintenance Mechanic**
Responsible for the setup and performance of preventative maintenance on a range of machines such as Bliss Punch Presses, Kaufman Mill & Thread machines and Cincinnati Injection Molders. Handled the fabrication of equipment modifications to upgrade systems.

U.S. Navy, San Diego, CA                    2002-2006
**Hull Maintenance Technician / Ship Fitter**
Conducted a wide range of ship repairs in accord with OSHA and NAVOSH regulations. Performed welding, cutting and grinding on materials such as carbon steel, stainless steel, aluminum and copper-nickel.

## EDUCATION:

College of DuPage, Glen Ellyn, IL
Successfully completed classes in Schematic Interpretation and Basic Electricity.

# ALBERT M. LENS

2270 Madrid Court
Hanover Park, IL 60103        lensman@aol.com        630/555-0871

## *PHOTOGRAPHY / FILM*

**PROFILE:**

- Skilled in creative photography, film and video production from concept to final editing, including promotional and art shots in color and B&W, with 35 mm, medium and large format cameras.
- Experience with Hasselblad and Mamiya (medium format) cameras and 4"x 5" view cameras; handle creative developing and darkroom procedures; experience in PhotoShop 4.0 and Avid.
- Featured in various galleries and publications, including **Photographer's Forum Magazine's** hardbound edition, *The Best of College Photography, 2008.*
- Fluent in Spanish; traveled extensively throughout Europe, 7/08-9/08.

**PHOTO EXHIBITS:**

**Group Exhibitions:**
New Works Gallery, Chicago, IL
University of Illinois, Champaign, IL        5/08, 12/07 and 10/07

**FILM & VIDEO WORKS:**

Personally wrote, produced and directed:
- Faith: (Experimental, 2006) Examination of elements in a church, 3.5 minutes.
- Maestro de Guitarra: (Documentary, 2007) Guitar performances, 12 minutes.

**INTERNSHIPS:**

Paul Elledge Studio, Chicago, IL
Kevin Banna and Frederic Stein Studios, Chicago, IL
Summer, 2007 Summer, 2006

**EDUCATION:**

University of Illinois at Chicago, Chicago, IL
**Bachelor of Fine Arts Degree**        Graduated 12/07
**Major:** Photography, Film and Electronic Media.
- Dean's List, 5 semesters. • Graduated with Honors.
- Golden Key National Honors Society and Phi Kappa Phi National Honors Society.

W.R. Harper College, Palatine, IL
**Associate of Arts Degree**        Graduated 12/05

**EMPLOYMENT:**

Illinois Shotokan Karate Clubs. Palatine, IL        1/02-Present
**Club Photographer / Instructor**
Document and instruct students of all ages, ranked up to black belt.

U.S. Marines:
Of a platoon of 86, one of only 5 recruits to graduate with Meritorious Promotion.
Stationed in Kuwait and Saudi Arabia during Desert Shield and Desert Storm.

**MEMBERSHIP:**

Member: American Society of Media Photographers.

**ALFRED A. KEYS**

6614 Glen Ellyn Road #205

Bloomingdale, IL 60108

708/555-2588

alfakey@aol.com

*COMPUTER OPERATOR*

A position where proven technical skills would be utilized.

**PROFILE:**  ►  Skilled in data processing with Windows 7 and all MS Office applications, including Excel, Word and PowerPoint for spreadsheets, professional correspondence and presentations.

►  Knowledge of PC setup and installation, as well as various peripherals, data entry and file updating.

►  Experience training individuals in system operations, as well as collections and customer service.

**EMPLOYMENT:**

U.S. Post Office, Forest Park, IL                          2004-Present

**Parcel Post Distributor**

Responsible for various post office functions including mail sorting.

Circuit City, Calumet City, IL                          2003-2004

**Computer Sales Representative**

Conducted training of staff and customers in computer system setup and operations.

Gained excellent experience in system operations and various types of hardware and software.

Rent-A-Center, Riverside, CA                          2000-2002

**Collections / Assistant Manager**

Directed and maintained collection operations related to past-due credit card accounts, including credit checks and status reporting. Assisted in training and supervising staff in all operations.

Provision Tech, Lansing, IL                          1997-1999

**Sales Representative**

Handled sales of credit cards and services via telephone.

**EDUCATION:**

Ivy Tech College, Gary IN                          1995-1997

**Major: Marketing**

Courses included business math, marketing, communications and human relations.

**MILITARY:**  United States Marine Corps, Japan/Korea                          1993-1995

**NCO Corporal**

Supervised a crew of 10, including the inventory of small arms and record keeping.

Earned various awards for excellent service.

# INDEX

CPSIA information can be obtained
at www.ICGtesting.com
Printed in the USA
LVHW061614140121
676490LV00009B/722